A PATENT LIE

Also by Paul Goldstein

Errors and Omissions

A PATENT LIE

A NOVEL

Paul Goldstein

DOUBLEDAY

New York London Toronto Sydney Auckland

DOUBLEDAY

Copyright © 2008 by Paul Goldstein

Published in the United States by Doubleday, an imprint of The Doubleday Publishing Group, a division of Random House, Inc., New York.
www.doubleday.com

DOUBLEDAY is a registered trademark and the DD colophon is a trademark of Random House, Inc.

This book is a work of fiction. Names, characters, businesses, organizations, places, events, and incidents either are the product of the author's imagination or are used fictitiously. Any resemblance to actual persons, living or dead, events, or locales is entirely coincidental.

Library of Congress Cataloging-in-Publication Data
Goldstein, Paul, 1943–
  A patent lie / by Paul Goldstein. — 1st ed.
    p. cm.
  1. Trials—Fiction. I. Title.
  PS3607.O4853P38 2008
  813'.6—dc22

                        2007050536

ISBN 978-0-385-51718-8

PRINTED IN THE UNITED STATES OF AMERICA

10 9 8 7 6 5 4 3 2 1

First Edition

To Jan

A PATENT LIE

ONE

The last time Michael Seeley saw his brother it was in a hotel kitchen in San Francisco and Leonard was arguing with the hotel's catering manager over the bill for his wedding reception. Workers were cleaning up and the pulsing bass from the dance band in the next room echoed over the clatter of silverware. Seeley had to catch the red-eye back to New York City, but the caterer was implacable and Leonard wouldn't let up, even when Seeley signaled that he was going to leave. Only after Seeley started out the door did Leonard stop, flinging his arms open to pull him into an awkward embrace.

"Let's stop being strangers, Mike." Leonard's breath tickled his ear.

Seeley broke away without answering. He loved his younger brother in the sense that he cared about his well-being, but he neither liked nor trusted him.

In the nine years since the wedding Leonard had called three or four times and sent his annual Christmas card. There was a printed announcement when he moved his medical practice from Palo Alto to San Francisco, and another last year when he took a job as chief medical officer at a biotech company in South San Francisco.

The announcement, mailed to Seeley in Manhattan, caught up with him in Buffalo, where he had moved his law practice. His first job out of law school had been in Buffalo. However, this time he was practicing not in the city's largest firm but by himself, and not in a steel-and-glass office tower but in a small office in the Ellicott Square Building, an ancient pile of bricks in the center of the city's half-deserted downtown.

Seeley's feet were up on a corner of his desk. Behind him, the single window looked out onto Swan Street, four stories below. His large shoulders hunched forward as if he was trying to warm himself against the chill scene outside. Rudy, the building's boiler man, was maneuvering a giant wrench beneath the decrepit steam radiator by the door and offering his views on whether the radiator was the oldest in western New York or in the Western world when a movement of yellow and gold flashed by the open door.

Seconds later, Seeley's part-time receptionist leaned into the office. "Someone to see you." There was an unfamiliar thrill in Mrs. Rosziak's voice, as if the visitor were a celebrity, or at least a client more prosperous than the ones who usually came to the office. "*From California.*" She underlined the words. "Your brother."

It was Leonard's sandy hair and the lemon V-neck under a brass-buttoned blazer that created the impression of yellow and gold. The wariness in Leonard's eyes when he came into the room didn't match the broad smile and outstretched arms. His arms dropped when he saw Seeley's frown. Leonard transferred a thick manila envelope to his left hand and reached the other across the desk. Seeley's single thought as he took his brother's hand was how quickly he could get him out of the office. He had already planned his day: reviewing client files, preparing for two court appearances in the early afternoon, visiting a jailed client who had been unable to make bail.

Rudy packed his toolbox and, going through the door, saluted Seeley with a promise that the radiator would be fine for at least another century. Seeley gestured for Leonard to take the client's chair across from him.

"It's nice to see you, Len, but I'm busy, and if you flew out here to pitch your case, you wasted your time."

"I left a message with your girl that I was coming."

The thought of Mrs. Rosziak being called a girl amused Seeley, but not enough to make him smile. "She told me."

Leonard had been leaving messages with Mrs. Rosziak for a week. His company, Vaxtek, had filed a lawsuit against St. Gall, the giant Swiss drug producer, for infringing the patent on Vaxtek's entry in the race for an AIDS vaccine. With the trial three weeks away, Vaxtek's lead lawyer suddenly died. Seeley understood that the company's future depended on winning the lawsuit, but he also knew that any one of hundreds of lawyers could try the case. Leonard was looking for something more.

"Why didn't you call back?"

"I didn't want to encourage you."

"Always looking out for your little brother." Leonard smiled around the words. "Still the college quarterback. A little thinner, maybe, but still a full head of hair." He patted the top of his own head where, Seeley guessed, the hair had been carefully barbered to hide a bald spot. The color, though Leonard's as a boy, now surely came from a bottle.

Leonard's eyes moved around the office, taking in the metal bookshelf stuffed with a worn, black-bound set of McKinney's New York Code, the half-dozen vintage prints of the Buffalo harbor that leaned against the bottom shelf waiting to be hung, two ancient file cabinets, and the window with its gray outlook.

Leonard was perspiring. Was he wearing a great deal of gold, or did it just seem that way? It struck Seeley that the charm on which Leonard survived as a boy had lost some of its polish.

"This is your kind of case, Mike. Little guy takes on big guy. David against Goliath. You get to be David's lawyer."

"Your little guy is a publicly held corporation. I don't represent corporations anymore. I sue them."

Leonard said, "In a single day, St. Gall makes more off its cure for erectile dysfunction than we make on all of our products in a year. They're a thousand times our size. In broad daylight they steal our biggest patent, and do you know what they say? I'm at a conference in Miami, giving a presentation, and when I finish, St. Gall's vice president for research—an MD, the guy with the same job as me—comes up and says, 'We're going to crush you.' That's it. He doesn't say hello, or I slept through your speech, or your patent's no good. Just, 'We're going to crush you.' Then he walks away."

Across the room, the radiator banged as if it had been struck by a hammer. The hiss of steam that followed had a rusty, boiled smell.

"You could take them down, Mike. I followed every one of your cases when you were in New York." He patted the hidden bald spot again. "You didn't know I did that, did you? I took subscriptions to a couple of legal newspapers just so I could keep track."

That wasn't the kind of thing Leonard would do.

"I clipped out the stories and gave them to Mom."

"That's the past, Len. I don't do that kind of case anymore." His brother's persistence was making Seeley repeat himself, and he resented it.

"I went out on a limb for you. I had to sell you to our general counsel, and then the two of us sold you to our chairman. He's counting on you."

"Then he's going to be disappointed."

"I thought that if I could make you understand how important this is to me, you'd take it."

Leonard removed a handkerchief from an inside pocket of his jacket and wiped his forehead. When he unbuttoned the jacket, Seeley saw that he had put on weight since the wedding nine years ago. Seeley felt a moment's sadness for Leonard and for his brother's dream of repairing a family that was broken from the start.

Seeley said, "I never saw you as a corporate type. I pictured you in a white coat, healing the sick."

"Or telling them they're going to die. I spent four years doing that. Half my patients in San Francisco were HIV positive. The other half already had AIDS. It's why I took the job at Vaxtek. What we have is as close as anyone's come to a real AIDS vaccine. Do you know how many lives this is going to save when we get our FDA approval? Here. Africa. Around the world. How many lawyers get the chance to defend a patent like this?"

"How did he die?" If he changed the subject, Seeley thought, Leonard might give up and leave. "The lawyer who was trying the case."

"Bob Pearsall was a fine lawyer. He was in your league, Mike. He orchestrated the case like Beethoven. A family man, too. Everyone loved him."

What Seeley heard was, a beloved family man, unlike Michael Seeley.

Leonard waited, and when Seeley didn't speak, said, "He threw himself in front of a train."

"How do you know that?"

"How else does a fifty-eight-year-old man end up dead on the railroad tracks?"

"Do you know why?"

"Who knows? His health was perfect—I know his doctor. He was an outdoors nut. Camping. Bird-watching."

"What do the police say?"

"What I said. Suicide. One of life's mysteries. Who knows what's beneath the surface?"

When Leonard read in the legal newspapers about Michael Seeley's courtroom triumphs, could he have imagined the dark corners that his older brother was navigating on his own precipitous slide? Trying big cases back to back, winning trials that he had no right to win, all the time retreating deeper into shadows that were visible only to him. It was no mystery to Seeley that despair could so engulf someone riding the crest of his career that he would decide to end his life.

"What time of day did it happen?"

"Early in the morning. Before dawn. Why would it matter?"

Seeley said, "I was wondering if anyone saw him do it." He could almost hear the wheels turn as Leonard calculated whether the lawyer's death might be the hook that would bring his brother to San Francisco. "Where did it happen?"

"A half hour south of San Francisco. He lived in the city. There weren't any witnesses."

"Why would he go that far from home? Was it close to a station?"

"Somewhere between stations, I think. Would it make any difference for you taking the case?"

"I was just wondering why someone would go so far out of his way to take his own life."

"Like I said, who knows what he was thinking? Look at the photographs in the obituaries. Half the time, a guy kills himself and in the picture he's got a big smile on his face."

"In Pearsall's photograph—was he smiling?"

"Like he was having the time of his life."

Leonard leaned forward and with his index finger pushed the thick manila envelope on the desk toward Seeley. "What can I say to get you to come to San Francisco?"

Two questions fought in Seeley's mind, one asking why he would let himself slip into his brother's plans for him, the other, why he wouldn't. When Leonard first called, Seeley turned him down at once, making the decision even before his brother could describe the lawsuit. After that, from the messages Mrs. Rosziak passed on to him, Seeley knew that, although the case was big, it could be tried in less than a month. For that short a time he could easily arrange continuances for his few cases in Buffalo. Wasn't this why he left his large corporate firm in New York City—not just to pick his clients and have no partners to answer to, but to be free to take cases of moral consequence. How many of his current cases came close to the heft of this one? Vaxtek was hardly the helpless victim that Leonard painted, but the multinational St. Gall was a war machine, and if Leonard was telling the truth his company's survival depended on this patent.

Seeley said, "I'm not admitted to practice in California." If Leonard was in fact following his career, he knew that his brother regularly tried cases outside New York State. A simple motion to the court, granted virtually as a matter of course, was all that it would take for him to appear.

"You've done it before—practiced in other states."

Seeley said, "Why are you smiling?"

"Because you're—"

"I didn't say I'd take the case."

Leonard lifted his hands, placating. "I was just going to say I'm glad you'll consider it. That's all I'm asking for. Willingness." He pressed his palms against his lap and rose. "Let me take you to lunch. Give me a chance to find your weak spot."

Leonard's confidence annoyed Seeley. "I have to be in court at two."

"My flight's at three-thirty. Is the Hatch still open?"

"The places on the lake close down after Labor Day."

"Let's go and look. It's worth a try."

The Hatch was little more than a lunch counter on a built-up part of the Lake Erie shore, locally famous for its grilled bologna sandwich—a massive slab of meat tucked into a hard roll along with a pile of grilled onions and a slathering of bright yellow mustard. Seeley remembered childhood outings when Leonard would inhale the sandwich as greedily as if it were a communion wafer.

Seeley again thought about motives—Leonard's in pursuing him, his in resisting—as he lifted the camel-hair coat from the stand by the anteroom door and handed it to his brother. He took a maroon scarf from the other hook and threw it around his neck. At her desk, the surface filled with a collection of creams and lotions, Mrs. Rosziak beamed. The office's exterior walls were the original lath and plaster, but the partition that divided Seeley's office from the receptionist's anteroom was thin wallboard, and from the officious bustle of papers Seeley knew that she had eavesdropped on the conversation. As soon as the door closed behind him, she would be on the phone to the airlines, checking on flights to San Francisco.

The sky had been a muddy gray since the beginning of October, and Buffalo wouldn't see the sun again for months. Over the past week, an errant snowflake or two would materialize out of the crisp air and as quickly disappear. Any day could bring the first snowfall. But more than the snow and bitter cold, it was the prospect of this unrelenting, joyless sky that defined the season for Seeley.

The cold slowed Leonard's chatter as they walked, and he seemed almost contemplative. The three or four blocks that radiated south and west from the Ellicott Square Building resembled a bustling downtown, but once the brothers passed the city's police headquarters, a squarish afterthought of dirty yellow brick, the office buildings gave way to a grim patchwork of low anonymous structures, weed-choked lots behind chain-link fences, and here and there a darkened church. The bundled-up pedestrians disappeared, and closer to the thruway overpass the downtown traffic dwindled to the occasional car cruising Erie Street, hip-hop blasting from behind rolled-up windows. In the shadow of the overpass, the temperature suddenly dropped ten degrees. Thruway traffic drummed the vaulting concrete.

Leonard huddled into his topcoat. "One thing I'll take to the grave with me is the bleakness of this place. I can be at the beach in the middle of July, but if I think about Buffalo, I feel the cold in my bones."

Seeley said, "Austerity has its virtues."

"And that's why you left New York? Not enough austerity? This city is falling apart, Mike. It's no place to live."

"You know as much about Buffalo as the tourists on their way to Niagara Falls." Apart from a terrifying childhood, he and Leonard had little in common. As a boy, Seeley was the explorer, taking his bicycle to every corner of the city while, other than on the occasional family outing, Leonard rarely strayed outside their dark immigrant neighborhood on Buffalo's far east side. "What California architect can match Louis Sullivan? H. H. Richardson? Daniel Burnham? Your idea of a boulevard is a street lined with strip malls."

Leonard said, "I'm surprised you came back. You're not the kind of person who comes back."

Even when you left home, Seeley finished his brother's thought. When Leonard Seeley Sr., the drunkard who was their father, stormed through the house in his underwear, railing at the boys and their mother, waving a loaded revolver and firing live rounds into the ceiling, it was Seeley who hurried his brother behind the living-room sofa or under the bed and faced his father alone. By the time Seeley was fifteen, and almost as heavy-framed and strong as he was today at forty-seven, it was inevitable that the confrontations would one day turn more violent. He couldn't explain this to Leonard at the time—he barely understood it himself—and for his twelve-year-old brother, Seeley's leaving must have seemed nothing less than a callous abandonment.

Leonard said, "And this is the law practice you dreamed about? Nickel-and-dime cases. A receptionist in a housedress. No offense, Mike, but your office is a dump."

Seeley said, "It's a work in progress." He had left New York and the big-stakes corporate cases that fueled the life of his law firm at the bottom of a long alcoholic slide that undid not only his practice but his marriage. The rent in the Ellicott Square Building was reasonable and Mrs. Rosziak worked for little. But the paying clients were few and, with the recent county budget cuts, court appointments, even for felony cases, barely paid for the paperwork. The irony was that it had been easier for Seeley to attract $100 million intellectual property cases in New York City than it was to get a client to sign up for a no-money civil rights case in Buffalo. More than once it occurred to him that the rivers of alcohol which had brought him to the bottom had also flattened his acuity the way water smooths a stone.

A single snowflake, as thin as a wisp of smoke, landed on Leonard's collar and, in the same instant that Seeley felt the impulse to brush it off, dissolved.

"You're in cold storage, Mike."

"It's a transition."

"Purgatory's a transition. This is a rut. No matter how good you are, you never hit better than the guy you're playing against." Leonard's sport had been tennis, Seeley's football; Seeley drilled hard passes over center while Leonard's every return had a topspin on it. "Who do you go up against here? Government lawyers counting the days until they retire? Kids two years out of law school?"

Was this was why Leonard had come—to rescue him? As a boy, Seeley protected his younger brother, then abandoned him. Now it was Leonard's turn to be the hero.

"You're afraid you've lost your edge, aren't you? That you're not up to handling a big case."

Leonard was here to save him, and to remind him that no one knows your fears better than a kid brother.

Two joggers in velour suits, mufflered against the cold, passed them on the asphalt path that traced the contours of the lake. The brothers continued past the Naval and Military Park where a guided missile cruiser, a destroyer, and a submarine as black as carbon clustered like tamed, implausible beasts. It had taken years for Seeley to observe the incongruity of it: none of these oceangoing vessels, now mothballed, would ever have seen action on Lake Erie.

Out on the lake, a few rubber-suited kids were hotdogging hydroplanes, oblivious to the cold, and a tugboat made its careful way through the small sailboats that flitted across the water. Farther out, a low unmoving barge could have been of a piece with the horizon, and on a deserted jetty was a Chinese-roofed pavilion, its former painted brilliance now a rusty gray. One of Seeley's aunts, or sometimes a neighbor family, would bring Leonard and him here for evening picnics as children, and the pavilion, its lively dance music audible on the shore, had embodied for Seeley all of the exotic possibilities of grown-up life. Years later, he learned that it was a weekend dance hall for workers from the Bethlehem Steel and Chevrolet plants in nearby Lackawanna.

Leonard was thinking about the past, too, because he said, "Was it really that bad for you?"

"I don't think about it much."

"Mom does." Leonard checked for a reaction, but Seeley's eyes were fixed on the horizon. Leonard's last Christmas card reported that their mother had moved to a retirement home in Palo Alto, not far from where Leonard and his wife lived in Atherton. Other than at Leonard's wedding, Seeley hadn't talked to her since he left home.

Leonard said, "She still feels sorry about your leaving."

If that was true, his mother had changed. "Feel" and "sorry" had never been part of her vocabulary.

Finally, Seeley said, "Some wounds can't heal."

"I'm a doctor, Mike. I like to think they can."

An iron railing and a narrow strip filled with concrete picnic tables separated the Hatch from the lake. The squat cinder-block structure was locked and shuttered, closed for the season. The tables were empty, except for one at which three ancient, animated black women, dressed as if for church, were holding on to their hats against the gusts coming off the lake, shooing the gulls that swooped over the tall thermos and sandwiches from their picnic basket.

The brothers leaned on the railing, looking out at the water. Seeley knew he had no good reason to ask, but he did anyway. "When does your case go to trial?"

"October twenty-sixth. Two weeks from today."

"You're kidding, right?" Except that, for all his smiles, Leonard rarely joked.

"The case is in shape to go to trial tomorrow. Our law firm has a whole team working on it. It's a purring engine, just waiting for you to shift it into drive."

"Who's your firm?"

"Heilbrun, Hardy."

Heilbrun, Hardy and Crockett had roots in post–gold rush San Francisco and was known for its strong litigation practice. Seeley said, "Pearsall must have had a second chair. Why can't he take over?"

Leonard didn't understand.

"A lieutenant. Another lawyer at the firm who helped him run the case."

"There's a young partner, Chris Palmieri. I'm sure he's competent, but he doesn't have the experience to take the lead on a case this size. We need someone with your instincts. Your judgment."

"San Francisco's a trial lawyer's town. There have to be two dozen lawyers there who could do the job."

"You don't know our general counsel. There are only four lawyers in town Ed Barnum thinks are any good. Two of them are already booked, and another's a prima donna who won't work with a team that some other lawyer put together. The fourth one is representing St. Gall."

Seeley turned his back to the lake. "I've handled big patent cases, but most of them were mechanical inventions. Railroad couplers. Dumpsters. Stents. I've done some electronics and chemicals, but vaccines are science." By the time biotech suits were first reaching the courts, Seeley's law practice in New York had already collapsed.

"Do you think Bob Pearsall knew anything about immunology? You can learn the science the same way he did. We wouldn't want you if we weren't certain you could do it. We have an expert witness from UCSF who can fill you in on anything you can't figure out for yourself. If you want, I'll tutor you."

A gull came in low past the railing, distracting Seeley. Ignoring the gloved, shooing hands of the three ladies, it snatched a crust from their table and continued on, out over the lake, all in a single sweep. A warning stenciled on the railing read DO NOT FEED THE BIRDS. To himself, Seeley filled in the punch line: BECAUSE THEY CAN FEED THEM-SELVES.

"When your lawyer, Pearsall, got hit by the train, Lenny—you didn't push him, did you?"

Seeley didn't know why he asked the question. Maybe it was Leonard's lecturing him about the poverty of his life in Buffalo, or maybe it was Leonard's having an answer for every excuse Seeley could give for not taking the case. Seeley knew the excuses were weak. Who was he angry at, Leonard or himself?

Leonard said, "You wouldn't even have to drop your practice here. The trial won't be more than three weeks. You don't seem particularly . . . busy."

"Why are you pushing so hard on this, Lenny?"

The look Leonard gave him could have been part of the landscape, it was that parched.

Seeley said, "This dream you have about the family. Let it go."

Leonard looked at his watch. It was a relief to Seeley that his brother now wanted their meeting to be over as much as he did.

"I left the envelope in your office. A paralegal at Heilbrun, Hardy put it together. Everything you need is there—witness list, deposition summaries, Chris Palmieri's number. Ed Barnum's number is there so you can work out the details—your fee, whatever you want. My number, in case you've lost it."

They walked to the short line of taxis on the corner where two sweeping marble slabs made up the city's Vietnam memorial.

"I didn't say I was going to take the case."

Leonard reached over and touched the lapel of Seeley's jacket. "Do you still have some good suits you can wear to court?"

Seeley's suit was from Brooks Brothers, like all his others, and no different from what he'd worn for years. He said, "I can remember when you were happy to wear the clothes I grew out of."

Leonard rested a hand on the open taxi door. "Another thing,

Mike. When you get to San Francisco, it's Leonard. Not Len or Lenny. Leonard."

Leonard Sr. would say the same to anyone who used the diminutive. With their father, though, it was a demand, not a request, and the sanction for disobeying was a vicious pummeling. Seeley wished his brother a safe trip home.

At the time it was built in 1896, a grand birthday cake of granite, brick, cast iron, and terra-cotta tile, the Ellicott Square Building was the largest building in the world. Daniel Burnham's masterpiece was located at the center of the city's downtown, not far from the Y where Seeley lived from time to time after moving out of his parents' house. As impressive as the building's ornately figured exterior was, it was the vast interior courtyard, rising to a glass-paneled dome ten stories above, that instantly captured the fifteen-year-old's imagination. The potted tropical greenery that filled every corner, the colorful storefronts opening onto the courtyard, couples at café tables, men rushing to significant business engagements—the space was a Turkish bazaar out of an adolescent's storybook. When Seeley left his New York firm to return to Buffalo, there was never a question about where he would set up his one-man practice.

The heavy fragrance of lavender greeted him in the anteroom. Mrs. Rosziak worked half days and Seeley hadn't expected to find her at her desk, massaging yet another lotion into her hands. She was long retired from a bookkeeping job at a car dealership in the suburbs, and her familiarity with the details of litigation papers and procedures suggested that the dealer had more than passing encounters with the legal process. She was bossy and her manner sometimes crowded Seeley, but she was smart and efficient and brought an order to the office that had escaped his own halfhearted efforts. Most important, she depended on him for nothing.

She nodded her head in the direction of the office, anticipating Seeley's question. "Whatever he did to the radiator, he didn't fix it. I was going to stick around until he's done."

Seeley looked into the office. The radiator cover was off and tilted against the wall. Hanging from a corner was a blue jacket with "Rudy" woven in red script beneath the letters "ESB." Work boots and white socks extended from behind the radiator.

"I thought he was finished."

"It was making noise when you were in there with your brother."

"What else did you hear?"

"I think you should take your brother's case."

Seeley took the chair next to her desk. "Why would I want to do that?"

"How long can a trial take—two weeks? Three?"

She hadn't only listened in on the conversation, and she hadn't just taken Leonard's telephone messages. Mrs. Rosziak and Leonard had talked; they had conspired. Leonard was a natural seducer, someone who would know exactly how to pluck the strings of this practical woman's sympathies.

"AIDS, San Francisco. Suing a big company. You could use the publicity, taking on a case like this."

"You know what the Chinese say, Mrs. Rosziak: The nail that sticks up is the one that gets hammered."

"I'm not talking about making a TV commercial. What can you lose if someone sticks a microphone in front of you? I bet your brother wouldn't run the other way."

Seeley understood her frustration. But if his legal career wasn't headed in the direction of redemption, she would have to accept that.

"Harold and I are grateful for what you did for him."

Mrs. Rosziak's cut-rate services were Seeley's reward for winning a modest settlement for her bachelor son who was beaten by three uniformed patrolmen in a downtown duplex where he had gone to meet a friend. A part-time housepainter with a rap sheet for getting into fights at the local 7-Eleven, Harold was white and overweight with a sour disposition, which meant there was nothing about him to win sympathy from the local press or political activists—or, Seeley feared, from a law-and-order jury. Seeley persuaded the city to settle the civil case when no one could explain how a handcuffed man managed to sustain a broken nose, six cracked teeth, and a gash across his forehead requiring twenty-four stitches without having his civil rights violated. The settlement was large enough to keep Harold in twelve-packs for years to come. Seeley also got the DA to drop the resisting charge.

"I'm sure all your clients are grateful to you for winning their cases. But if you started getting clients who could pay you what you're worth, would that violate your principles?"

As she spoke, Mrs. Rosziak smoothed more lotion onto her hands, one hand wringing the other. It occurred to Seeley how little he knew of women's habits.

"How many lawyers can say they're doing what they want to do?"

"Whatever dark cloud you have hanging over you, it's not going to go away by your hiding out here. Down at the cafeteria in the county building they say you're the mystery man. You lost a big case in California and someone died who shouldn't have."

Buffalo, though a city of 300,000, was in many ways a small town.

"Tell your friends they watch too many crime shows." He just wanted her to leave. "Thanks for sticking around," Seeley said. "I'll keep an eye on Rudy."

"You have a court date at two." She started collecting the bottles from the desktop to drop into her oversized purse. "You know, to look at the two of you, you wouldn't think you were brothers."

"Leonard takes after his mother." Fair, soft Leonard, always the victim. And, Seeley thought, I take after my father. Large and coarse-boned like him, but chased by my own demons.

"I wasn't just talking about your looks."

"I wasn't either," Seeley said.

"With the holidays coming, you want to be with your family." That had been Leonard's unspoken plea: Come for Thanksgiving. Christmas.

"I'm sure that whatever happened between the two of you, he's forgiven you." She was watching Seeley carefully to see if she had overstepped. When he didn't respond, she said, "Why else would he call? Why would he fly out here and beg you to take his case?"

To rescue me, Seeley remembered. Do the conditions of my life look so disastrous that I would need to be rescued? He put a laugh in his voice. "You should have been a trial lawyer."

"And you're not going to find the answers hanging around here.

You could use some sunshine. The one time Mr. Rosziak took me to San Francisco, everyone was smiling."

Sure, Seeley thought, even when they throw themselves in front of commuter trains.

"Are you going to go?"

Seeley said, "You'll be the first to know."

She gave him a resigned look and finished collecting her creams and lotions and keys from the desktop. Seeley had been married for eight years—and divorced for less than one—and he had been in relationships with women before and since, but the unfairness of the imbalance still galled him. As profound as his ignorance was of what they were thinking and of what drove them, women knew exactly where the buttons and levers were that could turn or twist him in any direction, giving him no choice but to resist. Not just Mrs. Rosziak; women.

He went into the office to get ready for court and to find out from Rudy what the spread was for the Bills game on Sunday.

TWO

Heilbrun, Hardy occupied five floors of an office tower on Battery Street, off the Embarcadero at the edge of the city's financial district. In the conference room adjoining the office that before his death had belonged to Robert Pearsall, Michael Seeley shifted comfortably in a leather-cushioned chair. Thirty-eight stories down, sailboats scudded across the sun-speckled bay and the Golden Gate Bridge was a cupid's bow across the water. To Seeley, the scene was as flat and trite as a picture-postcard.

Fat loose-leaf binders labeled *Vaxtek, Inc. v. Laboratories St. Gall, S.A.* filled the conference room's wall-to-wall shelves. The black binders held the deposition transcripts of witnesses who would be testifying at the trial; the red binders collected patents and scientific papers related to the development and efficacy of Vaxtek's discovery, AV/AS; and the blue binders contained legal research memos. The black and red binders outnumbered the blue binders fifty to one, confirming the trial lawyer's truth that in litigation facts count more than law.

The footwork for a case this size entails months of depositions, reviewing mountains of interrogatories, camping out in chilly warehouses to examine documents, researching the applicable law, and arguing motions in court. St. Gall had overstaffed the case the way giant companies usually do, with lawyers drawn from firms in Zurich, New York, and Chicago, as well as San Francisco. Pearsall, by contrast, had staffed the case leanly, with no more than two dozen lawyers, paralegals, document clerks, and typists. Although Seeley and Chris Palmieri, Pearsall's second chair, would be Vaxtek's only trial lawyers in the courtroom, the team from the office would feed them facts, research, and law as needed.

Running big cases had not been part of Seeley's dream when he set out for law school, but, like the conference room in the sky, responsibility for a case like this offered a reassuring familiarity. He was still uncertain about his motive for coming to San Francisco. It could have been to prove that Leonard, and Seeley's own deepest fears, were wrong, that his professional edge was as sharp as ever. Or perhaps it was no more complicated than escaping the onset of another gray Buffalo winter which, if it was like the last one, would hold a perfect mirror to his soul. In either case, coming to San Francisco was the only way he was going to find out.

Before leaving Buffalo, Seeley spent a week of eighteen-hour days working through the binders that Palmieri express-shipped to him, all the while arranging continuances for his cases in the state and county courts. By the end of the week, as he began to connect the jigsaw pieces of Vaxtek's case, Seeley had a good measure of Pearsall's qualities as a lawyer. He would not have assembled the case the same way, but neither could he find anything to fault in the shrewd care with which Pearsall had gathered his facts and witnesses.

Pearsall's secretary, assigned to Seeley for the duration of the trial, came into the conference room while he was rechecking the witness list to locate a misplaced deposition binder. Christina Hoff couldn't have been more than twenty-two or twenty-three, young to have worked for a partner as senior as Pearsall, and in her neat skirt and oxford shirt with the sleeves rolled up, was mostly elbows and knees. She had shown him around the firm's five floors of offices when he arrived earlier in the morning, and although she had touched up her makeup, it still failed to mask the bleariness in her eyes, from fatigue, Seeley thought, or grief.

"I just wanted to see if you needed anything." She had a nice voice.

"Should I call you Christina or Tina?"

"Tina. How'd you know?"

She was almost six feet tall, just an inch or two shorter than Seeley, and he guessed that, as a gawky adolescent, the shortened name might have helped inch her toward invisibility. There was a vulnerability about her that, along with the earnestness, seemed out of place amidst the hard polished surfaces of the conference room.

Seeley said, "Have you seen the deposition binder for Lily Warren?" Warren was a St. Gall vaccine researcher, and she should have been deposed along with the others on St. Gall's witness list. But the binder was missing. The last transcripts Seeley reviewed in Buffalo had traveled on the plane with him as freight and were now back on the conference-room shelf with the others. He had called Mrs. Rosziak, but she said he hadn't left any Vaxtek papers in the office.

"We have a sign-out system for them." Tina took a slender file from the credenza at the far end of the room and quickly paged through it. "No one's checked it out."

That meant nothing. Litigators, meticulous about observing court procedures, regularly overlook office protocol, particularly as they get close to trial.

"How long did you work for Mr. Pearsall?"

"It would have been one and a half years next month." Her fingers fluttered first at the file, then at a few stray hairs at her neck. She didn't seem to know what to do with her hands.

"Did he keep a trial notebook for his cases? You know, his thoughts about the case, the way he planned to try it." Sooner or later someone would return the binder containing the transcript of Warren's deposition, but if there was anything important in it that needed attention at trial, Pearsall would have mentioned it in his notes.

Tina shook her head. "He never said anything about a trial notebook."

A lawyer with Pearsall's experience would not prepare for a trial of this size without outlining his strategy, setting down the main points for his direct and cross-examinations, noting whether a deposition witness seemed overly forgetful or remembered events that had not occurred. By this point in his preparation, Pearsall also would have sketched out his theory of the case, the story interweaving fact and law that would, or so every lawyer hoped, give the jury no choice but to decide for his client.

"After Mr. Pearsall died, who moved his things out of the office?"

"I did. Any documents related to the case, I sent down to the workroom." One floor down, the workroom had been part of Tina's office tour that morning. The size of three conference rooms, it was where the paralegals working on the case had their cubicles. The storehouse of last resort, the workroom was also where the team kept the correspondence files and documents that were not in the conference room.

Tina said, "I gave the papers for his other cases to Chris."

Palmieri had evidently been Pearsall's lieutenant on other cases, not just *Vaxtek*. The young partner had been in the workroom talking with one of the paralegals when Tina and Seeley came through, and he seemed annoyed at the interruption when Tina stopped to introduce Seeley.

"What about his correspondence file?"

"I have it, but it's only letters."

"Briefs?"

"Mr. Pearsall didn't write them. Usually one of the associates did, or sometimes Chris. Mr. Pearsall marked them up, crossed things out and wrote comments on them. Sometimes he rewrote them. But someone in the pool typed them."

"Was anything else removed from his office?"

"I filled some boxes with personal things—you know, diplomas, family pictures." She remembered something and gave Seeley a small, tentative smile. "There were the steno pads he used to draw in. Sometimes, late in the afternoon, I'd come in and he'd be looking out the window with a stenographer's pad open, drawing."

Boats on the bay, Seeley imagined.

"I put them in the boxes along with the other stuff and had them delivered to Mrs. Pearsall."

Papers and belongings dispersed, Seeley thought, how long would it take Pearsall's partners to forget him completely? He was thinking about his own former partners in New York, some of whom, he was sure, were still working hard to forget him.

"Could you leave me her telephone number and address? And tell Chris I'd like to see him."

"She'll appreciate that," Tina said.

"What's that?"

"Mrs. Pearsall. Your visiting her. Paying your respects."

After Tina left, Seeley continued working down the list of witnesses, preparing for each a brief summary of his or her testimony, the first draft of his order of proof.

Other than the travel-poster view, the conference room was virtually identical to the dozens in which Seeley had spent a good part of his professional life, plotting strategy with his trial team, taking or defending depositions, negotiating settlements. Law firm interior designers all had the same shopping list: dark gleaming wood for the bookshelves and conference table, plump leather-and-steel chairs, chrome carafes and ice buckets to sit next to the telephone on the sleek credenza. On one off-white wall was a generic painting, neither offensive nor banal, that looked as if it had been ordered by the yard.

Seeley was near the end of the witness list when there was a knock at the open door and Chris Palmieri came in. In a firm where the younger lawyers went without ties and jackets, Palmieri wore a trimly cut gray suit, starched dress shirt, and silk tie. A pale pink pocket square was carefully folded to look like a casual afterthought, and his light hair was cropped close.

"Tina said you wanted to ask me about something."

Seeley had wondered about Palmieri's prickliness not only when Tina introduced them in the workroom but also in their telephone conversations the week before. He assumed it was the young partner's resentment at being passed over to run the case when Pearsall died. But it could also have been ill will toward any lawyer who tried to replace his mentor and, probably, friend.

"Do you know where the Warren deposition is?"

"Warren?"

Seeley slid the witness binder down the conference table to where Palmieri was. "Lily Warren. The scientist who St. Gall says invented AV/AS first." Vaxtek's case turned on its claim that one of its own scientists, Alan Steinhardt, invented AV/AS. If St. Gall could prove that Warren invented AV/AS first, it would win.

"Oh, her." He left the binder on the conference table, unopened. "We didn't depose her."

Seeley waited. Not to depose a key witness was unthinkable.

"St. Gall dropped her. It turns out she's a crackpot. They were afraid her testimony would backfire on them."

In a deposition, the deposing attorney—for Warren it would have been Pearsall or another Heilburn, Hardy lawyer—gets to ask the witness anything he wants. If, on questioning, Warren said something that hurt Vaxtek's position, the deposition transcript would be there to warn the lawyer against asking the same question at trial. However, if Warren said something that was favorable to Vaxtek and later contradicted herself at trial, Vaxtek could introduce the deposition transcript to impeach her testimony. Otherwise, no member of the jury would ever get to see the deposition. From Vaxtek's viewpoint deposing Warren was a no-lose proposition. Why, then, hadn't its lawyer done so?

"So there's no record of her story?"

"I think she talked to one of the newspapers, maybe the *Chronicle*, but after St. Gall dropped her, there wasn't a story." Palmieri tilted his chair back from the table and closed his eyes. "No deposition, either."

"Do you know how we can reach her?"

Palmieri was looking at him again, but made no effort to hide how boring he found this. "I think St. Gall fired her right after they cut her from the witness list."

"You'd think Pearsall would want to get her story down, for the record. She could still turn out to be a problem for us."

Palmieri flushed. He half rose and leaned over the table. "Warren was St. Gall's witness, not ours." For the first time, he looked squarely at Seeley. "Bob never missed an angle that mattered."

"I'm not saying he did. He may have been planning to depose her when he died." Seeley didn't mind that Palmieri idolized his mentor; he admired loyalty. But if they were going to work together, the young partner would have to calm down. "Did Pearsall seem any different before he died? Had he changed?"

Palmieri drew back. "You mean, what happened that he would throw himself in front of a train?" He started to answer his own question, but changed his mind. "Bob was as passionate about this case as he was about all his cases."

That told Seeley nothing. What looks like passion can in fact be nothing more than a driving fear of failure. In his last years in New York, even as he was winning most of his cases and favorably settling the others, Seeley could never shake the conviction that he had failed his clients by not obtaining a larger damage award or more generous settlement terms.

"Maybe Warren isn't a problem," Seeley said, "but I want to nail this down. If there's someone out there with a halfway legitimate claim that he—or she—made this invention before Steinhardt did, I need to know it before I put him on the stand. I'm seeing him this afternoon, but I want you to go through his lab notes and mark anything that could raise a question."

Again Palmieri reddened, and this time Seeley caught the meaning at once.

"This is too important for an associate. If it weren't important I wouldn't ask you to do it. I'll look at whatever you come up with tomorrow morning."

Palmieri pushed back to leave.

"Look, Chris, when Vaxtek asked me to take this case, I told them they should let the second chair run it, but they wouldn't listen."

"What did they say?"

"That you didn't have enough experience."

"And you believe that?"

"It wasn't my decision to make." Seeley remembered the missing trial notebook. "Did you get a look at Pearsall's trial notes?"

Palmieri said, "Look, Mr. Seeley—"

"The people I work with call me Mike. What about the notebook?"

"He didn't keep one."

"You're sure of that."

"I worked for Bob from the day I started here. Eleven years. He never kept a trial notebook. Maybe it's something New York lawyers do."

Seeley was growing tired of the barbs. "Did he talk to you about his theory of the case?"

"Sure. Except he didn't call it that. For him it was the 'path to victory.' We worked it out together."

"And what does it look like—Vaxtek's path to victory?"

"Nothing that would surprise you: Vaxtek's a small American company that has nothing going for it except the brilliance, creativity, and dedication of its handful of scientists and the protection of the American patent system. St. Gall is a multinational octopus that knows nothing about science, lacks any creative aptitude or spirit, and survives by poaching on the hard work of small companies like Vaxtek."

"And what's Emil Thorpe's 'path to victory' going to be?" Thorpe, St. Gall's lead trial counsel, was a legend of the San Francisco trial bar and, for major cases like this one, was at or near the top of the list of preferred counsel for any company that could afford him. Seeley guessed that Vaxtek would have hired Thorpe if St. Gall didn't already have him on retainer.

"Bob and I never got the chance to talk about it." Palmieri was at the conference-room door, looking down the corridor.

Seeley wondered if he was like this with everyone, or reserved his detachment for interlopers.

"You're running this case," Palmieri said, "so you get to choose your second chair. If you want to work with someone else, that's fine with me. I'll do everything I can to support him."

Seeley had reservations about Palmieri, but he knew that if he hesitated for a moment he would lose him. "You're the one I want sitting next to me at counsel's table."

"Thanks"—Palmieri turned back into the room—"but you'll have to talk to the client about my being at counsel's table."

"Why?"

"Ask Ed Barnum when you see him."

As Vaxtek's general counsel, Barnum was the person Seeley was supposed to answer to.

"It doesn't matter what Barnum says. I want you there."

"Just ask him." Palmieri started out the door.

"Have you taken care of the pro hac papers?" Because Seeley wasn't a member of the California bar he would have to be admitted, just for this trial, pro hac vice.

"One of the paralegals is taking care of it."

"Good. If I don't get admitted, you'll be sitting at counsel's table all by yourself."

For the first time since he met him, Palmieri smiled.

Seeley checked his watch. Vaxtek was in South San Francisco, a half-hour drive from downtown. On his way out, he stopped at Tina's desk. She wasn't there, but had left a message slip for him with Judy Pearsall's address and phone number on it.

Lawyers occupy forty-story office towers to inscribe their presence on the skyline. Scientists stay closer to the ground. Vaxtek's building in South San Francisco was two floors of glass and polished stone, one of dozens of such façades along the commercial boulevard that exited from the freeway. Signs on some of the buildings indicated biotech companies, but others were more mundane—a restaurant-supply firm, a marble-and-granite works, outlet stores for several big retail fashion brands. A temp agency was next door to Vaxtek. For a long stretch of boulevard, the grass was overgrown and clogged with windblown debris, but the lawn in front of Vaxtek's building was neatly trimmed. Low hedgerows separated the parking lot from the street.

Seeley signed in at the security desk and let the receptionist clip a laminated visitor's pass to his lapel. The sparely furnished lobby could have been an airport waiting area with its empty walls and industrial gray carpeting. A slender potted tree guarded two chairs and the carpet gave off a chemical smell as if it had been recently installed. There was no movement in the broad corridor on the other side of the glass double doors leading into the building's interior. After a while, an attractive middle-aged woman in jeans and a turtleneck sweater came through the doors to take Seeley to Leonard's office.

Seeley had heard somewhere that cramped quarters were common in biotech, even for senior executives, and Leonard's office was no larger than Seeley's in the Ellicott Square Building. The desk was a slab of blond wood, part of a combination cabinet-bookshelf. The desktop was empty and the bookshelf nearly so. A beefy man in chinos and polo shirt had propped himself against the desk's outer edge, facing the open door. His bulk partially obscured Leonard, who was sitting behind the desk. There was a tension in the room, as if the two had been arguing.

"Ed Barnum," Leonard said, introducing them. "Michael Seeley."

Barnum studied Seeley unhurriedly through aviator glasses and said nothing while Seeley walked around the office. The photographs were mostly of Leonard on vacation, posed against a ski slope or beaming under a baseball cap on a fishing charter. A woman was with him in the photographs. The view out the wall-sized window was of a succession of mud-brown hills, relieved in their monotony only by a bright ribbon of cheap-looking houses.

Leonard started to speak, but Barnum said, "Ray Crosetto sends his regards. So does Sandy Eyring." The two were well-known trial lawyers, Crosetto from Los Angeles and Eyring from Salt Lake City. Seeley had litigated against them in a couple of long trials before he left his New York firm. This was Barnum's way of letting Seeley know that he had asked around before agreeing to take him on as his new trial counsel.

"They said you're a good lawyer, but that you have an independent streak. I don't know if Leonard impressed on you how important this case is to our company."

"All my cases are important."

Barnum moved so that Seeley could no longer see Leonard's eyes. "I don't think you understand. St. Gall already has its product on the market. If we lose this patent the generics will flood the market with knockoffs inside of a year. We've sunk almost half a billion dollars into AV/AS. If you lose this case, we'll never see a dime of it."

From behind Barnum, Leonard said, "We have other drugs in the pipeline, Mike, but AV/AS is why Wall Street loves us."

Barnum's large pink face was just inches from Seeley's. "If you lose our case—"

"I'm not planning on losing your case," Seeley said. "But you're the ones who came looking for me to run this trial. If you changed your mind, now's the time to tell me."

Barnum paced the small room. He had a sluggish way of responding, and Seeley didn't know if the silence was deliberate or if he was just slow.

Leonard leaned back in his chair. "What Ed's saying is, we're betting the company on this case. If—"

Barnum said, "How does the case look to you?"

"Bob Pearsall did a good job putting it together."

"That's why I hired him. I don't want any loose ends."

When Seeley didn't respond, Leonard said, "There aren't any loose ends, are there?"

"There's Lily Warren."

Annoyance crossed Barnum's face. "Who?"

Leonard said, "The woman who thinks she invented AV/AS."

"Oh," Barnum said. "The crackpot."

It was what Palmieri had said, but Seeley thought it was more likely that the description came from Barnum.

Leonard said, "Why should that be a loose end?"

Seeley said, "Even if she's not on St. Gall's witness list, she could be a problem."

"There won't be a problem." Barnum's impassive face moved in front of Seeley so that he again lost eye contact with his brother. "St. Gall already stipulated that Alan Steinhardt invented the vaccine first."

The information stunned Seeley. When two companies flog their researchers around the clock to come up with a cure for the same disease, it is no accident when they arrive at virtually identical drugs, sometimes within days of each other. Often the margin of difference is so thin that, outside a courtroom, no one can say for sure which team produced the invention first. Alexander Graham Bell's competitor, Elisha Gray, got to the patent office on the same day as Bell, forcing Bell to prove that he invented the telephone first. And, like Bell, whoever reaches the finish line first not only gets the prize they were all competing for—a patent—but, with that patent, the power to stop anyone else, including the runner-up, from producing or selling the invention.

For St. Gall to concede priority was no less than for a country to cede half its territory to a despised foe, and without a shot being fired. There were still important issues to be litigated at trial, among them, whether the discovery of AV/AS was sufficiently novel to deserve a patent. But for St. Gall to stipulate that Vaxtek won the race even before the trial began was startling. It also bothered Seeley that, if he hadn't asked about Warren, Barnum might never have told him about the stipulation.

"Why did they concede priority?"

"Probably," Barnum said, "because we were first."

"If you were first, why are they already in the market, and you're just starting phase-three trials?"

"Resources," Leonard said. "They got a late start, but their money and connections got them through the FDA in half the time we could."

That still didn't explain St. Gall's stipulation of priority—particularly if they thought one of their employees made the discovery first. "What about Warren?"

"I told you," Barnum said, "she's a crackpot."

St. Gall's concession that Steinhardt invented AV/AS first would explain why only two lawyers, Thorpe for St. Gall and Pearsall for Vaxtek, were present when Thorpe deposed Steinhardt. For a witness this important, the deposition room would usually be crowded with lawyers and experts from both sides to advise the two principal lawyers as Thorpe pressed the scientist to pin down the exact moment that he completed the invention.

Barnum said, "Is that your only loose end?"

"So far," Seeley said. "I still have two more shelves of depositions to read."

"Did you get your pro hac motion granted?"

"Chris Palmieri's taking care of it."

Barnum gave him a doubtful look. "What do you think of him—Palmieri?"

"Why?" Seeley remembered Palmieri's uncertainty about joining him at counsel's table.

Barnum said, "It didn't seem to you that he's maybe . . . a little light in the loafers?"

As he spoke, Barnum moved and Seeley caught a warning look from Leonard. It took him a moment to understand what was on Barnum's mind. The trim build, the close-cropped hair, the pink pocket handkerchief.

Seeley said, "That's none of my business."

"If you want to win this case, you'll make it your business. The jury's impression of Vaxtek, what kind of company we are, is what they see when they look at counsel's table. I don't want them to see a queer sitting there."

Seeley decided not to ask Barnum how many jury cases he'd tried. "If you count up who a lot of the AIDS victims are in San Francisco, I'd think having him at counsel's table would be an advantage." It was a cheap tactical point that Seeley regretted as soon as he made it.

"There's a big difference between the San Francisco you read about in the newspapers and the San Francisco that sits on a federal jury."

Leonard had come around to the front of his desk. "Mike has a great track record with juries. I'm sure he'll pick his jurors carefully."

"Not before Ellen Farnsworth, he won't." Barnum's eyes hadn't moved from Seeley's. "She runs her own voir dire. She picks the jury."

Seeley reminded himself that he hadn't yet done his research on District Judge Ellen Farnsworth, who would preside at the trial.

Seeley said, "Palmieri's the only one on the team who knows where the evidence is. He has all the exhibits and depositions indexed and cross-indexed on his laptop. If he's not next to me, I can't cross-examine witnesses."

"Get someone else on the team up to speed."

"No. I already told Palmieri it's going to be him."

Barnum turned to Leonard. "Your brother's a real piece of work."

"I already told you, if you don't want me to run your trial, I can be on a plane tonight."

"I'm going to be up there with you at counsel's table."

Barnum would use his bulk, Seeley thought, to hide Palmieri from the jury. "That's fine," Seeley said. "So long as there's room."

"I might as well tell you now, I'm not like other GC's you've worked for. They see a trial coming and they run the other way. My first job out of law school was in the San Mateo County DA's office. I like going to trial and, when I get there, I keep a tight grip on the wheel."

Seeley said, "I'm sure you've taken the company's trial work to a new level."

After Barnum left, Leonard said, "You haven't lost it, have you? Your talent for pissing off a complete stranger."

"My only interest is in winning this case. But I'm not going to let your general counsel abuse my team."

Leonard unfolded and buttoned a sleeve of his sport shirt. "Ed's okay. Give him some room." He buttoned the other sleeve. "Steinhardt's waiting for you. I'll take you to his office."

Seeley followed Leonard down a carpeted corridor lined with rows of cubicles, only a few of them occupied.

"Once we scale up and go to market, every one of these desks is going to be busy with marketing and backup."

They crossed a wide corridor, and linoleum tile replaced the carpeting.

"What you told Ed, that there aren't any holes in the case—you're sure?"

Seeley said, "There's no case that isn't a crapshoot. Things come up. But, as far as I can see, you're in good shape."

Leonard put a hand on Seeley's arm, pleased. "We can crack open a bottle of champagne tonight."

Leonard's dismay when Seeley told him that he'd decided to stay at a hotel and not at his house in Atherton left Seeley no choice but to accept his brother's dinner invitation.

The walk to Steinhardt's office took them past laboratories that looked little different from the high-school labs at St. Boniface, where he and Leonard were students thirty years ago. There were more plastic containers than Seeley remembered, and there hadn't been laptops on the scarred black lab counters, but the shelves lined with reagent bottles were the same, as were the spaghetti of tubing that looped down from fat-globed flasks into glass beakers and the neatly labeled drawers, the refrigerator posted with black-and-yellow warnings, and the exhaust hood under which the class clown manufactured his stink bombs. White lab coats hung from hooks along the walls. Somehow science had made all these extraordinary leaps using little more than a high-school junior's lab tools.

Seeley said, "How closely did you monitor Steinhardt's work?"

Leonard heard the concern behind the question. "You just told me there weren't any loose ends." His good humor had evaporated.

"I want to make sure Warren isn't a problem."

Leonard took Seeley's arm and steered him around a jumbo-size doormat at the entrance to one of the labs. The white vinyl mat looked as sticky as flypaper and was clotted with shoe prints. "Real high tech," Leonard said. "It's to get the crud off your shoes when you go into the lab."

He continued on, holding Seeley's elbow. "I review Steinhardt's work as closely as anybody's. When he started getting results, I looked even more closely. But remember, Mike, I'm running seven fully staffed labs here."

"Did you review his lab notes?"

Leonard gave him a hard look. "You're not listening, Mike. If I get three or four hours at night to review the science we do here, I've had a good day. Most of my time I spend explaining to the FDA why AV/AS is safe and effective. Do you know how many trips I had to make to Washington to get us on track for phase-three trials? It's a full-time job just convincing our insurance companies that they're not going to be defending liability lawsuits the day after we go to market. The World Health Organization's watching us. So are the nonprofits. And there's the AIDS activists. You'll see them when you go to court."

"I'd think they'd be supporting you."

"This is the globalization crowd. They say we're going to use our patent to gouge the Africans on price. We haven't told them, but in sub-Sahara we're prepared to price AV/AS as low as fifteen dollars a dose."

"Why don't you tell them that? The AIDS group."

"Because then I would have to explain to the American AIDS groups how, if we can go to market for fifteen dollars in Kenya, we can justify charging two hundred fifty dollars here. They don't understand that fifteen dollars doesn't support this kind of research."

Seeley wondered where the money went. Vaxtek certainly wasn't spending it on offices or laboratories.

They were at the door to Steinhardt's office. Leonard, his voice suddenly thick, said, "You don't approve of how I do my job."

"It's none of my business, Len, to approve or disapprove."

"I'm looking forward to dinner tonight. Renata, too." Leonard tried to make it light, the charming host, but the emotion in his voice reminded Seeley that, whatever his accomplishments as a physician and executive, part of his brother was still the kid hiding out behind the living-room couch.

The open box of imported chocolates on the marble end table, not a single piece removed, told Seeley everything he needed to know about Alan Steinhardt. The chocolates, the translucent silk drapes, Oriental rugs, antique furniture, and the scale of the room—the office was at least five times the size of Leonard's—were all for show. Steinhardt might at one time have been a dedicated researcher, but the surroundings made Seeley wonder how much of his energy he now invested at the laboratory bench. A recording of a string quartet played from speakers hidden in the ceiling.

A side door opened and Steinhardt entered the room, moving quickly but gracefully. He tilted his head and arched an eyebrow in the direction of the room he had just left. The scientist's fingertips no more than grazed Seeley's hand. "You must forgive me. There are always crises in the lab and—I am sure someone told you—I must be on a plane to Paris in three hours. You will excuse me if I keep our meeting brief."

"That's up to you," Seeley said. "We can go over your testimony now or the day before trial."

"I don't think a rehearsal will be necessary."

Steinhardt's narrow face, the neatly trimmed goatee and mustache, the slicked-back gray hair were moderately forbidding. Seeley imagined that it was a long time since anyone had called him Al. Still, he thought that with some sandpapering he could turn the scientist into a passable witness—not lovable but authoritative. A juror who was looking for a father's approval might be persuaded to believe in him.

"As I said, it's your decision. But I'd recommend that you leave yourself some time. Right now, you're my lead witness and St. Gall is going to go after you on cross-examination like you're the only thing that stands between them and a profitable fourth quarter. If you're not prepared, you're going to wind up looking look like a real horse's ass." He stopped to make sure the scientist was paying attention. "The press loves it anytime a prominent witness gets torn apart on cross-examination."

"The press?"

"The local papers will be there. I'm sure the *Times* and *Wall Street Journal* will send stringers. This is a big case. *Time* should have someone. Maybe *Newsweek*."

Steinhardt's expression darkened. He shot the cuffs of his white lab coat. The coat looked like it had been custom-tailored to his small, trim frame. "What would I need to do?"

"You can start by telling me what AV/AS is about."

"If you need me to explain that to you, I'd say you're not the man to conduct my case."

"This isn't for me," Seeley said. "It's for the jury. You're the one who's going to have to explain the science to the jury."

Steinhardt considered that, and for a moment stood even more erect. He gestured to Seeley to take one of the antique upholstered chairs and took one himself. Then he checked his watch and appeared to change his mind. "I could give you the five-minute version, but I expect you will have questions. This will have to wait until I return from Paris. I promise you, it will be a brief trip."

"If I were you, I'd cancel the trip."

"You obviously fail to understand. I have an important paper to deliver. Not to go would be out of the question."

Seeley had worked with scientists before, and it was a puzzle to him why anyone would spend good money to put these people on airplanes and lodge them at luxury hotels just so they can read papers to each other that they could more conveniently and at less expense read at home. Steinhardt could at least answer one question for him. "What does AV/AS stand for?"

"AV is standard nomenclature. AIDSVAX. One of the first vaccines tested—this was years ago—was AIDSVAX B/B." Steinhardt's smug expression told Seeley he didn't have to ask what AS stood for.

"And this was entirely your work? No one else contributed to it?"

The scientist didn't flinch. "Of course it was. I have people working for me, assistants, but their work is entirely routine, on the order of cleaning test tubes. None of them does any science."

"And Lily Warren?"

Steinhardt frowned, and Seeley expected to hear yet again that Warren was a crackpot.

"She was my graduate student at the university."

"Which university is that?"

"UCSF. The University of California at San Francisco. I had my laboratory there before I brought it here. Surely, you've read my résumé."

"And Warren worked with you at UCSF."

"*For* me. We only did the most basic science there. Nothing patentable. In any event, she was little more than a glorified lab technician."

Seeley had seen Warren's résumé in the black witness binder, as he had Steinhardt's. She did her undergraduate work at Johns Hopkins, took her doctorate at Rockefeller University, and then got a postdoctoral fellowship in Steinhardt's lab at UCSF. She wasn't just his graduate student, as he said; she was a postdoc. And she was not someone who cleaned test tubes.

"You're aware, she's made a claim that she discovered AV/AS."

"I'm also aware that no one, not even St. Gall, has displayed the poor judgment to take her claim seriously."

Was it possible, Seeley wondered, for this man to utter one word

without condescension? In theory, Pearsall's decision to make Steinhardt Vaxtek's leadoff witness was correct. Corporations may pay for
the research and development that it takes to produce a new drug, but
jurors want to see the invention's human face, the scientist whose genius and tireless effort produced a miracle out of nothing more than
an idea and a few cell cultures. Seeley revised his estimate of Steinhardt's prospects as a witness. In the hands of a capable trial lawyer,
which he knew Thorpe was, arrogance like this was going to destroy
Steinhardt in the courtroom. If Seeley kept him as the leadoff witness,
the damage to Vaxtek's case could be irreparable.

Seeley said, "If new facts come out, St. Gall can still change its mind
and call Warren to testify. I need to know if we're going to find her
fingerprints anywhere near AV/AS."

"I can assure you, Lily Warren has no claim to my discovery."

Steinhardt saw that this didn't satisfy Seeley, and with a curt gesture
motioned him closer. "You are my lawyer, is that right? Anything I
tell you is confidential?"

"I'm Vaxtek's lawyer, not yours."

"A technicality." Steinhardt drew closer. The eyebrow arched; the
shoulders shrugged. "You are a man of the world, Mr. Seeley, so you
will understand. This young woman was infatuated with me. Such
things happen. She is attractive, and she can even be charming, but
of course it would have been unprofessional of me to take an interest.
This ridiculous claim of hers is revenge, nothing more."

"Did you tell Leonard about this? Ed Barnum?"

"What is there to tell? As I said, I don't want to injure her professional opportunities."

Even if Seeley believed Steinhardt, Warren must have had a sub-
stantial enough claim to the invention that St. Gall had not initially
thought her a crackpot. Why, then, had they so precipitously dropped
her and stipulated that Steinhardt was the sole inventor?

"Is there anyone else who might make a claim to AV/AS?" Seeley
knew the question would infuriate Steinhardt.

Steinhardt shook his head.

"You are the sole inventor of AV/AS?"

"Of course I am!" He came out of the chair, directly at Seeley, his face twisted in anger and dark from the rush of blood. "What have I been telling you?"

"You're going to have to learn to control your temper. I'm being gentle with you. Emil Thorpe, who will be cross-examining you, will not. The jury will turn against you if you can't do better than this. But, if it's a consolation, the press will love it."

"Have you looked at my laboratory notebooks?"

Seeley remembered asking Palmieri to review Steinhardt's notebooks.

Behind Steinhardt, a slender woman came into the office. Her suit and the way she wore the scarf knotted at her neck told Seeley that she was either European or had mastered the look. She had a small stack of euros in her hand and a slender envelope.

Steinhardt took the bills and envelope and placed them on the desk. The exchange was wordless, and she left.

"You need have no concerns, Mr. Seeley. I will return from Paris on Sunday, in ample time to testify. It is imperative that I be the one to explain my discovery to the court." He started to unbutton the starched white jacket. "You do have me on your list as the lead witness?"

Pearsall had already told him he was. The man's insecurity was as staggering as his ego.

"He left you instructions to put me first, didn't he—the poor fellow who jumped in front of the train?"

"Rest assured," Seeley said, "you will be the most important witness in the trial."

THREE

The last week before the start of a major trial rises and falls on ocean swells of crisis—exhibits to be readied, last-minute motions to be filed, witnesses to be prepared—but the crises had become predictable over the years, their resolution as inevitable as their occurrence, and Seeley had left to Palmieri all but the most daunting of them: where to place Alan Steinhardt in the lineup of witnesses and how to rebut any last-minute claims by Lily Warren.

Still, Seeley knew that he could make better use of his time than chasing down Highway 280 after a gold BMW with Leonard, one hand on the steering wheel, the other resting on the open window, deftly changing lanes three and four cars ahead of him. Leonard had promised that his house in Atherton was no more than twenty minutes from Vaxtek's offices and gave Seeley rapid-fire directions in the event they lost each other in traffic. "I want you to get to know Renata and me," Leonard said. "You've changed. I want to get to know you."

Seeley was curious about Renata. He had met her at the wedding nine years ago, a period when he was drunk or hungover most of the time, and he remembered only fragments of the event. He assumed that the attractive woman in the snapshots in Leonard's office was Renata, but could not connect these images to the young bride who had pressed her body into his as they moved across the ballroom floor.

One other memory stood out. As Seeley was leaving to find Leonard in the hotel kitchen, Renata took his hand and, rising to her toes, whispered a message—a goodbye? a wish? a secret?—in his ear. With the music and the noise, Seeley had not made out a single word. From Renata's expression when she drew away, he at once saw the urgency and consequence the words had for her, but he was too drunk or embarrassed, for her or for himself, to ask what she had said. From time to time in the years since, when he passed a wedding party or saw couples dancing, Seeley thought about what Renata's words might have been. He wondered, too, whether he owed her an apology for not fulfilling whatever promise his silence had implied.

Leonard's street in Atherton, when Seeley found it, was a well-shaded cul-de-sac. Magnolia, eucalyptus, and chestnut trees, even an improbable palm here and there, formed a canopy over the narrow lane, and there were no sidewalks. Seven-foot hedges hid lawns and houses from view. Seeley asked himself what these people were hiding and what they were hiding from. The evening had turned cool, and the dusty medicinal scent of eucalyptus filled the rental car.

Leonard's house was at the end of the lane and, from the boundaries marked by hedgerows, was more modest than its neighbors. Leonard was waiting at the front door.

"You didn't get lost, did you?" He already had a drink in his hand.

Seeley said, "I had your directions."

Leonard put an arm around Seeley's shoulder and led him through the hallway into a tall room that, with its floor-to-ceiling windows and encompassing skylight, could have been a solarium or a greenhouse. Set into the one wall that wasn't glass was a massive stonework fireplace. In front of it, a slender figure crouched, adjusting logs. Seeley had the sense of a cat ready to spring.

"Well, here he is," Leonard said. "The prodigal brother."

Renata turned to face them and, after staring at Seeley for a moment, gave him a hasty, vexed smile. "I'm just setting a fire." She struck a kitchen match against the stone, put it to the newspaper crumpled beneath the logs, and replaced the screen. The tinder flared behind her and, rising, she momentarily lost her balance. Seeley steadied her with the hand he had extended in greeting.

Leonard gave Renata an unhappy glance. He said, "I'll get the champagne."

Seeley took a chair close to the fire and Renata sank into the hassock beside it, drawing her knees up and positioning herself so she could watch both Seeley and the flames. Fair and fine-boned, with a mass of dark hair that fell to just below her shoulders, she was more glamorous than in the photos. Yet, even this close, Seeley had no memory of her as the bride on tiptoe with an urgent message.

She gave Seeley an amused, quizzical look and he wondered if she, too, was thinking of the whispered words.

"Time flies," she said, not inviting a reply. She seemed to be comfortable just sitting there, watching him and the fire.

A painting crowded with nude figures hung on the wall above the fireplace. The figures were clustered in groups of two and three and, although the faces were indistinct, the painter had artfully used the bodies to convey emotions of sadness, joy, repose. It was far from the bold abstract expressionism that Seeley liked, but there was a sensual quality in the painting that intrigued him.

Renata said, "With all the glass, there aren't many places to hang paintings."

"Who's the artist?"

"Do you like it?"

The way she asked told Seeley that the painting was hers. "Very much." The words surprised him.

"I stopped a few years ago. Orthopedic surgery doesn't leave much time for painting."

Seeley had thought she was a nurse.

She must have seen his confusion. "I was still a nurse when I met you." She gave him a crooked smile. "That's what a girl did in those days if her father was a doctor and her mother was a housewife. I met

Leonard at a med-school mixer at Stanford. There weren't enough women, so they brought in nurses. We discovered we were the only ones there from upstate New York. In California, that's enough of a reason for two people to get together."

"You're from Buffalo?"

She shifted on the hassock to see him better and tugged at her skirt, where it had ridden above her knees. "Schenectady."

"Like Daisy Miller."

"You don't look like a Henry James fan."

"I'm not," Seeley said. "I read it in a college lit class. What would a Henry James fan look like?"

"I don't know. Thin, neurotic. Maybe pale and bloated. Anyway, not like you."

In the kitchen a cork popped.

Even before he stopped drinking, wine was at the very bottom of Seeley's choices. He didn't mind the taste as much as he did the inefficiency, the whole bottles he had to consume just to come within striking distance of the oblivion that three or four quick tumblers of gin could deliver in far less time. It was more than a year since he'd had a drink; Buffalo's enveloping familiarity had cosseted him well. Sometimes he went whole weeks without thinking about alcohol. Other times he could think of nothing else. The smallest mishap could set off the craving. He successfully navigated a long and difficult disbarment proceeding that threatened to finish off what was left of his career without once having the urge to drink. But, a week later, a shoelace broke and all he could think of was alcohol. A sound, like ice being scooped into a glass, could set off the craving. Or a cork popping.

From the doorway Leonard gestured at the painting with the open champagne bottle. "It's good, isn't it?" He set the glasses on the coffee table, filled them, and handed them around, touching his glass to Seeley's—"A toast to Mike on his first visit to our home"—and then to Renata's. Renata tipped hers in Seeley's direction.

Leonard sipped at the champagne, his eyes on Renata.

Renata drained her glass and said to Seeley, "Which is more important to you, to be loved or to be admired?"

Leonard said, "What kind of question is that?"

Seeley laughed. "Why would I have to choose?"

"It's always a choice," Renata said.

Seeley said, "I never thought about it. What about you?"

Renata touched the empty champagne flute to her lips. "You really should think about it. You'd be amazed how much the answer will tell you about yourself."

"Right now," Leonard said, "I just want Mike thinking about one thing—our case. He told me there's no way we can lose."

"Then you're in good hands," Renata said.

"Drink up, Mike. Can I give you a tour of the house?"

Seeley was aware that Renata was watching him. "Thanks, I'm fine here."

Leonard said, "How do you like it? The house."

Seeley looked around. "It's a lot of glass."

"You mean, too much for earthquake country."

Seeley hadn't meant anything.

"The structure is cantilevered," Leonard said. "It was designed by a student of Frank Lloyd Wright. Do you want to hear a story? Wright designed a house a couple of miles from here on the Stanford campus, and when the owners discovered it was on top of the San Andreas fault they sent him a frantic letter. Do you know what Wright sent back? A telegram: 'I built the Imperial Hotel in Tokyo'! This house is the same. The earth would have to split to its core before you even heard a rattle."

Seeley knew nothing about earthquakes, and didn't know if this was the usual California bravado or just his brother's.

Leonard lifted the bottle and Seeley thought he was going to fill Renata's glass, but instead, he started back to the kitchen.

"Make the steaks rare," Renata called out. "Not dead." She turned back to Seeley and, so Leonard could hear, said, "My husband used to be a fine doctor, but he doesn't know the first thing about broiling meat."

She placed her empty glass on the coffee table next to Seeley's still-full one, asking his permission with a look before lifting his glass.

"To Henry James," she said.

It occurred to Seeley that Renata's drinks had started much earlier. The scariest drunken times for him were when he was aware that, behind his rigid mask of sanity, he was entirely out of control, and he wondered now if that was how it was for Renata. Stone-faced drunk, he had once called a sitting justice of the New York Supreme Court a toad. A pompous toad. Other lawyers had called the judge worse, but not to his face, and not in his chambers. The incident had brought him to the brink of being disbarred.

"Your mother says you've had an amazing career, that you win all your cases."

Seeley wondered how much Leonard told her about their life growing up.

"I didn't know she was keeping track."

"She subscribes to a couple of legal newspapers just so she can see how you're doing."

Seeley remembered Leonard telling it differently in Buffalo.

"Whenever there's something about you, she clips it out for Leonard. She's tremendously proud of you, but I don't think she knows how to tell you." She sipped at Seeley's champagne. "She told me about your wanderlust, how you left home when you were fifteen."

In the fireplace, a log dropped and sent up a shower of sparks.

"She says you're like mercury, that you're impossible to grab hold of. First you go to New York, then you go back to Buffalo. She didn't say it, but I got the impression she thinks you waited until she left Buffalo before you moved back."

"I moved to New York because I wanted more challenging cases. I went back to Buffalo because I wasn't getting the kind of cases I wanted."

Renata emptied Seeley's glass. "Did Leonard tell you she's in Mexico with her church group? Somebody dropped out at the last minute and she took her place. I think she was afraid you wouldn't want to see her."

This was the kind of conversation women liked, and Seeley lacked the words, the grammar, even the tone of voice it required. "I only came here to try a case." He took the empty glass from her and returned it to the end table next to him. "Did you know Robert Pearsall?"

She followed his lead as closely as if they were dancing. "Do you mean, do I think he killed himself?"

Now that Renata had turned on the hassock to be closer to him, Seeley found it unsettling, the way she looked directly in his eyes as she talked.

"When I was an intern, I tried out a psychiatry rotation for three months before I decided to be a real doctor. There's something about suicidal patients that you don't see in the others, even the most depressed ones. There's an emptiness in the back of their eyes that just goes on and on; there's nothing there."

"And Pearsall?"

"I don't know. I saw him at one or two parties up in the city and a couple down here. His wife's on the board of a private school we support. He always seemed agreeable, but you could see he had a deeper, serious side." Renata hesitated. "No," she decided, "there was always a light in his eyes. He didn't have that hopeless look."

Leonard called out that dinner was ready, and Seeley followed Renata into another glassed-in room. Three chairs were at the end of a long table, and place mats, silver, and glasses were set in front of them along with a green salad and an open bottle of Bordeaux. The steak, sliced and heaped on a platter, was rare.

Renata said, "We were just talking about Bob Pearsall."

Leonard filled no more than a quarter of Renata's glass, and Seeley waved him away from his.

"You only had a glass of champagne."

"I have an early meeting tomorrow." Leonard didn't need to know that the meeting was with Pearsall's widow, to search through the lawyer's belongings for a missing trial notebook, anymore than he needed to know that it was Renata, not he, who had emptied the glass. It was a reflex. He did the same when they were boys, protecting Leonard from anything that he thought might upset him.

"One of the mysteries of the human soul," Leonard said. "You look at a guy like Pearsall, he seems fine to you, but you never know what's going on inside."

Seeley said, "I was thinking about what you said, that the train was between stations when it hit him."

Renata sipped at her wine. "Why should that be important?"

Leonard said, "You wouldn't believe my brother's sense of humor. When I went to see him in Buffalo, he asked me if I pushed him. Pearsall."

"Mike!" Renata laughed.

It was the first time she had spoken his name, and the sudden cry felt as intimate as if she had slipped her hand into his.

Leonard speared a slice of steak from the platter. "Do you remember Billy Elrod, Mike?" He turned back to Renata. "Elrod was a little hoodlum when we were at St. Boniface, the kind of kid who picked wings off flies. Once, for a week, he went around the playground with what looked like one of those narrow jars olives come in, but filled with a clear liquid. Billy swore it was nitroglycerin, and that if anyone told the teachers, he would drop it and blow the place up. We all knew he was lying, but still with Billy you couldn't be sure. Finally, my brother here—how old were you, Mike, ten? eleven?—goes up to him and says, 'Hey Billy, look up in the sky, there's a blimp' "—Leonard pantomimed, pointing to the ceiling—"and when Billy looks up, Mike pokes a finger into his stomach"—again, Leonard playacted the move—"so that he drops the bottle and it smashes on the ground. Of course it was just water. That's my brother's sense of humor."

After that, the conversation drifted to Renata's childhood in Schenectady, the challenges women faced as surgeons, stories about her work as one of the Stanford football team's on-field physicians, and the constant temptation to go into research.

Leonard said to Seeley, "You didn't tell me how your meeting went with Alan Steinhardt. He's impressive, isn't he?"

"A legend."

"Alan can be a pain in the ass, but he's a talented scientist. He's won all the prizes but the Nobel. It takes vision like his to design this kind of research, much less pull it off. Looking for an AIDS vaccine is like running a marathon, except no one gives you a map to show you the route or even how far it is to the finish line. If there is a finish line."

Seeley said, "I need to be sure he got there all by himself, and that Lily Warren wasn't there, too."

Renata said, "Lily Warren?"

Leonard said, "Twenty years ago, if you asked the best scientists in the business how long it would take to come up with a true AIDS vaccine, they would have told you ten years. If you asked them the same question today, do you know what they'd say?"

"Ten years?"

"AV/AS is as close to a real vaccine as anyone's come. It's not like a polio vaccine or measles. It's not a cure-all. Maybe in ten years we'll have a vaccine that is. But right now, this is the best chance we have to save some of these people. Maybe the only chance."

Renata said, "Do I know Lily Warren?"

"She worked with Alan at UC, before he came to work for us."

"And," Seeley said, "she went to work for St. Gall."

Leonard said, "St. Gall used her to try to get a look at Alan's notebooks. They were desperate to develop a vaccine strategy. From the papers he was publishing, they knew he was onto something, but they didn't know what."

Seeley said, "How do you know that?"

"One of our security guards found her in Steinhardt's lab alone, after hours." Leonard chewed as he spoke. "You've got a first-year lawyer on your team who made herself a hero on this. She was going through our security reports, trying to find evidence of industrial espionage, and when she sees Warren's name on one of the reports, she remembers that she was on St. Gall's witness list. That's why St. Gall agreed to stipulate priority. They'd look like common thieves if this came out at the trial."

First the stipulation, then the story behind it. What else was his client hiding from him? "Barnum never told me this."

Renata had finished her dinner and risen from her place. "I have an early day tomorrow. Like Mike."

Leonard didn't hear her. "Ed must have forgotten. Our deal with St. Gall is, they don't challenge our priority, we don't go to the DA with criminal charges."

Seeley felt Renata standing behind him. "Did Pearsall know about the deal?"

"Of course he did," Leonard said. "He brokered it."

"I'm glad you came," Renata said. "Are we going to see you tomorrow night?"

Before he could answer, Leonard said, "Joel Warshaw's having a benefit at his house tomorrow night. He wants to meet you."

Warshaw was Vaxtek's chairman, but that didn't mean Seeley had to go to parties at his house. "I have a trial to prepare for."

"Joel doesn't come in to the office," Leonard said. "He works out of his house. This is a command performance."

All the more reason not to go, Seeley thought.

"Come by here first," Renata said. "We'll drive over together. It's just a few blocks."

"I'll see if I have the time."

Leonard gave Renata a brusque wave as she left the room. Seeley, although she hadn't touched him, had for the briefest moment the sensation of her hands lifting from his shoulders.

In the living room, Leonard added a log to the fire and took the easy chair across from Seeley. "This is how it used to be, isn't it? The Seeley boys, taking care of each other."

Seeley didn't know if it was the wine, or the end of what was probably a long day, or maybe just the person Leonard had become—altogether, they hadn't spent more than two or three days with each other in the thirty-two years since Seeley left home—but it occurred to him, as it had in Buffalo, that there was an unquenchable hole at the center of his brother's life, one that for some reason he thought he could fill with family.

"I haven't done anything for you yet. The thought of Steinhardt on the witness stand bothers me."

"And that's the only problem?"

"I don't like how broad your patent is." Patents can be broad or narrow, and Steinhardt's patent claimed that the invention included not only AV/AS but anything remotely similar to it. The problem was that, like any other target, the broader a patent is, the easier it is for a competitor like St. Gall to shoot it down in court.

"That wasn't Steinhardt's call. The decision came from the top. Joel."

Warshaw was an entrepreneur, not a scientist. From a business-magazine cover story two or three years ago, Seeley knew that Warshaw had founded and sold three software companies in less than ten years. Six months before the dot-com crash, when everyone in Silicon Valley, including the guys who waxed and detailed his car, were making paper fortunes on Internet stocks, Warshaw sold all of his holdings and with part of the proceeds bought a controlling stake in Vaxtek. At the time, it was a struggling biotech with neither products nor patents, but with huge sums of money invested in research. Seven years later, with a small portfolio of patents and two drugs on the market that hadn't yet paid back their investment, Warshaw was beginning to realize that the human immune system is considerably more resistant to quick fixes than computer software.

"Joel wants a blocking position. That way, if anyone comes within a mile of us, we can nail them. If all we got out of our investment in AV/AS was a patent that anyone could copy if they made the smallest change, we'd be out of business anyway. Joel knows it's a crapshoot. All or nothing."

"What happens if you lose?"

"We have other drugs, but, like I told you, this is the big one. If we lose, the stock will take a hit and Joel will sell the company to one of the big pharmas—Pfizer, Merck, Novartis—for whatever he can get."

"And if you win, you'll be rich."

"Believe it or not, Mike, this isn't about money. If we wanted to get rich we wouldn't have gone after a vaccine. The real money is in therapies. A therapy you can sell to a patient week after week, but a vaccine's a onetime deal. How many times did you have to get vaccinated for measles? Once, and that was it. Even the flu vaccine you get only once a year. Clinical trials take longer for vaccines than for therapies. It's almost impossible to get insurance. Give a therapy to a patient who's sick and he's so grateful he won't complain about the side effects. But give a vaccine to someone who's healthy and ten years later, if he has a stomachache, you've got a lawsuit on your hands."

The glass room had grown dark, illuminated only by the fire, but neither man moved to switch on a light. For some time they sat by the fire without speaking. Backlit by the moon, the branches of a giant oak that overhung the skylight danced in shadows across the polished floor.

On the other side of the glass wall, moonlit figures moved slowly through the yard, first together, then apart.

Leonard turned to see what Seeley was watching. "Deer," he said. "They love the roses. By the end of the summer, there's nothing left to eat in the hills, so they come down to forage. Two, three in the morning, you'll find them walking down the middle of Atherton Avenue like they owned it."

Seeley was thinking about how much Leonard had and hadn't changed from the twelve-year-old boy he'd left at their parents' house. Somewhere he had acquired a passion to help people—even in the 1980s, no one went to medical school to get rich—and Seeley admired him for this. Still, Leonard was someone who never stopped manipulating people and events to get what he wanted.

Leonard said, "Do you ever think about the distance we've come? Leroy Avenue. St. Boniface. The Broadway Market with the old ladies in their babushkas. And here we are, talking about a drug that could save tens of millions of lives, two professional men, one who had a hand in creating it, the other who will be defending it in court."

"The American dream," Seeley said.

Leonard was almost invisible in the dark. When he rose, Seeley saw the reflection of firelight in his eyes. He came around to behind Seeley's chair. "You were what—fifteen? That's a long time ago." As he spoke, Leonard kneaded his brother's shoulders with soft fingers. "If we're going to win," Leonard said, "we need to be working as a team, everyone pulling in the same direction."

Seeley wondered what else his brother and Barnum had forgotten to tell him. "Sure," he said. "That would be helpful."

FOUR

Seeley let down the window as he backed out of Leonard's driveway and the fragrance of eucalyptus again flooded into the car. Turning onto the main road back to the freeway, he thought about how careful Leonard had been with his money long before he haggled with caterers over wedding bills. Into a pickle jar in their bedroom closet he would deposit the coins and dollar bills that he collected from babysitting neighbors' children and making deliveries for the corner grocer. The squat barrel-shaped jar left the closet only when the little miser carried it to the grocer's to change coins for bills. So when, one night, Lenny offered Seeley every penny, the entire hoard, in return for his help, Seeley knew that his easily panicked brother had this time truly blundered into catastrophe.

It was late spring, Buffalo's most temperate season, and close to the end of the school year. Even in this sullen neighborhood of Poles, Litvaks, Ukrainians, and Germans, where resentments hung in the sooty haze like a premonition of bloodshed, neighbors called to each other from stoops and porches, and modest hopes stirred around the patchy, sprouting flower gardens. Seeley, freshly showered from baseball practice, was stretched out on his narrow bed, reading for a history final. Lenny was at his end of the card table that the boys used for a desk, fidgeting with a pencil and pretending at his math homework. In the half hour since Seeley came in Lenny did little more than trace the wood-grain pattern of the vinyl tabletop with a fingertip while a foot tap-danced ceaselessly below. Seeley was certain his brother was going to piss his pants.

It was the dinner hour, as their mother called it, even though the hour itself usually stretched past six o'clock to eight or nine or even later. The rule, cast in iron, was that no one in the Seeley household sat down to dinner before Leonard Seeley Sr. returned from the Germania Social Club to take his place at the head of the kitchen table. Seeley's father had for years worked on the assembly line at the Chevrolet plant, but, with the plant's closing, the after-work detours to the Germania grew longer, filled with complaints to anyone who would listen that the new job, assembling windshield-wiper arms at the Trico plant, was depleting his soul. The Germania was in truth little more than a bar with stuffed stag heads and the heraldry of several German provinces on the wall, and on those rare evenings when her own boiling resentments had sufficiently stoked Mrs. Seeley's courage—a church group meeting might have required that the family eat at a normal hour—she would send Mike to the Germania to collect his father. The stale reek of smoke and beer permeated Seeley's memories of those trips, memories painted in the varnished yellow light of the place.

Once, when Seeley was eleven or twelve and searching through his parents' bureau and closet shelves for some key to the secrets that enshrouded the small, dark house, he found in a compartment of the carved box on top of his father's dresser a stamped brass key, the kind that might open a suitcase or a trunk, and a worn envelope with a translucent plastic sleeve the size of a postcard inside. The stained sleeve contained what Seeley took to be an identity card or visa. It bore the photograph of a man in his twenties—from the steep jaw and violent eyes, it was unmistakably his father—and the name Lothar Seelig.

That mystery lasted until, exhausted by her sons' pestering, their mother explained that, when he arrived in the United States in 1951, Lothar Seelig had changed his name to Leonard Seeley to escape the vilification of Germans that persisted even after the end of the war; indeed, during the war her own family had sloughed off the name Hüber to become the Hubbells. The explanation only complicated Seeley's sense of his father's depravity. Even on his finest days, pitching a shutout or topping the school record for completed passes, Seeley's awareness of himself was that he was the son not of one but of two madmen. Alone in their room, he and Lenny entertained each other by walking about like cartoon monsters, legs goose-stepping, arms straight out and frozen into sticks, abjuring the other to beware, I am *Lo*thar! I *vill* seize you and destroy you!

Beneath the card table, both of Lenny's feet tapped wildly.

"For God's sake, Lenny, go to the bathroom if you have to pee."

"You've got to help me, Mike." The boy's lips trembled. "I'll give you all the money in my jar. You have to get rid of this for me."

It was past eight o'clock and the aroma of roasting meat loaf had long since faded. Their mother had by now settled in the parlor and was knitting or mending or on the telephone with one of her church friends. In the empty kitchen, the television played at top volume; on the evidence of the laugh track, it was tuned to a sitcom. In Seeley's memory, the television, though rarely watched, was always on. It could have been a fifth member of the family and the only one to be counted on for laughter.

From under the card table, Lenny brought out a package and pushed it toward his brother. When Seeley only looked at it, Lenny, his voice breaking, said, "Take it, Mike. You have to get rid of it."

The bag, an ordinary lunch sack creased and stained from his brother's handling, was tightly wrapped around the object inside, and the moment Seeley lifted the package, he knew from its heft what it was.

"Does he know you took it?"

Lenny shook his head.

"Put it back before he gets home."

"I can't." Beads of moisture had formed on his brother's upper lip. He nodded at the bag. His voice pleaded. "Open it."

Seeley emptied the bag onto his bed. In the bright light of the room, the chrome barrel glowed. The gun was intact and the cartridges, which Lenny had emptied from the cylinder, were all there. Then Seeley saw why Lenny couldn't return the revolver to their father's dresser. The barrel was scarred and abraded as if it had been smashed repeatedly with a rock. Black shards of some hard material clung to the cartridges. Seeley looked at the gun's grip. Lenny's efforts with the rock had shattered the cast black rubber. The larger pieces he had reattached with rubber bands and what looked like library paste.

"What were you trying to do?"

His brother emerged from the closet with the half-full pickle jar. "I wanted to break it and throw it down the sewer."

"Why didn't you?"

"I was afraid. Take the money, Mike! You have to help me."

"I don't want the money."

"You *have* to get rid of it!"

It seemed to Seeley that he had shielded his brother since before Lenny learned to walk. A table lamp shattered on the floor; grape juice splashed from a glass onto a lace curtain. It was easier for Seeley to absorb the blame than to have to listen to his brother suffer a beating. The logic that the role of the strong was to protect the weak was too ingrained for him to do anything else.

Their father could arrive home at any moment, and Seeley thought quickly. Outside it was still twilight, but even if the neighbors had gone indoors, the narrow backyard offered no place to hide the revolver. There was the shadowy cellar where his father spent long hours drinking beer and working on his hunting and fishing gear, but the man knew every spider-filled corner of the place. The living and dining rooms were hopeless: the sofa and easy chairs, covered in stiff transparent plastic, were impenetrable and the cabinet with his mother's collection of porcelain figurines was mostly glass. The two small dressers in the boys' bedroom were the first place his father would look. It seemed odd to Seeley that a house so filled with secrets should have no hiding places.

When Seeley opened the pickle jar and carefully shook the coins and currency onto the table, Lenny misunderstood. "Take the jar! You can have it! Just get rid of the thing."

On his own forays into his father's bedroom dresser, Seeley had examined the revolver more than once. The grip and barrel now appeared shorter than he remembered and, in proportion, the trigger and guard seemed outsized. For some reason that difference now underlined for him the weapon's deadliness. He pressed open the cylinder and, one by one, inserted the six loose cartridges. The smooth movement of the parts—he clicked the cylinder back into place—was almost comforting in its precision. He quickly covered the bottom of the jar with coins, placed the revolver in the center of them, and distributed the rest of the money on top of the revolver and around it. He screwed the top back onto the jar. The hard black crumbs he gathered up from the bedcover and dropped in the wastebasket. Even if his father were to look there, drunk as he was by the time he got home, he would not connect them to the missing gun.

Seeley examined the jar doubtfully before returning it to its corner in the closet. "I'll toss the gun on the way to school tomorrow."

Leonard said, "Maybe he won't come home."

That was Lenny's fantasy, but Seeley had his own version. At around this time, the U.S. Justice Department had, with much publicity, initiated the prosecution in nearby Cleveland of a local autoworker for fraudulently entering the United States by failing to disclose that he had been an SS guard at two death camps in Poland. It took no great forensic leap for Seeley at age fifteen to conclude that Lothar Seelig, also an autoworker and immigrant, had himself been an SS camp guard. Surely the brass key in the carved box would unlock the incriminating evidence. Some day, like the Cleveland autoworker, neither of the two madmen would come home.

One sitcom had replaced another on the television when a slamming door shook the house. Seeley's mother must have come into the kitchen because his father's ancient tirade—booming, guttural, unforgiving—at once filled the house with its complaint of incompetence and betrayal. The sentences had lost their meaning long ago, but the fact that the words were English, not German, momentarily loosened the knot in Seeley's chest. When his father spoke English in the house it meant that his drinking had not yet carried him past the last edge of decency.

There was a heavy *thump* and again the house shook. From experience Seeley knew that his father had hurled his mother against a kitchen wall. Her cry, if there was one, was drowned out by the television. There was a long silence before the heavy boots staggered down the hallway, stopping at the closed door behind which, Seeley on his bed, and his brother at the card table, neither breathed nor moved. The boots turned into his parents' bedroom. Lenny started shaking and, though terrified himself, Seeley was astonished to discover, peeking out from some corner of his soul, a spark of mischief, even glee, anticipating the roar of the dumb, confounded beast pawing through drawers of socks and underwear as he discovered that his gun was gone.

Drawers opened and slammed shut in the next room. Then, as Seeley expected, the mindless, anguished cry. *Wo ist es? Wo ist mein Revolver?*

The door to the boys' room swung open—the latch had broken long ago—and the massive figure, all chest and gut, a blown-up version of the boys' pantomime monster, crashed in, the fierce stench of alcohol filling the room. He didn't ask who took the gun. The bloodshot eyes that locked onto Seeley's announced that he had already been convicted of the theft. Wordlessly, his father ripped one drawer from Seeley's dresser, then another, flinging them against the wall, before doing the same with Lenny's. Ignoring Lenny, who was frozen in his chair, the monster seized the table by a leg and flipped it over. The wastebasket he flung against the wall, and black shards rained onto the floor. He didn't notice. Pants, shirts, jackets, followed by wire hangers flew from the closet. The monster again turned to Seeley and glared at him.

To avoid the man's gaze, Seeley's eyes swept past Lenny and the telltale closet, fixing instead on the ocean scene that decorated the wallpaper directly opposite his bed. Against a blue-gray ground, horizontal rows of sailboats alternated with parallel rows of tropical fish. The sailboats were the same color as the sea, separated only by a thin red outline tracing the hull and sails. The fish bore pastel stripes and spots, but, like the boats, were otherwise transparent to the color of the sea. Improbably, the fish were three times the size of the boats. The gross unreality of the images cemented Seeley's terror, as if the fact that these forms could coexist on his bedroom wall implied that any horror was possible; that in this house so rarely visited by outsiders, anything could happen.

The gun's discovery was inevitable. The house was too small, the furnishings too spare, to hide the smallest secret from this man's rage. As if reading Seeley's thoughts, his father swung back to the closet. For an instant, the single swiping movement of his boot threw him off balance but then shoes and sneakers hurtled out into the room. Bracing his bulk against the doorframe, the man leaned in and brought out the squat glass jar. He twisted off the top and, staggering across the room, emptied the jar onto the foot of Seeley's bed. Propped against a pillow, Seeley watched as his father pawed the coins, quickly uncovering the revolver. With a startling delicacy, he lifted the gun so that the scarred weapon rested in his palms. He could have been cradling some small injured animal.

Beneath Seeley's pounding blood, the perverse sense of mischief peered out again, taunting. "Lothar," Seeley said. His brother shot him a horror-stricken look. "Lothar," Seeley said again.

If his father heard, he gave no sign. "This is what you do to my possessions?" The voice was heavy with alcohol. "The man, your father, who gives you a roof over your head"—he aimed a thick finger at the ceiling—"who feeds you? This is how you repay me? *Dolchstoss!* A stab in the back!"

A hand the size of a baseball mitt seized Seeley by the collar, and he didn't resist when it pulled him off the bed, onto his feet. The flat of his father's hand propelled him through the door and down the narrow hallway, the tip of the gun barrel pressed into Seeley's skull, behind his ear. Lenny remained in the bedroom. He must have pried himself from the chair because Seeley heard the door close behind him.

"Let's show your mother what a fine son she bore me." They were in the kitchen, where Seeley's mother had pressed herself against the far wall. On the stove, a pot boiled violently and the evening's dinner congealed in its roasting pan. As in the bedroom, the raw smell of alcohol filled the room. Formerly a student of wallpaper, Seeley now fixed on the television screen. Two women his mother's age, but elegantly dressed, chatted amiably in a stage-set living room.

Seeley's father cried out, "This is the ungrateful monster you raised." He threw Seeley against the stove, and brought the gun up to his son's face. "How are you going to pay for this?"

Inside Seeley, the snapping spark of mischief fired into something fiercer. His eyes, when they caught his father's, turned defiant. As if on its own, his hand shot up and in a single swift motion seized the gun. His other hand, clenched into a fist, swung forward, striking his father high on the jaw. Seeley felt every whisker of the man's stubble. As much from surprise as from the force of the blow, his father dropped in an instant, crashing onto the floor, blood pouring from his nose. Seeley stood above the sprawling figure, his heart throbbing, but holding the gun steady with both hands. He aimed at his father's heaving chest. He heard himself shouting, "What kind of bully threatens his family with a gun? What kind of coward does that?"

His mother came away from the wall. "Don't speak to your father like that! You put that gun away and apologize this instant!"

Squeeze the trigger. Seeley remembered the seasoned cop instructing the rookie on some long-ago television show. *Squeeze, don't pull.* Seeley tasted metal at the back of his mouth. Carefully, he pointed the barrel toward where he imagined his father's heart would be, inches from the center of the man's chest. He squeezed. Nothing happened; the trigger, locked by the safety catch, failed to move.

His father lay motionless, the blood now bubbling from his nostrils onto the linoleum. Seeley's mother came away from the wall and grabbed for the gun, but Seeley caught her by the wrist, wrenching her arm upward. An emotion flashed behind her pale eyes that Seeley had seen before, but this time he didn't know whether it was hatred or fear, or both. Her look stopped him as he realized what he had almost done. He had never struck his father before nor stopped his mother from striking him. Now everything had changed in an instant. He felt an overwhelming sense of relief, but at the same time he understood that when he seized the gun, when he aimed it at his father, when he squeezed the trigger, he had crossed a line from which retreat was impossible. He could no longer live in his parents' house.

Seeley took a room that night at the downtown Y and for the remaining years of high school he shuttled between the Y and couches
in his teammates' homes. He went to a local college, Canisius, on an
athletic scholarship and took a one-room apartment off Chippewa
Street, downtown, supporting himself from tutoring and part-time
jobs. He did much the same when he left Buffalo to go to Harvard
for law school.

Thirty-two years later, adjusting the heater vent in the rental car,
Seeley could still smell the fumes of his father's alcohol. He could
see the four of them frozen there in that afflicted house: him holding his mother's arm aloft, as if he were a referee and she a victorious
prizefighter, her mouth locked in a wordless *O*; his father, sprawled
dumbstruck and bleeding on the linoleum floor; and Lenny hiding in
the bedroom behind the closed door. It was at that moment, Seeley
now remembered, that a burst of canned laughter exploded from the
television.

FIVE

There is a quality to the early-morning light in San Francisco that exists in no other American city. The sun shines silver, burnishing the stone-and-brick buildings like a jeweler's cloth. Only in the medieval quarters of old European cities had Seeley seen such light. Stepping out from the lobby of the Huntington Hotel, he smelled the scent of freshly mown grass from the pocket park across California Street at the top of Nob Hill. A large bird crowed, and the breeze coming off the bay mixed the smells of roasting coffee and just-baked sourdough.

Seeley hadn't taken a break from work for years; he had no talents as a tourist and idleness made him irritable. Setting out for the halfmile walk to the Pearsall apartment on Vallejo Street on a morning like this was all the vacation he needed. The day bristled with challenge, starting with Alan Steinhardt. Seeley had no reason to believe that St. Gall's corporate ethics were above industrial espionage, but he was also certain that neither Leonard nor Ed Barnum had told him the full story of Lily Warren's visit to Steinhardt's lab or her attempted theft of Vaxtek secrets. If, as Leonard said, Vaxtek had caught her alone in Steinhardt's lab, it would have given the story to the DA and to the press—unless Vaxtek, too, had something to hide.

What mattered right now was that St. Gall had dropped Warren as a witness, which meant that Seeley was free to talk to her without going through the company's lawyers. Before leaving the hotel he left a message for Tina to track down her telephone number.

The apartment building on Vallejo was 1930s Art Deco, and the lobby, which rose two stories, was all dark wood and ceramic tile the color of sandstone. The plaster molding along the ceiling was a maze of geometric designs, Aztec in their complexity. Seeley could imagine that, however warm it was outside, the temperature in the lobby never rose above the coolness of a crypt.

At a small desk, the doorman was talking to a girl. Seeley asked for the Pearsall apartment and, before the man could respond, the girl stuck out her hand.

"You're Mr. Seeley. I'm Lucy Pearsall, Robert Pearsall's daughter."

In her green plaid school uniform, the girl was of a piece with the morning: clear-eyed, bright, self-assured. Seeley studied her face for some sign of loss or sorrow, but other than the dark shadows beneath her eyes, found none. Her hand, when Seeley took it, was small, but the grip was a young athlete's.

"My mother's expecting you. She said you're taking over Dad's case." It was a statement of fact. Nothing in her voice or her expression asked for sympathy. "He was the best."

"That's what I heard."

When she leaned to look around him, Seeley turned. A yellow school bus had pulled into the space in front of the building.

"It was good to meet you," she said. She swung a bulky backpack over her shoulder and was out the door.

"Impressive kid," Seeley said to the doorman.

"Mr. Pearsall's death was a knockout blow to the two of them." The man was looking at the school bus, not at Seeley. "But neither of them would ever let you know that."

"Could you call up to the apartment for me?"

The man talked as he dialed the apartment telephone. "Since it happened, Mrs. Pearsall won't let her wait for the bus outside. She has to stay in here with me."

A voice came on the line, and after the man finished and put down the receiver he said, "You know, Mr. Pearsall wasn't the kind of man that can be replaced."

Seeley thought to tell him that he hadn't come courting. Instead, he just thanked the man for his help.

"Apartment 7C," the man said. "Second door on your right."

When Judy Pearsall opened the door, Seeley saw at once the source of Lucy's forthright manner. The face was handsome and intelligent and her handshake was the same firm grip as her daughter's. She wore no makeup and had made no effort to disguise the lines at the corners of her dark green eyes. Her sandy hair was cut short.

She led Seeley into a living room with tall French windows looking out onto Vallejo Street, busy with traffic. Seeley declined the offer of coffee and quickly surveyed the room. Any one of the three upholstered chairs could have been Robert Pearsall's favorite. He took a corner of the couch.

"I'm sorry about your loss."

"I appreciate your saying that." The words were measured, honest. "But, you know, I can't just curl up into a hole and disappear. It wouldn't do my daughter any good, or me."

Already, Seeley thought, she had fallen into the habit of the singular. *My* daughter.

"I know you're here to look through Bob's papers, and I'm glad to help you if I can. But, so you don't waste your time, you need to know right off, Bob did not kill himself."

When Seeley called to arrange the visit, he told her that he was looking for her husband's trial notebook. There was no reason for her to connect this to an interest in how Pearsall died other than that, in Judy's mind right now, everything was connected to his death.

"What do the police say?"

"You don't look like a foolish man, Mr. Seeley, and if you're a trial lawyer, you've had experience with the police. The police don't know anything. Whatever they say is speculation. It's not factual and it's not based on anything they know about Bob."

The framed black-and-white photograph on the side table showed an erect, wide-shouldered man in corduroys and denim shirt. Binoculars were slung around his neck and he was smiling broadly. In the distance behind him, the face of a mountain was split by a waterfall of astonishing height. Pearsall looked like a grown-up Eagle Scout.

"Did he seem different in any way?"

"That's what the police asked."

"What did you tell them?"

"He seemed to be distracted the last few days before he died."

"He was in the middle of preparing for a trial," Seeley said. "That wouldn't be unusual."

"I've seen Bob through a lot of trials, and that was one of the things about him: he was totally devoted to his cases, but only in the office or the courtroom. He never brought any of that home."

"And you didn't ask what was bothering him."

"Just once. He said he couldn't tell me, and left it at that. I knew better than to ask him what he meant."

Judy didn't strike Seeley as a woman who could be dismissed so easily.

She must have seen the skepticism in his expression. "You have to understand, Mr. Seeley, in our marriage there was nothing we couldn't talk about, unless it was something to do with one of Bob's cases. Bob would never betray a client's confidence."

"So you think that, whatever was bothering him, it was something a client wouldn't want anyone to know about."

"That would seem logical, wouldn't it?"

Sure it would, Seeley thought, along with at least a dozen other possibilities, including a romance gone wrong, money problems, blackmail, drugs, or—he looked again at the good-humored face in the photograph—a despair so profound that living no longer made sense.

"Is it possible that someone made a threat on his life?"

"I don't know. The police asked me that. It's not the kind of thing Bob would talk about. Bob was old school. He thought his role was to protect his family, not worry us."

And, if Seeley's speculation about despair was right, to put on an upbeat front even though he was in the most excruciating pain.

"And that's why you won't let your daughter wait for the school bus outside the building. To protect her."

For the first time, there was a break in Judy's composure. She pressed her hands against the arms of the chair, as if to steady herself. "A mother's instinct," she said. "Bob and I didn't marry until late. He was already in his forties when Lucy was born. She's our only child." She rose. "This isn't helping with why you're here. I'm sure you have a great deal to do. Let me show you Bob's study. It's where I had them put the boxes from the office."

There was a desk in Pearsall's study with a computer and what looked like a fax machine. Books filled the ceiling-high shelves and spilled over into piles on the floor. Seeley examined a precarious stack of hardcover and paperbound books next to a well-used leather recliner. Kant's *Critique of Practical Reason* was on top, works by Hume, Rawls, and Dworkin beneath it.

"Moral philosophy," Judy said. "It was one of Bob's hobbies. Like his bird pictures."

Seeley hadn't noticed the photographs of brilliantly colored birds lining the one wall where the bookshelves were only chest-high. The pictures were close-ups taken with a long lens and, Seeley imagined, a great deal of patience. They weren't snapshots, either. Each photograph was carefully composed and captured its subject in full light. Pearsall had an artist's eye.

On the floor, at the foot of the shelves, were six corrugated bankers boxes with HEILBRUN, HARDY AND CROCKETT printed in large block letters.

Judy said, "Those are the boxes the firm sent over." She hadn't moved from the doorway. "Let me know if you need anything."

Seeley cleared away a corner of a library table piled with still more philosophy books and set a box on it. On top, when he opened the box, was a silver-framed photograph of a younger Lucy in a bathing suit, seated on her mother's lap. Beneath this was a stack of framed certificates acknowledging Pearsall's good work for the Legal Aid

Society, the Sierra Club, the San Francisco Bar Association, and a prisoners' rights project in Chicago. A certificate attesting to Pearsall's membership in the exclusive American College of Trial Lawyers reminded Seeley that he had misplaced his own certificate long ago.

He tried the next box, and the one next to it, but found nothing that looked like a trial notebook. In the fourth box, under a layer of bar association magazines, he found the stenographer's pads that Tina said she saw Pearsall sketch in at the end of the day. Seeley selected one. "U.S. v. Gunnison Oil, 6-17-95," was printed neatly in ink on the cardboard cover, and when Seeley flipped the cover open, the notebook gave off the musty smell of old paper. He riffled quickly through the pages. The book was a sketch pad filled with pen-and-ink drawings. Some were of sailboats on the bay, as Seeley expected, but most were portraits.

Seeley turned back to the first page. On it was a quick but accurate sketch of a well-known university economist who often testified as an expert witness in antitrust cases. Then Seeley saw that in the same loose hand as the drawings—which is why he had at first missed it—Pearsall had written, "Theory of lost profits has hole in it. Check with WFB." Paging through the rest of the notebook, Seeley found similar comments, no more than a line or two on any sheet, written with a flourish beneath, or sometimes above, the portraits.

From Pearsall's comments, and two or three recognizable faces, Seeley immediately understood what the steno pads were. *U.S. v. Gunnison Oil* was an antitrust case in the 1990s and here, in pictures of the key players—witnesses, lawyers, the trial judge—Seeley had found Pearsall's trial notebook. Pearsall knew what any experienced trial lawyer knows: not only are cases mostly about facts, but no facts are more important than the personalities of the participants. Instead of writing extensive notes to himself, Pearsall did what an artist would naturally do: he captured the theory of his case, and the holes in his adversary's, by sketching the cast of characters, with the strengths and weaknesses of each.

Seeley rapidly searched through the fifth box, but the notebooks went no further than the 1990s. Only at the bottom of the sixth box—Tina had organized the notebooks in reverse chronological order—did he find three stenographer's pads labeled "Vaxtek v. St. Gall." The notebooks, like the one from the Gunnison case years earlier, had a few street scenes, but were mostly filled with pen-and-ink sketches of witnesses and lawyers. Some pages had only pictures, not words. On one of these, a cluster of three spare drawings of Chris Palmieri revealed not only the young lawyer's intensity but also Pearsall's affection for him. On most of the pages, a sentence or two connected the portrait to a concern Pearsall had about the case or a trial tactic he planned to employ. A head-and-shoulders portrait of a woman in judicial robes took up a whole page in the second Vaxtek notebook. *Ellen Farnsworth. First patent trial. Build legal foundation slowly.* Pearsall probably made the drawing during an early hearing. The information on the judge, and the caution, though mundane, would be useful.

Several drawings of St. Gall's lead lawyer, Emil Thorpe, were scattered through the second notebook. From the changing backgrounds, it appeared that Pearsall had sketched the portraits over a period of time, each portrait depicting Thorpe's dissolute features from a different angle. Studying the images, it struck Seeley that Pearsall had made them with the same patience and keen observation as he had given to his bird photographs. The trial lawyer made the sketches to gain a purchase on his adversary, to understand what was driving him.

The early pages of the last notebook were sketches of St. Gall witnesses made during their depositions, each with a name and a comment or two beneath the portrait. Following these was a single portrait of Alan Steinhardt. With features that verged on caricature, Pearsall had uncannily captured the man's self-absorption and pomposity. An eyebrow arched ever so slightly; the ears elongated and sharpened; the goateed chin pointed, as in life. For a glancing moment, the portrait could have been of the devil himself. The words beneath were, *What else is A.S. hiding?*

Seeley put the steno pads back in their boxes, keeping out the three that Pearsall had filled with sketches for the Vaxtek trial, and returned the boxes to their place beneath the shelves. He sank into the worn leather recliner and leafed through each of the Vaxtek notebooks a second time, looking . . . looking for what? Easing the recliner back, he stared for several minutes at the ceiling, letting his thoughts slide back and forth past each other. Then he pulled the chair upright and looked again at the bird portraits on the wall and the volumes of moral philosophy stacked on the floor and on the table. His right hand resting on the small stack of stenographer's pads, like a witness about to take an oath, Seeley decided that Pearsall had not taken his own life.

In the hallway he called out to Judy to let her know he was leaving.

She came into the front hall, drying her hands on a towel. "Did you find what you were looking for?"

"I think so," Seeley said. "Your husband had a fine eye." He showed her one of the notebooks. "Would it be all right if I borrowed these for a few days?"

"Of course," she said. "Bob called them his doodles." Then the firm voice wavered, as if something had caught in her throat. "I know it's not why you came, but did you find anything that shows the police are wrong?"

"All I found were the drawings," he said. How many times had he lifted others' hopes to the level of his own, only to let them down? He was not going to make that mistake with Judy Pearsall. "I'll let you know if I come across anything."

The doorman was still at his desk in the lobby, and Seeley found a corner out of earshot where he could call the office. Tina picked up the phone on the first ring.

"Did you find Lily Warren?" If, as Pearsall's question indicated, Steinhardt was hiding something, perhaps his postdoc—and alleged thief—could tell him what it was.

"I checked the local directories. There's a number in Half Moon Bay, but it's unlisted."

"Chris said there was something about her in the *Chronicle* a few weeks ago. See if you can find it. Maybe there's a copy in the workroom. Call the reporter and ask him if he has her phone number."

"Do you really think he'll give it to me?"

"No. Just see if he kept the number. And ask Boyd McKee to meet me in my office in half an hour." McKee was the Heilbrun, Hardy lawyer who had prepared the application for the AV/AS patent. Like Warren, he might be able to explain to Seeley how Steinhardt made his scientific breakthroughs.

Pearsall's office, which had been assigned to Seeley along with the conference room, was one floor up from Heilbrun, Hardy's reception area. Seeley passed his key card over the electronic lock to the double door and took the private corridor to Tina's cubicle. She handed him an orange message slip.

"It's the number for the reporter at the *Chronicle*."

"Did he have a number for Lily Warren?"

"He's a she. A business reporter."

Seeley looked at the slip. The reporter's name was Gail Odum.

"She said you can call her at the paper anytime before six."

Seeley folded the slip and put it in his pocket. "What about Boyd?"

Tina said, "He gave me the impression that he's too important to wait in your office." The crease in her brow told Seeley that McKee wasn't one of her favorite lawyers at the firm. "He said if I let him know when you got in, he'd see if he could find the time."

Patent lawyers had only lately ascended to the aristocracy of the American bar. Trained not just as lawyers but as scientists or engineers, and working in small, specialized firms, they were at one time rudely dismissed by corporate lawyers as gearheads in green eyeshades, not good enough at science to be scientists, nor sufficiently talented at law to be real lawyers. Then came the intellectual property revolution of the 1990s, and these onetime outcasts found themselves ruling the last vibrant corner of the American economy. Suddenly every large corporate firm like Heilbrun, Hardy had to have its own patent department. But even as the corporate firms sought mergers with the few remaining intellectual property boutiques, the tensions between the two camps persisted.

Seeley dialed the number Tina gave him for Gail Odum at the *Chronicle*. Her voice was hard to hear over the clatter of keyboards in the background.

She said, "Lily Warren is a source. I told your secretary, I can't give out a source's telephone number."

"I understand that," Seeley said, "but could you call her yourself and give her my number so she can decide if she wants to talk with me?"

"What would I tell her you want to talk about?"

Seeley knew the reporter would jump at any suggestion that a question had arisen about the trial. Still, he had to give her a reason to call Warren, and he had to give Warren a reason to call him.

"Tell her it's about a stipulation in the Vaxtek case."

"What stipulation?"

"Just tell her. She'll understand."

"And if I get her to talk to you, you'll give me the story?"

"I don't know that there is a story."

"But if there is."

"I can't promise that."

The reporter was silent and the sounds of the newsroom took over. After a few seconds, Seeley said, "Look, if it turns out there's a story, and if I can give it to you, it's yours. You'll have an exclusive."

There was another silence. Then Odum said, "I'll tell her you want to talk to her."

Seeley gave her his phone number and hung up. He opened the loose-leaf litigation binder he was assembling—a trial notebook, but without pen-and-ink sketches—and removed the copy of U.S. Patent No. 7,804,438: Human Neutralizing Monoclonal Antibodies to Human Immunodeficiency Virus.

Like all patents, this one had begun as a somewhat different document, an application for a patent prepared by McKee. If the application followed the usual back and forth between the patent lawyer and the examiner in the U.S. Patent Office, it had been revised repeatedly, the patent examiner insisting that McKee narrow the scope of Vaxtek's claimed invention and McKee pushing back to get the broadest scope of protection he could. After two years of these negotiations, the patent that finally issued was a compromise that described precisely how far Vaxtek could go to stop anyone else from making, using, or selling a vaccine that was similar to AV/AS, much as the legal description for a parcel of real property describes the landowner's boundaries.

Seeley was reading the patent for what felt like the hundredth time when McKee walked in.

"Hey," McKee said, "what's up?"

Seeley guessed that the patent lawyer was in his early thirties, which meant that he couldn't have been a Heilbrun, Hardy partner for more than a year or two. The tennis shirt and jeans showed off a good build; McKee's head was shaved as smooth as a billiard ball.

Seeley said, "I wanted to talk to you about the Steinhardt patent."

McKee dropped into the chair across from Seeley and draped his arms over the sides, looking as exhausted by the effort if he had just finished a triathlon. In another minute, Seeley thought, he's going to put his feet up on the desk so I can admire the soles of his high-tech running shoes.

"AV/AS?" It was a groan, not a question. "You don't think it's a little late?"

Instantly Seeley felt older than forty-seven, and the day that had started so brilliantly turned dark. "Did you review Steinhardt's lab notebooks before you filed the application?"

"Of course I did." He sat up straighter. "It's standard procedure."

"Was there anything to indicate that Steinhardt wasn't the sole inventor?"

"He's the only one who signed off on the entries."

A bench scientist's lab notebooks should be as precise and complete as a ship's log. If some of the hardest-fought patent battles are over which of two competing inventors completed the invention first, it is the laboratory notebooks, witnessed by others in the lab who understood the invention, that provide the indelible fingerprints of priority.

Seeley said, "When was the last time you wrote an application for a drug patent that named only one inventor?"

Mousetraps have sole inventors, as do windshield wipers and railroad couplers. But pharmaceutical inventions are team efforts. Seeley had reviewed dozens of other patents to see how close their subject matter was to AV/AS, and none listed fewer than three inventors.

McKee said, "When was the last time you wrote a patent application?"

The accent and attitude were pure New York—Brooklyn, Seeley guessed. McKee knew as well as he did that trial lawyers litigate patents, they don't apply for them. "Did you interview any of Steinhardt's witnesses?"

McKee swiped a hand over his shaved head as if he were brushing back a lock of hair. He was sitting erect now and the other hand was a fist in his lap. "Steinhardt said I didn't have to. He said he was the one signing the inventorship oath, so it wasn't my problem. Even if I pushed him on it, he'd never let me talk to his witnesses."

"Vaxtek's your client, not Steinhardt." Seeley made no effort to hide his anger. "You realize, because you let Steinhardt intimidate you, St. Gall can destroy our inventorship claim."

"You try talking to Steinhardt."

"He's in Paris. That's why I'm talking to you."

Business clients will roll right over their lawyers anytime it suits their purposes. But evidently no one had taught McKee that the lawyer's first duty is not to let that happen.

McKee shifted in the chair and worked his jaw. "You know, there's a difference between patents on monoclonal antibodies and patents on garbage trucks."

"What's that supposed to mean?"

"This isn't Brigadier Dumpster."

Seeley hadn't thought about *Brigadier Dumpster Corp. v. DeSimone and Sons, Inc.* for years. It was the first patent case he had tried after making partner at his old Buffalo law firm, and remarkably the case had made its way into two or three law school texts. Brigadier, a Decatur, Illinois, manufacturer of truck bodies and rigs, owned a patent on the front-end loader that garbage trucks use to lift dumpsters over the truck cab to empty their contents into the hopper in the rear. Brigadier had sued its way around the country, bullying payments from manufacturers that lacked the money or the will to fight its patent in court. The DeSimones, who owned a foundry and fabrication plant in Cheektowaga, outside of Buffalo, had little cash to defend a lawsuit, but when Brigadier sued them for copying their rig, they refused to settle and hired Seeley to defend them.

McKee said, "The guy who taught me patents at NYU thought your defense was brilliant."

It was clear from McKee's tone that he didn't agree.

"And you?"

"Too much flash, not enough engineering."

The DeSimones needed more than engineering to win their case. Vincent DeSimone, the older of the two sons, stood with Seeley in the company's parking lot in a driving sleet storm, discussing the litigation to come. The two were watching the company's foreman test a DeSimone rig before it was crated for delivery. Vincent shook his head in disgust at the thought that the government had granted a patent to a device as simple as the Brigadier lift. He said, "My three-year-old could've dreamed one of these up with his Tinkertoys."

Seeley watched the rig's two robot-like arms swing out over the cab, grab a bin, jerk it up, then toss it in a single, smooth arc backward over the cab. "A catapult," he said to Vincent.

"A what?"

"The rig is nothing more than a catapult."

After that, preparation for trial was straightforward. Seeley paged through histories of ancient siege weaponry until he found a diagram for a thirteenth-century advance on the catapult, called a trebuchet, that bore a striking resemblance to the Brigadier rig. He hired a local cabinetmaker to build tabletop operating models of both the trebuchet and the rig. "Just the rig," Seeley told the man. "I don't want the jury to see the truck chassis or body. And make the two models exactly the same size."

"Do you want me to paint them?"

"Sure," Seeley said. "Paint them whatever color Brigadier paints their rigs."

Three months later, Seeley's entire case consisted of demonstrating to the jury how the structure and operation of the Brigadier rig was virtually identical to that of its medieval predecessor. It took the jurors less than an hour to return with a verdict that the Brigadier patent was invalid. Most of that time they spent composing a note to the judge asking whether there was some way he could order Brigadier to reimburse the DeSimones for their attorney's fees and the expense of building the two models.

Seeley said to McKee, "Are there any catapults out there that St. Gall's going to surprise us with?"

Vaxtek wanted the broadest patent it could get, and McKee had accomplished that by referring in his patent application to only a few prior inventions. But that meant St. Gall could in court come up with another invention—a catapult—that, even though it was not exactly like AV/AS, would be close enough that a jury would vote against the patent.

McKee shrugged. "Steinhardt told me what inventions to cite."

"And you didn't do your own research to see if there were others?"

"Hey, back off. My instructions were to limit myself to what Steinhardt gave me."

"That's what Steinhardt told you?"

"No, the chief medical guy. Leonard Seeley."

It was odd hearing a stranger refer to his brother by name.

A sly smile spread across McKee's face. "You two are related."

Seeley said, "When was the last time a company's head of research told you what prior art to cite?"

"When was the last time you tried a pharma case? All the drug companies have committees that review the R&D and decide if they want broad patents or narrow ones."

Seeley said, "But, once a company decides what it wants, did you ever have the company's head of research tell you how much prior art to cite?"

McKee looked unhappy. "No."

"And because you didn't cite the prior art, St. Gall can argue there was fraud on the Patent Office. The court could invalidate the patent."

Seeley thought about Leonard and his deceptions. It's one thing to lie that you clipped stories about your brother from legal newspapers. But to bully a young lawyer into deceiving the U.S. Patent Office was dangerously wrong and, by not telling Seeley what he had done, Leonard had exposed him to judicial sanctions for perpetuating that fraud in court. The equation, he knew, was lopsided: when Seeley held facts back from Leonard it was to protect him, and when Leonard held facts back it was to protect himself. He and his brother had that in common—they were both protecting Leonard Seeley.

McKee said, "St. Gall's complaint didn't say anything about fraud."

"But they can make the argument at trial, and I don't want to be blindsided if they do. Make me a list of all the prior art you would have cited if you hadn't listened to Steinhardt or Leonard Seeley."

"I've got a lot on my desk."

"I want the references by the end of the day."

McKee rocked back on the balls of his feet, chest out, jaw working. "You're not even a partner here."

Seeley didn't get up. "I'm trying a case for a client of this law firm, and I'm not going to lose it because one of the firm's lawyers was too lazy or insecure to stand up to a client and tell the client that what it was asking him to do was wrong."

"They would have fired us."

"You've got it backward, Boyd. You should have fired them. If you can't stand up to a client, you might as well turn in your bar card."

McKee reddened. "Like I said, I'll get to it when I can."

Seeley watched McKee's back go through the door. He had made no friends at Vaxtek yesterday, and it seemed that he wasn't making any at Heilbrun, Hardy, either. But it was none of his business what these people thought of him. Sitting at Pearsall's desk, Seeley sensed that he was doing exactly what Pearsall himself would have done were he alive. What he didn't know was whether that was a good or a bad thing.

The telephone rang.

"Mr. Seeley?"

"Yes."

"This is Lily Warren."

SIX

Over the course of his practice, Seeley had read the résumés of dozens of scientists—mostly expert witnesses testifying for or against his clients—men and women in their fifties and sixties at the top of careers filled with academic appointments, government consultancies, and awards, including in two cases a Nobel Prize. From the résumé Seeley found in the witness file, Lily Warren was at thirty-six on the same path as these other scientists, one of those rare individuals who can set a goal and then pursue it undistracted by physical or emotional limits. When he explained to her on the telephone that he was Vaxtek's lawyer and that there were facts about the discovery of AV/AS he needed to confirm, the pleasantly husky voice at the other end had the measure of authority. Seeley also thought he detected a British accent.

"If you're their lawyer, you know that everyone's decided that Alan Steinhardt got there first. Whatever I did, it doesn't matter."

Seeley had said only that he wanted to confirm facts about the discovery, not her role in it. "I also know about your visit to Steinhardt's lab."

"I promised I wouldn't talk about this to anyone."

If she didn't want to talk, she wouldn't have returned his call. "Did you sign a confidentiality agreement?"

"There's nothing in writing." She sounded surprised that he didn't know. "They didn't make me sign anything."

If St. Gall didn't think it was necessary for her to sign a secrecy agreement, that meant the company had some grip on Warren stronger than a lawsuit for breach of contract.

She said, "You're taking over for the lawyer who killed himself."

"Robert Pearsall. I won't ask you anything he didn't already know." Seeley would take it one fact at a time. "I know St. Gall conceded that Steinhardt was the first to invent AV/AS."

"That's what St. Gall and your client agreed." Seeley imagined a foot tapping with impatience.

"And at the time Steinhardt made his discovery, you had already stopped working for him."

"*With* him. I worked with Alan, not for him. When he left UC to go to Vaxtek, I went to St. Gall."

"Before St. Gall and Vaxtek made their agreement, did someone from Pearsall's law firm interview you?" Seeley was still a long way from what a St. Gall employee was doing at a competitor's laboratory alone, after hours, but he was certain that Pearsall wouldn't have accepted the stipulation unless he had satisfied himself that no one had coerced Warren.

"Pearsall interviewed me himself."

"What did you talk about?"

There was a long silence. "You're persistent, aren't you?" The tone wasn't unfriendly, but it wasn't amused, either.

"I just want to know what you told Bob."

Again, silence. Was she calculating, or had she concluded that it was a mistake to have returned his call?

"I'd prefer not to do this, Dr. Warren, but I could get a subpoena requiring you to testify."

Seeley would not subpoena Warren. Forced to testify, she could easily say things that would damage his case. But if he didn't know why she went to Steinhardt's lab that night, he also wouldn't know why St. Gall so unexpectedly surrendered its claim to have invented the vaccine first. That lack of knowledge could turn out to be even more damaging. "I promise you, nothing you tell me will go any farther."

Finally, she said, "How do I know I can trust you?"

"You don't. But if you think about it, you really don't have a choice." Seeley gave her some time to take that in. "Just tell me what you were doing alone in Steinhardt's lab."

"I'll meet you, but I won't promise to answer your questions." She seemed about to say something more, but stopped.

Seeley looked at his watch. It was past noon. He hadn't eaten since an early breakfast, before seeing Judy Pearsall. "Anywhere you like. Just make it someplace we can get lunch."

She gave him the name of a restaurant in Princeton-by-the-Sea, off the coastal highway south of San Francisco. Seeley wrote it down and hung up.

On his way out, Seeley knocked at the open door of Palmieri's office. The young partner looked up from a thick stack of deposition summaries. There was no sign of the laboratory notebooks that Seeley asked him to review.

"Did you go through Steinhardt's notebooks?"

"I'm almost finished. When do you need them?"

Seeley wondered if he had even looked at them. "Did you find anything?"

"Nothing unusual. The trail of invention is seamless. All the experiments and results look like they're logically connected."

Palmieri's office had no windows, but the lighting was indirect and the museum-white walls were hung with neatly framed posters. The one Seeley was looking at advertised a benefit concert at a San Francisco arena two years ago and was in the style of a World War II recruiting placard. The colors and lines were classic Norman Rockwell, but the girl, in halter top and tight shorts with a sailor's cap askew on auburn curls, was strictly pinup art. JOIN US the top line read and in the same large letters at the bottom, FIGHT AIDS.

Seeley said, "How far back did you look?"

"All the way to the beginning, with the basic science he was doing at UC."

"Was there anything about co-inventors?"

Palmieri shook his head. "Some of the UC entries are signed by Lily Warren, but none of them are concrete enough to qualify for a patent. Steinhardt did all the patentable work at Vaxtek."

Do your basic research at a university, Seeley thought, but when you're ready to turn it into something you can get a patent on and make some money, move to the private sector. "And after UC, the entries are all Steinhardt's?"

"Every one of them." Palmieri hesitated and studied Seeley for a long moment before continuing. "There was one strange thing. The UC notebooks look like what you'd expect—lots of mistakes and cross outs. But the ones from when he started at Vaxtek are different."

"No corrections?"

"They're as buttoned-down as Steinhardt himself. Not a line crossed out, not even a sentence fragment or grammatical error." Palmieri held his thumb and forefinger the smallest fraction of an inch apart. "Every word in his teeny-weeny handwriting."

Seeley said, "Maybe his lab methods suddenly improved when he got to Vaxtek. Or—"

"Or," Palmieri said, "maybe when he didn't have his postdoc looking over his shoulder, his methods changed."

"You think he kept two sets of books." Seeley thought of the words below the portrait in Pearsall's sketchbook: *What else is A.S. hiding?*

Palmieri closed his eyes and pushed back from the desk.

Seeley said, "If they're as perfect as you say they are, he may have kept rough notes as he went along and then transcribed them later."

"Sure, and dated his discoveries to before he made them."

If Steinhardt kept two sets of books, and Thorpe found that out, it would open another door for Thorpe to prove fraud on the Patent Office—that Steinhardt's dates of discovery were in fact later than he claimed. It would be the end of Vaxtek's case.

"Are all the entries witnessed?"

"Every one of them."

The fact that each day's notebook entry was signed not only by

Steinhardt but by a witness from his laboratory meant nothing. A scientist of Steinhardt's eminence could, if he wanted, get an assistant to swear that he had watched the great man map the human genome single-handed.

"When can you finish with the notebooks?"

"Hey," Palmieri's forced a smile, "I have fifteen lawyers and paralegals to get ready for trial. My hands are full just keeping this crew on course."

Since arriving in San Francisco, Seeley had been so absorbed with his client and the case, and so out of practice at running a large-scale trial, that he failed to do what he automatically did at the start of a case, big or small: meet with his trial team. "I'll ask Tina to get everyone together for a meeting."

"They'll appreciate that," Palmieri said. "Right now, you're still the mystery man from back East."

Seeley glanced at his watch. "Let's talk when I get back. I'm meeting with Lily Warren."

"What for?"

"The usual pretrial diligence." Seeley tried to make it sound offhand. Then he thought about what they'd just discussed. "If she told St. Gall's lawyers how Steinhardt keeps his notebooks, I don't want to be hearing about it for the first time when Thorpe cross-examines him."

"Where are you meeting her?"

"Some place down the coast. Princeton-by-the-Sea." Seeley fumbled in his pocket for the note he had written. "Barbara's something."

"Barbara's Fish Trap."

That was it.

"Order the tempura oysters. One bite and you'll never come back."

Seeley wondered whether that was in fact what the young partner wanted.

Barbara's wasn't a shack, but it was close. Neon tubing in the windows traced the logos of popular beer brands and outlined caricatures of fish, lobster, and crabs. At the far end of the low red building, a window was open for takeout. A man and woman, both in shorts and hugging themselves against the cold, waited for their orders, and a well-dressed Asian woman sat at the single outside table. Behind her, stairs led down to a parking lot and, beyond that, to an intricate network of piers and ramps. Pleasure and fishing boats crowded the harbor, white hulls rocking in the black water.

Seeley went through the door into the restaurant's front room, little more than a screened-in porch with electric-coiled heaters hanging from the ceiling against the chill, and from there into the dining room. Couples and families were at the oilcloth-covered tables. There were a few tourists, but most of the customers, in unfashionable jeans and flannels, appeared to be locals. None looked like a thirty-six-year-old immunologist named Lily Warren. Seeley went back outside to wait. The couple at the takeout window had gone and the Asian woman came toward him.

"Mr. Seeley?" It was the assured voice from the telephone, and she smiled tentatively when he nodded. "You're embarrassed. Don't be. People are always surprised. Warren's not a very Chinese name is it?"

She was slender and slim-hipped, but buxom in a way that made Seeley think of the recruiting poster in Palmieri's office. What most struck Seeley was the erect dancer's posture. Care had gone into Lily Warren's makeup, and her hand, when she extended it, was marble smooth and perfectly manicured.

They went into the restaurant, and a waitress led them to a corner table, leaving them with menus. There was the faintest hint of something savory in the air, less a fragrance than a memory for Seeley of some fine meals in the past. The window looked out onto a small patch of sand and, beyond that, the Pacific. At the next table, a sheriff's deputy in sharply pressed khakis was having a solitary lunch.

"Thank you for meeting me," Seeley said. "Can we talk about why you went to see Alan Steinhardt that night?"

Warren said, "Let's look at the menu." She pushed his toward him and studied her own. "Everything here is good. The crab's better than anything you can get in San Francisco." She saw that Seeley wasn't reading the menu. "Why are you smiling?"

"I was hoping that if you met me, you'd see you could trust me."

"And maybe I will, after I get to know you. The fact that someone is direct doesn't mean he deserves to be trusted."

"But you came anyway."

"You told me you'd get a subpoena if I didn't."

Seeley said, "That's not what's worrying you. There's something you want to talk about."

She put the menu down. "I don't understand why you're making such a big deal about my going to see Alan at his lab. I knew him. I already told you, I worked with him at UC." When Seeley frowned, she said, "I know people think he's cold—have you met him?"

Seeley nodded.

"In fact, Alan is a kind man. Warm, too, in his own way. I went to see him because he offered to help me professionally."

The waitress returned. Warren ordered a crab salad and Seeley, remembering Palmieri's suggestion, ordered the tempura oysters. When the waitress asked about drinks, he glanced at the decorative rows of imported and domestic beers along one wall and told her water would be fine.

"So you went there at night, after the building was closed."

"It was the only time I had free. I was working full-time at St. Gall. There was nothing suspicious about it. Alan met me at the front door and let me in."

"So he could help you professionally." Seeley remembered Steinhardt telling him about her crush on him, but Warren didn't look like a woman who pursued men.

"The AIDS research community isn't very big, especially vaccine research." Warren was as erect sitting as she was standing, her posture accentuated by the way she thrust out her chin as she talked. In a face with conventional Asian features, one was not: a delicately hooked nose that made an otherwise pretty face achingly lovely.

"Alan knew what the bureaucracy was like at St. Gall. He knew they weren't going to give a young scientist, particularly a woman, credit for her work. So he offered to go over our experiments together at UC and co-author some papers with me."

Seeley didn't doubt that Steinhardt could be charming, or that he was capable of concealing his motives, whatever they were, behind a mask of amiability. But after more than twenty years litigating patent cases, it was inconceivable to him that two people working on directly competing research projects could visit after hours without one planning to extract information from the other, particularly when the two already knew each other well, and one was famous and the other was ambitious for fame.

She continued on about Steinhardt and the exciting work that they had done together at UC. There was an energy in the air as she talked about her science. It was as if someone had struck a tuning fork and the vibrations hadn't ceased.

The waitress brought their food, Seeley's a heaped pile of crisp-battered Pacific oysters, each as fat as a baby's fist. A mound of creamy coleslaw was on the side. Warren started on her salad, and he bit into an oyster. Palmieri was right. Seeley had not tasted anything like this before. First, there was the sensation of the grainy, almost buttery crust, and then the sudden astonishment of the oyster's intense flavor exploding and liquefying in his mouth like the essence of the ocean itself. There was a genius at work in the kitchen, someone who knew the secrets of frying seafood.

Seeley looked around the room with its corny nautical decorations hanging from the ceiling and walls. Behind the cashier's stand was a small open kitchen, with the cooks' busy white backs. Every fifteen seconds the booming of a foghorn punctuated the background buzz of conversation.

While they ate, Lily, with Seeley's encouragement, talked about herself. She grew up in China, came to the United States on a student visa for graduate and postgraduate work, married Warren, a Canadian software engineer living in the United States, and ended the marriage two years later when she failed her husband's expectations of a dutiful Asian wife and refused to give up her career to have children. By this time, she had already started publishing articles in immunology under her married name, and so continued using it after the divorce. When Steinhardt left UC for Vaxtek, he offered her a position in his new lab, but she went to St. Gall instead, converting her F-1 student visa to an H-1.

Unlike other lawyers, Seeley took little pleasure in recounting trial stories, but when Lily asked him about patent cases he'd worked on, she seemed genuinely inquisitive. He was telling her about a case seven years ago, involving a drug-coated stent that had so revolutionized cardiovascular surgery that demand from surgeons across the country overwhelmed his client's capacity to supply the market, when a shrewd light went on in her eyes.

"I bet that instead of trying to shut down the infringers, you just asked the court to make them pay a license fee."

Her quickness stunned him. "How did you know?"

"Greed is an unattractive quality. Your client couldn't supply the market by itself. Patients needed the stent. It would have been bad strategy to ask for more."

"If we said it was all or nothing, the court probably would have struck down the patent and given us nothing." For the first time in a long time, Seeley was enjoying a conversation.

"That's the difference between science and law," Lily said. "In law you can divide things up so everyone gets something. In scientific research there's only one winner and lots of losers."

The way she said the word told Seeley that Lily would not accept being one of the losers.

"Had a lawyer ever done that in a patent case—not try to shut down his competition?"

Seeley shook his head. "Sometimes the hardest part of a case is convincing the client to do the right thing."

"And you're always so confident about knowing the right thing to do?"

When Seeley returned her smile he realized that he was flirting with her. "In trials, sure."

The waitress cleared away their plates and flipped her pad open for dessert orders. "The Snickers bar pie is one of our specialities." Lily shook her head and said tea would be fine. Seeley asked for coffee.

"You enjoy eating, don't you?"

"Sure," Seeley said, "when the food's as good as this."

"Do you like dim sum?"

When Seeley nodded, she said, "In China people have it for breakfast or lunch. I like it for dinner. And mine's better than what you can get in a restaurant."

Seeley didn't know where this was going.

"Your reflexes outside the courtroom could be better. That was a dinner invitation."

"Just like that?"

"Why not?"

"I'm going to trial in three days."

"You still have to eat dinner. My apartment's in Half Moon Bay— it's only forty minutes from the city."

"Why?"

"I already told you. If I'm going to talk to you, I need to know you better."

"When you left UC, why didn't you go to Vaxtek with Steinhardt?"

"How about next Tuesday?" She had taken a leather-bound calendar from her purse.

"I'd like that. But finish telling me about you and Steinhardt." Tell me, Seeley thought, what your feelings were for this arrogant peacock.

"When he went to Vaxtek I'd already worked with him for three years. It seemed like a good time for me to move to a different lab."

"Did you have him over for dim sum dinners?"

The porcelain cheeks colored, and Seeley wondered how seriously he had overstepped.

But her voice was even; she seemed neither angry nor embarrassed. "I had a relationship with Alan, if that's what you mean."

Either Steinhardt was lying when he said that her crush was unrequited or Lily was. Seeley decided to believe her, even though he couldn't picture her in Steinhardt's arms nor him in hers.

She read his reaction as surprise. "Which stereotype are you sticking me with—cool, dispassionate scientist or chaste Chinese lady?"

"Neither. It's just that—"

She laughed. "I like discovering things, finding out what goes on behind the professional front that people wear. Alan is a very interesting man, and even though it didn't last long, I'm glad we had a relationship." This time she enunciated the word carefully, as if it might explode. She looked directly at Seeley. "You're an interesting man, too. Even enigmatic."

"How so?"

"You come on tough and in control, but when the waitress asked you what you wanted to drink, the way you looked at that row of beer bottles, you could have been a teenager mooning over a pretty girl."

Seeley reminded himself to be more careful the next time he took a scientist to lunch.

"I can understand your leaving Steinhardt's lab, but why'd you go to a place the size of St. Gall? I'd think you'd be afraid you'd get lost there."

She studied Seeley and waited a moment before she spoke. "That's what Alan said. But it was either that or get lost in his shadow. Alan's not the kind of person who shares credit."

This made more sense to Seeley than what she said before. "But when, out of nowhere, he tells you he wants to publish articles with you, you go to his lab to see him."

"I believed him. People change."

Sure they do, Seeley thought. In the case of people like Steinhardt they get worse.

"Alan was right about St. Gall not giving me the recognition I deserved."

"They were ready to have you testify in court that you invented AV/AS."

"That was only after Vaxtek sued them, and it was their lawyer's idea. They thought a woman scientist would play well to a San Francisco jury."

Emil Thorpe would know exactly what worked with a San Francisco jury. "So, before anyone knew there would be a lawsuit, you went to see Steinhardt and he left you alone in his lab—"

"He had to go to his office to get the UC notebooks."

"And a security guard found you."

"It wasn't a big deal. As soon as Alan came back he told the guard I was with him."

"But the guard wrote in his report that you were there alone."

She saw where Seeley's questions were going: that Steinhardt had set her up, creating an appearance of industrial espionage, with her as the spy. "No one would have known I was there if one of the lawyers in your office hadn't connected the guard's log and the witness list."

"And St. Gall dropped you as a witness because they thought you stole Vaxtek's secrets."

"Isn't that why you're asking all these questions?"

"Why did St. Gall make you promise not to talk about what happened?"

"They fired me, but they got me a job at a small start-up they're financing in Half Moon Bay."

"Are you happy there?"

"I'm in a holding pattern. It's mostly busywork. St. Gall wants to keep their eye on me until the trial is over."

"You could get a job anywhere. Dozens of companies would hire you."

"Not without a visa. All St. Gall has to do is call Immigration and I lose my H-1."

That was the hold that St. Gall had on Lily. Deportation. It was why they didn't need her signature on a secrecy agreement.

"You're a citizen of this country," she said. "You have no idea what it's like to live with the constant threat that, if you look at somebody the wrong way, you get deported."

"Is your family still in China?" If family was neither an attraction nor a consolation for Seeley, it might be for Lily.

"My parents are in their sixties. They live in Wuhan."

Seeley was certain she was going to tell him more, but she glanced quickly at a mirror in her purse and, after removing a business card, snapped the bag shut. "Have you ever done science, Michael?"

"Football practice got in the way of biology lab when I was in college."

"Then you have no idea how different my world is from yours." While she spoke, she wrote on the back of the card. "Whatever else is wrong with your country, America is still the best place in the world to do science. It's one of the few places where a woman can hope to get recognized for what she does."

The dining room had emptied. A lone waitress leaned against the cash register. Warren handed him the business card, on which she had written her address and Tuesday, 7:30.

Seeley said, "You must want something very much to risk having St. Gall see you with me."

She sipped her tea. "You're afraid that something is going to come out in court and ruin your case."

Seeley nodded, once again admiring how quick she was. "And you've told me what you're afraid of. So why don't you tell me what it is you want?"

"Look, Michael, we each have our own reasons, but the way things are arranged, St. Gall's not going to say anything, in court or out, and I'm not, either. So this secret you think I'm hiding is not going to be a problem for you."

Her logic was as impeccable as she was. But it was lawyer's logic, and for Seeley that had never been enough.

SEVEN

It felt illicit being in his brother's house with him not there. Renata told Seeley that Leonard was working late and would meet them at Joel Warshaw's party. "Leonard loves parties," she said. "Take your tie off. The only one there with a tie will be the headmaster."

"Headmaster?"

"It's a benefit for the Hill School. Joel's on the board." Renata's hands went to Seeley's collar and deftly loosened the tie, opened the top button, and slipped the tie from its knot. She let one hand stay flat on his chest. "Healthy heartbeat," she said and handed him the tie.

Seeley looked down at her, flustered.

A quizzical smile played on her lips. "Next time," she said, "I'll use an anesthetic."

It was late October, but the evening was balmy and Renata suggested walking the short distance to Warshaw's house. The light sleeveless dress clung to her slender figure, and she threw a sweater over her shoulders on their way out the door. "You made a conquest, you know."

Seeley didn't know who she meant, and didn't want to hear that it was her.

"Judy Pearsall called this afternoon and asked if you were going to be at Joel's. She's on the school's board—she's on lots of charity boards—but she doesn't usually come to these things."

"She said she'll be there?"

"No, but the way she asked about you, I'm sure she will."

Judy didn't impress Seeley as someone who chased strangers on a whim. He said, "She doesn't believe the police, that her husband killed himself."

"How could any wife believe that?"

"Especially if her husband's life insurance has an exclusion for suicide." Seeley didn't like to think that about Judy, but the apartment with its good address, high ceilings, and fine plaster walls was not cheap, nor was her daughter's private school tuition.

"I'm sure you have a soft spot for widows and children, but Judy doesn't need insurance money. She's from one of the old San Francisco fortunes—sugar, something like that."

They were crossing a broad avenue, and parked cars lined both sides of the street ahead. For some reason, in this flat, well-paved town, almost all of the vehicles were mammoth four-wheel-drive SUVs.

Renata said, "I'm sorry I never met your wife."

"Clare."

"Do you have a lady friend back in Buffalo?"

Before he could answer, Renata said, "Here's Joel's."

"No," Seeley said.

White-jacketed valets collected keys and cars at the entrance to the property. Warshaw's house, at the end of fifty yards of cobblestone drive, was two stories of light-colored stucco, flat-roofed and vaguely French, as if the architect had Versailles in mind with the rooftop balustrade and stacked quoins where the two wings joined the main part of the house. Contemporary sculptures, two of them brightly painted, dominated the sloping lawn. The other, of twisted rusting iron, Seeley recognized as the work of a former client in New York. The wail of a saxophone pierced the air.

With Renata, Seeley passed through a bright, high-ceilinged foyer to a flagstone terrace. The band, saxophone still soaring, was on the terrace, and more sculptures followed a gravel pathway that wound through three or four acres of lawn ending in a line of redwoods.

A striped tent the size of a house had a small stage and rows of folding chairs inside. An amateur-sounding auctioneer, his voice amplified by loudspeakers hidden in the trees, was soliciting bids for a spa weekend for two at Big Sur donated by a resort. Guests, wineglasses in hand, moved between tent and terrace. A few of the older men were in blazers and sport shirts, but most, like the younger ones, were in jeans or rumpled shorts, polo shirts, and running shoes. The women, glossy blondes, formal in skirts and heels, looked like they had dressed with more elegant companions in mind. The faces were lean, tanned, and, for all the smiles, fierce.

Renata touched Seeley's elbow and whispered, "Your new groupie." He turned to see Judy approaching them. Renata gave her a quick greeting. "I'm going to find the drinks," she said, and left.

"It's good to see you," Judy said. "Bob used to meet Joel here, rather than at the office." She frowned. "Apparently the CEOs down here like to stay close to home."

Like kids in a sandbox, Seeley thought. "Is this for Lucy's school?"

She shook her head. "Lucy goes to school in the city." She saw the question in his expression. "I went to Hill School when it was all girls. They started admitting boys fifteen years ago." Again, her expression told Seeley that she didn't approve.

"Was there a reason you asked Renata if I'd be here?"

Her mouth moved for a moment, but no words came—Seeley realized that he had been too direct—but she quickly recovered. "What does someone do if they think the police aren't looking sufficiently into a crime?"

"You could hire a private investigator."

She shook her head. "I don't think so."

"You could have a lawyer look into it. Have you talked to any of your husband's partners?"

"Heilbrun, Hardy's a San Francisco firm. That's where its influence is. They don't know anyone in San Mateo."

Seeley remembered Barnum saying that he had started out as an assistant district attorney in San Mateo. "Do you know Ed Barnum? Vaxtek's general counsel."

The noise from the tent had grown and Seeley noticed that more guests were crowding into it.

"He called me. He said he talked to the police and they were doing everything they could do. But——"

"But you don't trust him?" He knew what was coming.

"I know we've just met, but I trust you."

Why, he asked himself, hadn't Lily been as trusting. "I don't know anyone in San Mateo."

"I know this sounds silly"——her eyes didn't waver——"but you remind me of Bob, and I suppose that's why I trust you. I know you're busy with the trial, but I was hoping you might make a few inquiries."

Seeley could think of no way to say no. It wasn't the demands of the trial that concerned him; he could handle those. What he couldn't manage were Judy's expectations and the possibility that he would fail them.

"What have the police told you?"

"Nothing, really. Bob spent the day at his office. They're trying to track down who he had lunch with, but they know he had dinner with Chris."

"Palmieri?"

She nodded. "Would that be unusual?"

"They were preparing for a major trial. It would be unusual if they didn't have dinner together."

"They went to an Italian place in the Marina they both liked. Chris was the last person to see Bob."

Not the last, Seeley thought, just the last one the police knew about.

"Were there any new people your husband met who he talked about?"

She started to shake her head, then stopped. "When I took Lucy to the airport this afternoon——she's on her way to France with the school choir——she told me that once, when Bob picked her up from choir practice, she saw him sitting in the auditorium with the other parents, but when practice was over, he was gone. She went into the hall, and he was by the staircase, talking to another man, a stranger."

"When was this?"

"Maybe a week or so before Bob died."

"Did she describe the man?"

"No. Bob told her he was involved in a case he was working on." She looked away for a moment. "God, I miss him." It wasn't a complaint, just a statement of fact.

"Have you told the police about this?"

She shook her head. "I just learned about it."

"Do you think she could describe the man?"

"I suppose so. She comes home in five days. The trip was planned long before Bob died. We're trying to make everything as normal as we can."

"Did she tell you anything else about the man?"

For the first time since they met, Judy smiled. "Maybe it was going to France, her remembering."

"What's that?"

"Lucy said the man spoke English, but he had a French accent. Could that be a connection? That the man Bob was talking to was French?"

"I'll make some phone calls," Seeley said.

"That's all I was hoping for." Her eyes, filled with hope, told Seeley what he already knew—that he should have said no.

Seeley nodded in the direction of the tent. "Are you interested in the auction?"

"No," she said, turning to go. "I just came to see you."

The crowd now overflowed the tent and Seeley took a place by the entrance. He recognized the trim white-haired man on the stage as a former pro quarterback, and later coach, who had gone on to make a comfortable fortune with a string of auto dealerships. The white tennis shirt and light-colored slacks showed off his tan and he moved about the stage with an athlete's grace. He spoke softly into a handheld microphone about his connections to the Hill School—his daughter was a graduate and his grandson was the school's present quarterback—and then, raising his voice and blinking into the make-shift spotlight, he cried, "So let's do something for the kids!"

A younger man who had been waiting at the back of the small

stage came forward, took the handoff of the microphone with a flourish, and started the bidding. "Thanks to the generosity of the San Francisco 49ers organization, and our longstanding friendship with the coach, we're auctioning off a full game day, including access to the field and locker rooms, access to the press box, and dinner and photographs with the team. Bidding starts at $5,000!"

The bidding moved rapidly around the tent with hands gesturing eagerly. At the side of the stage, an older man in tie and blazer—the headmaster, Seeley concluded—watched intently, as solemn and self-possessed as the prime minister of a small country, his eyebrows rising at each $500 increment. Seeley saw Renata, her arm linked with Leonard's, behind the raised arm of a bidder. When the arm lowered she saw him and tipped her wineglass in his direction.

At $18,000, the bidding slowed, and when it reached $22,000, it stopped. The coach came to the auctioneer's side—Seeley saw at once that this had been planned; it was an act—and leaned into the microphone. The crowd was going to have to do better for the kids, he said, and, just to make it more interesting, he was throwing in travel to the game on the team's private jet, lodging for the night at the team hotel, and all meals with the team. "But," the coach said, "I don't want to hear any bids unless they go up a thousand dollars at a time."

A few feet from Seeley, just inside the entrance, a man's hand shot up. "Twenty-three thousand!" Under the youthfully cut gray hair, the man was red-faced and glassy-eyed, and it didn't surprise Seeley to see a large tumbler half filled with whiskey and ice in the other hand. The woman next to him, jewelry flashing, rubbed his back vigorously.

"Twenty-four!" The bid came from closer to the stage. The bidder rose from his chair and repeated, "Twenty-four!"

The bidding moved even more quickly than before, to twenty-five thousand, then thirty. The other bidders dropped out at thirty-five, and it became just the two men trading bids. The auctioneer turned to one man, then the other, before his rival even shouted his new bid. With each bid, the coach punched the air.

The bidder close to Seeley said to the woman, whose hand was still on his back, "I can't stop him. I knock him down, he just gets up." His face was bloodred. "Forty-two thousand!"

"Forty-three!"

"Well, just keep getting up and you knock *him* down!"

"Forty-four!"

The bidding stopped at $45,000 and the buzz in the crowd heightened. Faces turned to the man by the entrance. "Go," the woman barked into the man's ear. "Go! Go!" He wouldn't look at her, but just shook his head.

The coach stepped forward and this time he took the microphone from the auctioneer. His voice still mild, he said, "I want twice this money for the kids. I don't want to hear fifty thousand, I want one hundred thousand, and I know one of you men has it in you to do it."

There was a collective hum before the crowd went silent again.

"For my part of the deal, I'll double the pot: whoever wins gets to take his best buddy on the trip with him. But this time, the bids go up five thousand dollars."

"Fifty thousand!" cried the bidder by the entrance.

A heavy hand clapped Seeley's shoulder. "If he was smart," the voice said, "he'd offer to take the other bidder to the game. They could split the bid and the auction would be over. They'd each save themselves a bundle."

Seeley turned and at once recognized the face, pale and moonlike behind rimless glasses, from the cover of a business magazine. Joel Warshaw's only arresting feature was his melting, almost liquid brown eyes, the kind that gets beagles extra pats on the head.

"Fifty-five!" came the cry from close to the stage.

Warshaw said, "You know the Bible story, half a baby is better than none."

"If I remember right," Seeley said, "it's half a loaf." How deformed was the man's character that he would so profoundly mangle the point of the Old Testament story? "It's for charity."

Warshaw shook his head. "Charity's no excuse for stupidity." His hand touched Seeley's elbow. "Take a walk with me."

Seeley followed Warshaw down the gravel path. It had grown dark while he was watching the auction, and spotlights mounted in the trees now illuminated the sculptures and the grounds. The saxophone was gone, and the only sound was an occasional roar from the auction tent. Warshaw bent to adjust a pink-ribboned stake, one of dozens planted every twenty feet or so along the periphery of the property. He was a round man, and the effort of bending and rising showed in his face. The business magazine story put Warshaw in his late thirties, but the unlined face made him look younger.

"Deer," Warshaw said, wiping his hands on his trousers. "They knock the stakes over." He continued on toward the trees, not turning to see if Seeley was following, but speaking to the void in front of him. "You're thinking, it's been five, ten years since this property was developed, why does he keep the construction stakes?"

Seeley had worked for self-absorbed men like this before, but never comfortably.

"If you don't mark your boundaries," Warshaw said, "before you know it, you've lost your property lines and your neighbors are parking on your front lawn. Until the town fathers change the zoning and let me put up a fence, I have the gardener tie on new ribbons every spring." He prodded a stake with a toe to straighten it. "Leonard tells me you think my patent claims are too broad."

His claims, Seeley thought, not Vaxtek's or even Steinhardt's.

Warshaw said, "The claims are fine. St. Gall copied our invention. What's your assessment of the case?"

"Do you want my opinion, or are you going to tell me what it is?"

"I thought a lot about those claims." They had arrived at the wooded edge of the property and Warshaw walked along it, checking the stakes. "Everyone thought I made a big jump, going from electronics to biotech. What they don't understand is, it's all the same: you build a company and you sell it. The AV/AS patent is what makes this company valuable, and the broader that patent is, the more I can sell the company for."

The air was still, but there was a rustling in the shrubbery beneath the trees. Black eyes looked out and Seeley sensed, more than he saw, the presence of deer.

"You mean you want a monopoly."

Warshaw turned and looked at Seeley.

"Call it whatever you want. It's my property. It's why I made the investment."

"Broad claims are risky," Seeley said. "Juries don't like monopolies."

"Risk never bothered me. It's competition I don't like. If I wanted to compete, I'd be over there in the tent."

A gust of air blew past them and a pair of arch-backed dogs, anorexically thin, flew into the trees. The deer scattered. When the dogs returned, they went to Warshaw's side.

"Your brother's a better listener than you are." Warshaw bent to pet the dogs.

"Leonard's a fine salesman," Seeley said.

"Let me show you my sculptures. Leonard tells me you represent artists." Warshaw didn't wait for an answer but, as they walked in the direction of the house, lectured Seeley on each of the half-dozen pieces they passed. By the time they reached the terrace, guests were streaming out of the tent.

Renata was waiting for Seeley on the terrace, a full wineglass in her hand. "Asperger's syndrome," she said when Warshaw was gone. "High-functioning autism. People like Joel are usually brilliant at one particular thing, but they don't have what the psychiatrists call social pragmatics. It's the only disease known to medicine whose symptoms are being rich and powerful."

"And amoral."

Renata thought for a moment. "I suppose that, too."

"He seems to get on with his dogs."

Renata laughed. "I'm ready to go. How about you?"

"Where's Leonard?"

"He'll be the last one to leave. I have to be in the OR at seven-thirty."

Seeley remembered that she'd also been in surgery early today. "How many days a week do you do that?"

"Four, five. Leonard says I went into orthopedics as an excuse for not having kids."

"Did you?"

"I never wanted children and, whatever he says, Leonard doesn't either. He wants only one child in the house, and it has to be him."

"Why'd you pick surgery?"

"When I was a nurse, I knew that if I got through med school, it's what I'd do. All the parties I went to, the surgeons were always the ones having a good time."

"Are you having a good time?" Out on the street, the fragrance of grasses and lavender mixed with the familiar eucalyptus, like a magician's potion.

Renata said, "Even the best jobs get tedious. Doesn't yours?"

Seeley laughed. "I relieve the boredom by taking on cases that I shouldn't."

"For me it's being an on-field doc for the Stanford football team. I only work home games, but it's something to look forward to. Leonard said you played in college."

"It was a small Jesuit college in Buffalo. Strictly division three."

"Why don't you come to the Washington game next week? I'll get you a field pass."

"I'll be in the middle of trial."

He had said the same to Lily, but then agreed to dinner with her. At odd moments, driving back to the office from their lunch in Princeton-by-the-Sea and again driving down to Atherton this evening, fragments of his conversation with Lily drifted pleasantly through his thoughts. What had changed his mind about dinner—the need to discover what Lily was hiding, or the simple desire to see her again?

"It's just three hours on a Saturday afternoon. You'll need a break."

Seeley said he'd think about it.

They turned into Renata's street, where the sidewalks disappeared and the canopy of treetops became so dense that it obscured the night sky.

"Do you remember, at your wedding, when I was leaving, you whispered something to me?"

Renata gave him a blank look, then shook her head. "What did I say?"

"I don't know," Seeley said. "That's why I asked. But I had the feeling it was important to you."

Renata smiled and slid her arm through his. "I was probably just flirting with you."

"Did you do that a lot?"

They were at the front door. When Seeley turned to her, she was looking directly at him. "I still do."

Renata opened the door. "Do you want to come in?"

"You have surgery tomorrow," he said. "And I have an early meeting with my trial team." Until that moment, he had forgotten the meeting that Tina had scheduled for him.

She frowned. "You're afraid Leonard will come back."

"Maybe I'm afraid he won't." Seeley meant it to be light, but she didn't smile.

Renata said, "Let me know what you decide about the Washington game."

Before Seeley could answer, her lips brushed his cheek, leaving a scent of wine, and then she was gone, the door closed behind her.

EIGHT

At 7:30 in the morning when Seeley came into the office, Steinhardt's lab notebooks were in a neat pile centered on his desk. The two on top, marked "University of California," were clothbound, and the four volumes beneath them were unmarked and bound in black leather. Next to the notebooks was a message from Tina that Nicolas Cordier, Seeley's expert witness from South Africa, had arrived in New York and wanted to speak to him.

Seeley took the UC notebook from the top of the pile. The pages, lined horizontally and vertically like graph paper, were consecutively numbered and sewn into the binding to prevent an unscrupulous researcher from removing any that later turned out to be embarrassing. Paragraph after handwritten paragraph filled the pages, interrupted only by charts with numbers, symbols, and crisscrossing curves. At the end of each entry was the dated signature of the writer and, beneath that, of a witness. Most of the entries were in Steinhardt's small, meticulous hand, but some, in a loose, elegant script, were signed by Lily. The leather-bound books farther down in the pile were from Steinhardt's time at Vaxtek and, as Palmieri had said, were perfect, without an erasure or a cross out. All of the entries were signed by Steinhardt.

Remembering his promise to Judy to look into the police work on her husband's death, Seeley dialed the number for the San Mateo police headquarters, with little hope of learning anything that hadn't already been in the news. The receptionist told him that Lieutenant Herbert Phan was handling the investigation, but wasn't in yet. Why, she wanted to know, was he calling? Seeley hesitated. Palmieri's pro hac motion would cover Seeley's appearance in federal district court for this one case; however, not being a member of the California bar, he had no right to represent any other client. He bit his lip and told the receptionist that the Pearsall family had retained him to inquire into Robert Pearsall's death. She didn't sound impressed. Lieutenant Phan was busy, she said. Everyone in the department was busy, but she'd take his number and the lieutenant would call if he got the chance.

"What do you think about the notebooks?" Palmieri came into the office and took the chair facing the desk.

Seeley said, "When St. Gall served their discovery request, did they ask for Steinhardt's notes along with his notebooks?"

"Steinhardt told us there weren't any notes. Just the notebooks."

Palmieri was looking him in the eye today, and that relieved Seeley.

Palmieri said, "Do you think they went through Vaxtek's trash cans?"

"If Steinhardt had notes, I'm sure he shredded them—"

"They could still find someone who worked with him to testify that he kept a second set of books."

"Lily Warren," Seeley said. How far would she go to keep her visa?

"She only worked with him at UC." Then Palmieri remembered. "You mean the night she met him at Vaxtek."

There was a knock at the open door. It was Boyd McKee.

Palmieri turned and, seeing the patent lawyer, rose. To Seeley, he said, "Remember, we have a ten o'clock meeting with the judge."

Seeley put up a hand. "Let's see what Boyd has."

McKee ran a hand over his shaved head. "I have the prior art analysis you wanted." He remained in the doorway.

"Come on in," Seeley said. "Chris is as interested in this as I am."

Seeley had an instant's impression that, when McKee passed him, Palmieri tensed.

Palmieri said, "Is this the complete version, or is it still Prior Art Lite? I can't believe you let the client strong-arm you into hiding references—"

Seeley cut Palmieri short with a gesture. "Let's see what you have, Boyd."

McKee opened the manila folder and placed it on the desk. As Seeley read through the few typed pages, McKee said, "There really aren't that many discoveries that are close to AV/AS. Your brother was right about this being a pioneer invention."

Alexander Graham Bell's telephone patent was a pioneer patent. So was the patent on barbed wire. Courts regularly strike down broad patents like Vaxtek's, but they will sometimes make an exception for landmark inventions, because they open up a whole new field, and so deserve a wider range of protection than run-of-the-mill discoveries. If McKee was right, this could save Steinhardt's patent.

Palmieri said, "Did you check for foreign patents?"

"This is what I do, Chris. I checked *all* the prior art."

"Foreign publications? Unpublished papers?"

McKee's jaw clenched, and he massaged an earlobe. When he took his hand away, Seeley noticed three pinprick indentations, as if for earrings, and for a moment wondered about the young lawyer's nightlife.

The telephone intercom buzzed. It was Tina telling him that the trial team had been waiting in the workroom since 8:30. "Tell them I'll be right there."

Seeley rose. "This is good work, Boyd. Thanks." He tapped the folder. "This complicates the decision whether to keep Steinhardt as our lead witness. If he really was a pioneer—"

"You can't drop him," Palmieri said. "Do you know one patent case where the plaintiff didn't lead off with the inventor?"

Before Seeley could answer, McKee said, "Who would you use instead?"

Seeley said, "Nicolas Cordier. The South African. He's a physician, he can tell the frontline story of AIDS, and he can communicate better than anyone how important this discovery is."

"That's my point," Palmieri said. "It was Steinhardt who made the discovery."

Seeley added McKee's folder to the pile of laboratory notebooks, and nodded to the two lawyers to follow him out the door. "Steinhardt's a pompous ass. He's going to thump his patent like it's the Bible and he's God. That he created this field. The jury's going to hate him."

In her cubicle, Tina was on the telephone. When Seeley gestured to ask whether the call was for him, she shook her head and placed a hand over the receiver. "It's Mrs. Pearsall—about some partnership papers."

From behind Seeley, as they continued down the corridor, Palmieri said, "I think you're making a mistake."

Seeley stopped, and said to McKee, "What do you think, Boyd?"

"I think if you're going to use the South African, you should get him here real fast."

"He's in New York." Seeley remembered that he hadn't returned Cordier's call. As much to himself as to the others, he said, "I can work with him over the weekend."

After McKee left them, Seeley said, "Judy Pearsall told me you had dinner with Bob the night he died."

"And?"

"Did he say anything about the case that seemed unusual?"

"A long time ago, Bob taught me that when you're going to trial there's only one thing you should think about—"

"Sure," Seeley said. "The trial. And you think my looking into this is a distraction."

"That and chasing after Lily Warren."

"Steinhardt's notebooks are going to be a big part of the trial. She may know something about them that we don't."

"Okay," Palmieri said, "but shadowing a police investigation—"

"What if Bob's death is connected to the trial?"

"Connected how?"

They had arrived at the workroom.

"That's what I'm trying to find out," Seeley said.

Tina had sent an e-mail about the meeting to everyone involved in the case, and paralegals, secretaries, and document clerks filled the bare-walled workroom along with the lawyers, standing and talking in groups or perched on the low gray file cabinets, having their morning coffee. The moment Seeley came through the door, the room went quiet.

Seeley thought to apologize for keeping them waiting, decided that wasn't what they needed to hear, and instead explained the responsibility he felt, taking over a case that, working with every person in the room, Bob Pearsall had created. He then described the day-by-day path—he stayed clear of calling it a "path to victory"—that, building on Pearsall's plans but with changes of his own, he had laid out for the trial, and told them that they could expect continuing demands for exhibits, document review, and last-minute legal research over the coming days. He ended with the short speech he'd given dozens of times before. No one's job was too small to be critical to the team's success. If everyone did all that they were asked to do, and maybe ten percent more, victory was possible. This was supposed to be Pearsall's victory, he said. Now it's going to be yours. He saw no evidence in the coffee-sipping crowd that he had stirred or even connected with them. Palmieri motioned to him, tapping his watch, and Seeley said that they had to leave for a meeting with the judge. There was a sprinkle of applause, and Seeley was back in the corridor.

Judge Farnsworth was going to ask for his witness list at the meeting in her chambers, but Seeley still had not decided whether to keep Steinhardt as his lead witness or to drop him to a place in the lineup where he would do less harm. He forced himself to concentrate on the decision as he and Palmieri walked to the elevators. But, behind it, another question tugged at him: How many more potholes was he going to find in Robert Pearsall's path to victory?

NINE

The moment the taxi turned onto Market Street and Seeley saw the traffic backed up in both directions, he knew that they were going to be late for the meeting in Judge Farnsworth's chambers. The driver caught Seeley's anxious look in the rearview mirror and turned up the foreign-sounding music on the radio; zithers, it sounded like, and low chanting voices. Palmieri saw Seeley's expression, too. "I don't know about New York, but in San Francisco they don't hold you in contempt for being a few minutes late for a pretrial conference."

They arrived fifteen minutes late at the Phillip Burton Courthouse, a glass-and-granite high-rise that filled an entire block at the edge of the Civic Center, and spent five minutes getting through the security gate. On the nineteenth floor they had to wait for a buzzer to let them into a narrow corridor. Palmieri led Seeley past a warren of offices, courtrooms, jury rooms, more dim corridors, and, finally, to Judge Farnsworth's chambers.

The anteroom had the worshipful hush of a cloister. Barnum was already there. Ignoring Palmieri, he introduced Seeley to Rachel Fischler, who Seeley guessed was Thorpe's second chair, and to a young lawyer from St. Gall's headquarters in Switzerland. Barnum butchered the man's name, which Seeley deciphered as Philippe Dusollier.

Fischler was pear-shaped and had a frizzy thatch of black hair that looked as if no amount of effort would bring it under control. She apologized for Thorpe, who was finishing a trial in Akron, but would be back in time for jury selection on Friday. Her voice was high-pitched, almost a whine. The Swiss was slender and precise in a narrow-cut gray suit and steel-rimmed glasses; he had a porridgy complexion and, oddly, the otherwise thin face showed the beginnings of a double chin. He didn't speak, but the complacent gray eyes told Seeley that Dusollier was judging him, and would be throughout the trial for daily reports back to the home office in St. Gall.

The judge's secretary, who had been watching from a desk in the corner, asked if anyone else was coming. When Seeley told her no, she knocked on the door next to her desk, then opened it without waiting for a response.

Judge Farnsworth's office was softly lit and, with several easy chairs arranged in a semicircle around a sofa, looked more like a well-furnished living room than the heart of a judge's chambers. Fresh-cut flowers were on the end tables and Seeley recognized the framed prints on the walls as coming from small editions by contemporary masters. Floor-to-ceiling bookshelves filled with tan, black, and red volumes of the Federal Supplement and Federal Reporter—along with the American flag in the corner, the only government issue in the room—occupied one wall. Another wall, entirely of glass, framed the gray buildings and domed roofs of the Civic Center and, in the distance, glimmering behind a confusion of stalky construction cranes, the bay. It occurred to Seeley that, when they came to San Francisco, even government architects were seduced by the view.

Ellen Farnsworth rose from a small desk that, like her secretary's, was in an inconspicuous corner, and introduced herself to Seeley, greeting the others by name, pronouncing the Swiss lawyer's name fluently. She was attractive in a dark, heavy-featured way and her suit was elegantly cut; the skirt—shorter than Seeley would have expected on a federal judge—showed off long, well-shaped legs. Federal judges are usually smarter and more able than most of the lawyers who come before them and, with their lifetime tenure, possess a detachment not unlike the composure of a beautiful woman who knows the effect that her good looks have on men. Judge Farnsworth had both. Thorpe was shrewd to select Rachel Fischler for his second chair. Unlike any man he could have chosen, Fischler would implicitly stroke the judge's vanity.

The judge took the upholstered chair closest to the window and, after everyone found a place, said, "I suppose it's futile, but I'll ask anyway. Has there been any progress toward a settlement?"

"No, Your Honor," Fischler said. "There have been several discussions since our last meeting with you. As you ordered, the two CEOs talked. They met in New York City. But there hasn't been any progress."

Most patent cases, even major cases like *Vaxtek v. St. Gall*, would have settled by now. Seeley had seen violently adversarial parties reach agreement in the middle of trial. Twice, he had settled cases while the jury was out deliberating. Judges differ in how aggressively they encourage settlement and, from what Seeley saw in the files, Farnsworth had pressed the parties, but not hard. If she had met Warshaw, the entrepreneur who planted stakes to preserve the boundaries of his property, she would not have done even that. So long as Warshaw controlled Vaxtek, Seeley saw no possibility that the case would settle.

The judge took a pair of tortoiseshell half-frames from a drawer in the end table and opened the thick manila folder on her lap. Briskly leafing through the pages, she separated a single sheet from the pile. "I see you are visiting us from out of state, Mr. Seeley." She handed him the document. It was the printed form used for admission pro hac vice. "You will find us very hospitable here in the Northern District." She looked at him over the half-frames. "But if you want to be admitted, your motion will have to be in the proper form."

Seeley looked at the paper and immediately saw the mistake. Where the form asked for the name of the highest court of the state in which he was admitted to practice, whoever filled it out had typed in "New York Supreme Court." California calls its high court the Supreme

Court, but in New York it's the Court of Appeals. Seeley glanced at Palmieri, who had taken a legal pad from his briefcase and was writing rapidly.

"Our requirements are modest, Mr. Seeley, but punctilio, you will agree, is important."

Fischler was looking at the American flag across the room, jaw clamped to hide her amusement. Next to Seeley, Barnum put a hand to his mouth and cleared his throat, glaring at Palmieri. The coarse bully of two days ago was today disguised in a pinstriped suit and rep tie.

Seeley thought to say something clever, but decided to be safe. "I apologize, Judge. It was obviously an oversight." Irritation leaked out of his words. "I can assure you, we will have our motion in correct form no later than two this afternoon."

"The purpose of this meeting, Mr. Seeley, is to resolve all outstanding motions now, so we can get this trial under way."

The judge was letting him know that she had authority over him, and that it was Seeley's job to accept that. One of President Clinton's last judicial appointments, she had been a class action plaintiff's lawyer, specializing in securities fraud lawsuits. It wasn't Seeley's field, but he knew that courts had adopted several of the innovative theories she'd advanced for her shareholder clients, altering the balance of power in these lawsuits. She was the savior of the little guy while making a lawyer-sized fortune for herself. Seeley also knew that Farnsworth was toying with him; she would grant the motion even if he didn't hand in the papers until just before jury selection began.

Farnsworth turned to the chair across from Seeley. "Ms. Fischler?"

"If Mr. Seeley's proposal is acceptable to the court, Your Honor, we have no problem with it."

"Fine. You have until two o'clock this afternoon." Farnsworth was continuing through the papers in the file. "Do we have all the stipulations, or are there some surprises for me here, too?"

"No surprises, Your Honor."

"None," Seeley said.

"I see here that your client is stipulating priority of invention, Ms. Fischler."

"That's right, Your Honor. My client is aware of the court's interest in efficiency, and we thought it would help to move the trial along."

Fawning like this, Seeley knew, won a lawyer nothing but a judge's disdain. Thorpe would not have said it.

The judge looked over her glasses at the Swiss lawyer. "The court is very grateful, Mr. Dusollier. I'm sure your employer had its reasons."

The Swiss lawyer adjusted his tie and nodded, but said nothing.

The judge removed several paper-clipped pages from the folder. "I've looked at both of your witness lists—"

Fischler spoke before the judge could finish. "We have no changes, Your Honor."

Seeley said, "We have one change, Judge."

Farnsworth's frown told Seeley that he had misstepped. She wasn't interested in his witness lineup. She had been heading in a different direction when Fischler interrupted. Barnum either didn't see or didn't understand, and he leaned into Seeley. His whisper was hoarse. "What change? You didn't ask me." Seeley smelled the peppermint on his breath.

"The reason I was looking at your lists"—Farnsworth turned to include Fischler—"was that both of you, but particularly your client, Ms. Fischler, are going to have to thin out your witnesses. I've decided that we can try this case in two weeks. That means each of you has twenty-four hours of trial time to spend however you want, on opening, direct, cross, and closing argument. But unless your witnesses talk very fast, you're going to have to do some cutting."

Palmieri looked at Seeley before speaking. "We understood from our last meeting, Your Honor, that we had three weeks for trial, thirty-six hours for each side."

"Well, I changed my mind. I have three months of cases backed up on my calendar, all of them ready for trial. No one seems interested in settling their cases."

Fischler said, "All of our witnesses are prepared and ready to go, Your Honor. Each one's testimony is connected to the others'."

"I'm sure your witnesses have been well-prepared and orchestrated, Ms. Fischler, and I'm also sure that they have been well paid by your

client. But life is short and each of you can cut out three or four witnesses without inflicting a mortal wound on due process of law."

Dusollier whispered something to Fischler, and she shook her
head vigorously. "I was thinking about the record on appeal, Your
Honor."

"I appreciate your concern, Ms. Fischler, but if there's an appeal, this
case goes to the federal circuit and the record will be just fine there.
They haven't reversed me yet. I'll want to see your new witness lists
Friday morning."

Seeley had no problem with a two-week trial. But he should have
told Barnum about his decision to drop Steinhardt as their lead witness,
and it could take some time to bring the general counsel to where he
would agree to Steinhardt's testifying lower in the order. "We have no
problem with twenty-four hours, Judge." He'd find an opening later
to delay submission of the new witness list until Monday.

Farnsworth returned the folder to the end table and opened a
leather-bound calendar to a page marked by a blue ribbon. "We start
picking our jury at eight on Friday morning." She glanced at Seeley.
"I hope the hour doesn't come as a surprise to you."

Seeley said, "We have no problem with that, Judge." Palmieri had
already told him about Farnsworth's early hours.

"You understand that here in the Northern District, each side gets
three peremptory challenges and unlimited challenges for cause, but
the judge conducts voir dire. If you think I've missed any important
questions, you'll have the opportunity to let me know." She had been
looking at Seeley, but now took everyone in. "I'm sure Mr. Thorpe
knows all this. You can take as much time making challenges as you
want, but I've never recessed for lunch before a jury got picked, so
you will want to reflect on whether your objections are sufficiently
important to keep the jurors from their lunch."

Farnsworth snapped the calendar shut. "We will start with opening statements on Monday. I hear motions every day at seven thirty
and trial starts at eight. A week from next Monday, we'll recess at one
thirty so that I can attend a monthly district conference. A week from
Tuesday, I want to see your draft jury instructions. I'll give you my

draft instructions on Wednesday, and you submit your comments on Thursday. I'll instruct the jury the following Monday."

Click, click, click. Seeley was learning something new about women. They were better than any of the men he knew at bending their lives to a single object: Ellen Farnsworth, to efficiency; Lily Warren, to her research; and Judy Pearsall, to proving that her husband had not killed himself.

"Are there any questions?"

Seeley said, "We have no problem with a two-week trial, or with you picking the jury. But the two are connected. It's going to be hard to winnow out witnesses, not knowing what the jury looks like, and if we have no control over that—"

"An interesting point, Counselor. What are you suggesting?"

"That we give you our final witness list Monday morning at seven thirty."

"Do you have any problem with that, Ms. Fischler?"

"I don't know, Your Honor." The question flustered her. "I hadn't discussed this possibility with Mr. Thorpe."

"Why do you need Mr. Thorpe? Your client is sitting right next to you."

Dusollier shot her a puzzled look.

"It will be fine, Your Honor," Fischler said. "What Mr. Seeley proposes will be fine."

Farnsworth rose and gave them an amused but remarkably warm smile. "I will see you all Friday morning."

When they were in the brightly lit hallway outside the maze of corridors, Barnum gripped Seeley's arm, furious. Seeley pulled away as they went into the elevator. Palmieri came in behind them and said, "That was nice footwork in there."

Seeley said, "I don't like being put in tight corners."

"I'm sorry about the papers. I'll take care of it."

The elevator doors opened to the lobby. "Have them on the clerk's desk no later than one."

Barnum fumed silently until they were past the security station and out on the plaza. "Get clear on this," Barnum said. "I make the important litigation decisions—and the order of witnesses is an important decision."

"I've decided to lead off with Cordier, the South African. I'm putting Steinhardt on fourth, after Chaikovsky and Kaplan."

"Bob Pearsall was thinking that, too, but he had the good sense to come to me first. I don't care how good your track record is, I get to make that call."

Seeley wondered what Pearsall's reasons had been for moving Steinhardt. It was the scientist's arrogance that initially concerned Seeley, but since the lunch with Lily, he was also worried that there might be gaps that Steinhardt's well-buffed lab notebooks could not explain. He thought of the words in Pearsall's sketchbook: *What else is A.S. hiding?* What *else.* What had Pearsall already discovered when he wrote that, and what had he not yet discovered?

"Look, Ed, let's go over the list tomorrow and decide on which witnesses we can cut."

"Steinhardt comes back from Paris Sunday afternoon. If he hears you moved him, he'll go straight to Joel."

From what Seeley could see, Barnum was not a very good lawyer, but behind the bullying was a middle-aged man with few career prospects who was afraid of his boss. He was doing the best he could to keep his job, and all that he could see was Michael Seeley blocking his way.

"Joel Warshaw's not a problem. He'd fire Steinhardt if he thought that's what it would take to win the case."

This failed to console Barnum.

Seeley said, "Call me tomorrow and we'll talk."

"I got a call from Herb Phan this morning." The busy San Mateo police lieutenant had found the time to call the former county prosecutor. Barnum drew close and Seeley again smelled the peppermint. "Herb likes to focus on his investigations, and he doesn't like lawyers looking over his shoulder. You could take a lesson in concentration from him. Forget the widow. Let's win this case."

Barnum left, giving Seeley his first unhurried moment of the day. With jury selection on Friday, Steinhardt descending from Paris, Thorpe from Akron, and Cordier from New York—he again reminded himself to return Cordier's call—the quiet would be his last for the next two weeks.

Seeley surveyed the patchwork that surrounded the courthouse: parking lots, luncheonettes, a tire store, low-rise apartment and office buildings. Unlike the high-rise canyons of the business district two miles away and the grand, implausible architecture of the Civic Center next door, the jumble reminded him of nothing so much as the desolate heart of Buffalo's once-thriving downtown. The thought of his hometown pulled at Seeley as it did whenever he was away from it, perhaps because, as dark as the memories were, it was the one place where he felt entirely safe. He did not feel safe in San Francisco.

TEN

Click, click, click.

Jury selection moved forward like tumblers falling in a lock, Judge Farnsworth leaving no question about her complete control of the courtroom. On the benches in the first two rows of the gallery, the thirty or so prospective jurors talked quietly among themselves, waiting while the judge ruled on motions in other cases and on a last-minute evidentiary motion from Fischler. Thorpe was still absent, and the judge didn't ask why.

After she disposed of Fischler's motion, Farnsworth turned to Seeley. "Aren't you forgetting something, Counselor?"

The corrected pro hac papers had been filed, but the judge hadn't yet acted on them, and Seeley didn't enjoy being a supplicant. With a teasing smile, Farnsworth said, "Your motion for admission is granted."

At eight, the judge's clerk, a radiant black woman wearing gold hoop earrings, looked out to the gallery and read a name, Floyd Ramsey, from the paper in her hand, directing the prospective juror to the seat in the jury box closest to the judge. As he took his place in the front row, Farnsworth greeted him. "Good morning, Mr. Ramsey." She and the clerk continued on this way until they had filled all fourteen seats in the two rows of the jury box.

In a federal civil trial, a jury of as few as six can render a verdict, but the verdict must be unanimous. Palmieri had told Seeley that Farnsworth was going to impanel eight jurors, with the expectation that illness or an unexpected obligation over the course of the two-week trial might drop the number to seven or even six. This meant that, with each side entitled to three peremptory challenges, the judge was going to be strict in ruling on challenges to disqualify a juror for cause.

Surveying the courtroom as he waited for the first panel of jurors to take their seats, Seeley found himself thinking of *m* words: magisterial, medieval, murky. There were no windows in the courtroom, and the shadowy corners and dull reflections off the dark wood paneling made it easy to imagine a royal court or ecclesiastical hall from another century. The two heavy oak counsel tables were large enough for a banquet, and the witness box and desks for the clerk and the court reporter, a sharp stick of a woman with carrot-orange hair, clung like dependencies from the judge's bench. Only the polished granite behind the judge was amply lit, casting a halo around her robes.

The wooden gate separating the well of the courtroom from the gallery squeaked softly when someone passed through it, and Seeley and Palmieri turned when Thorpe came in. Everyone in the courtroom, even the judge, watched as the old lawyer shuffled to counsel's table, but Thorpe gave no sign that he was aware of the attention. Seeley figured his adversary to be in his late seventies, but the way his narrow shoulders locked into a shrug when he put his briefcase down and waited for a nod from Farnsworth to introduce himself had less to do with age, or even fatigue, Seeley thought, than with melancholy. His suit was well pressed, the white shirt starched; a silk tie was neatly knotted beneath a bloodhound's jowls. But sadness clung to him like a garment.

"Emil Thorpe for defendant, Laboratories St. Gall, Your Honor." The voice was of a piece with the man's appearance: gravelly, tired, sorrowful; the voice of a man who had been up too late, smoking too many cigarettes, pushing large boulders uphill. "I apologize for my tardiness."

"Your time is your own, Mr. Thorpe, and it is of no concern to the court"—she nodded in the direction of the jury box—"so long as you do not waste the time of these good people."

Fischler had left for Thorpe the same seat at the head of the table as Palmieri left for Seeley. In addition to Fischler and Dusollier, two men and a woman were at Thorpe's table. Seeley didn't know the men, but recognized the woman as a well-traveled jury consultant. From the jurors' personal and educational backgrounds, and from their body language as the trial progressed, the expert would—or so she promised the lawyers who hired her—tell counsel which questions, arguments, and exhibits would work and which wouldn't. For a case of this size, she would probably also assemble a paid phantom jury to mirror the actual jurors' traits, giving Thorpe the chance to try out his tactics. Seeley thought that these consultants were about as useful as astrologers, and was pleased that Pearsall had rejected Barnum's suggestion to hire one.

Farnsworth thanked the prospective jurors, both those in the jury box and those still in the gallery, for coming to court. Leaning over the bench, her hands clasped in front of her, she told them that the trial involved plaintiff, Vaxtek's, claim that defendant, St. Gall, had infringed Vaxtek's patent on AV/AS, a treatment for HIV/AIDS, and St. Gall's defense that the Vaxtek patent was invalid and, even if it were valid, St. Gall had not infringed on it.

"You will find this to be a fascinating case," she said, taking care to make eye contact first with those in the jury box and then with those still in the gallery. "It is an important case, too, in terms of its impact on the lives of people around the world. There's going to be some science for you to understand, but these are fine lawyers"—she nodded toward the two tables—"and, together with their witnesses, they are going to be your teachers. You may also hear some things about American patent law, but you needn't be concerned with these until the end of the trial, when I will instruct you on the law you should apply to the facts. This is, I promise, going to be a lot more enjoyable than your high-school biology class, and you'll be glad to know that there won't be an exam at the end"—two or three in the jury box laughed tentatively—"but you will, at the end of the trial, need to come to a verdict, a unanimous verdict."

Seeley had assigned an associate on the trial team to gather background on all of Farnsworth's cases from the time she was appointed, so he knew that she not only had fewer reversals than any other judge in the Northern District, but also that in her eight years on the bench, none of her juries had ever failed to reach a verdict. This was no accident. Judge Farnsworth lavished on the jurors in her courtroom a degree of attention and care that so exceeded their expectations, the jurors reciprocated with a loyalty of their own. If the judge wanted a unanimous verdict, they would find a way to give her one.

On an easel across from the jury box, questions printed on a poster-sized sheet of cardboard solicited the prospective jurors' name, residence, educational background, occupation, spouse or partner's occupation, hobbies, and whether any of them had previously been a juror or party in a lawsuit. As each of the fourteen in the jury box answered the questions, Seeley wrote the information on a lined white pad and Palmieri typed it into his laptop. Fischler and the jury expert did the same, but Thorpe, slumped in his chair, was absolutely still, giving no sign that his thoughts were here and not still in Akron.

Farnsworth told them that the list of excuses from jury service was short—"This is service to your country, and service requires sacrifice"—and only when she asked whether any of them had views on the patent system that might affect their ability to render a fair verdict, did a hand shoot up. In the second row, a pale middle-aged woman with flyaway gray hair rose from her chair. "The American patent system is a travesty! It's a criminal conspiracy by corporate America to raise prices and keep poor people from getting the drugs they need to stay alive."

There was nervous laughter among her neighbors and a few murmurs from the gallery. Seeley flipped through the lined pad, but before he could find the page, Palmieri pointed at his computer screen. Faye Simberkoff was single, a graduate of the UC Berkeley information science school, and now worked at a public library in Oakland.

When Seeley looked up, Farnsworth was waiting for him to challenge the prospective juror for bias.

Seeley knew that if he challenged Simberkoff, the judge would excuse her from the jury, but he didn't want to leave the thought hanging in the courtroom that patents are bad, nor did he want any juror to think that he had silenced the woman's views.

"It would help us decide whether to challenge for cause, Judge, if Ms. Simberkoff could expand a bit more on her thoughts about the American patent system."

Farnsworth saw what he was doing, didn't approve, but asked the librarian to continue if she wished. Vigorously gesturing with a raised fist, the woman enlarged her indictment of the patent cabal to include Wells Fargo Bank, Aetna Insurance Company, and the Roman Catholic Church. This time when Farnsworth said, "Mr. Seeley?," he asked that she be removed for cause, and the judge excused her.

Barnum had positioned himself at the side of counsel's table, where he would, as Seeley anticipated, obscure the jury's view of Palmieri. As the questions continued, Barnum regularly leaned his heft across the table, blind to Palmieri, who was between them, to whisper that Seeley should challenge the prospective juror for cause. Seeley nodded, as if weighing the advice. He had already decided to use one of his peremptory challenges for a pediatrician whose background would give him more credibility with the other jurors than he deserved. Usually physicians try to get out of jury duty, and it bothered Seeley that this one did not; he pictured him in the jury room explaining to the others how Steinhardt's discovery was entirely obvious, and thus unpatentable.

Farnsworth excused two jurors on her own—a woman with a job that made a two-week absence from work difficult, and a man with nonrefundable air tickets to London—and a third, a research employee of the world's largest patent owner, IBM, on a challenge from Thorpe. As each excluded juror departed, the clerk called out another name from the gallery, keeping the fourteen seats filled, until one prospective juror remained whom the judge had not yet questioned, a young-looking software engineer from a small Silicon Valley company.

Palmieri pointed at the laptop screen—Gary Sansone—but Seeley had already started to think of him as the "kid." With a blond ponytail and a jockey's wiry build, Sansone had an easy smile and the kind of natural authority that could move the others on the jury, even though all of them were older. At Thorpe's request, Farnsworth asked Sansone whether, as an employee at a start-up company, he might have a bias against a giant, multinational pharmaceutical company.

The kid grinned. "That would depend, Your Honor, on how evil and grasping a multinational it is."

The jury box broke into laughter, and for a full second a smile lit Thorpe's face as he joined in. The jury expert, seated next to him, tugged hard at the hem of his jacket, but he brushed her hand away. With a chuckle in his voice, Thorpe said, "We have no problem with this juror, Your Honor."

Thorpe had begun his own seduction of the jury. Farnsworth would use her solicitude to make the jurors feel that they were part of her team. Thorpe's tactic was more subtle. Having now seen the phantom of a smile from this austere, sorrowful man, the jurors would work to please him if that was the price to see him smile once more.

The jury liked Sansone, and they wanted Thorpe to like them, both of which meant that if Seeley tried to exclude the kid, he—and his client—would at once become the villains of the trial, even before opening statements. So far, he had measured each of the prospective jurors against a single question: How deeply would Steinhardt's arrogance offend this man or woman? Now, applying the same question to Sansone, he worried. According to the notes Seeley had jotted on the legal pad in front of him, the kid had taken premed classes, mostly in biochemistry, before switching to an electrical engineering major at Santa Clara University. His hobby was bicycle racing, and he read journals like *Science* and *Cell*. He might be sympathetic to Vaxtek as a small company but, like the pediatrician, he could also be the authoritative figure in the jury room who second-guessed Steinhardt and the science behind AV/AS. He could be the juror who kept Seeley from the unanimous verdict he needed.

Seeley decided not to fall into Thorpe's trap.

"We have no objection to this juror, Judge."

"Then," Farnsworth said, "if you each exercise your three peremptories, we'll have a jury."

Seeley tore off from the legal pad the remaining fourteen pages on which he'd written the names and backgrounds of the prospective jurors, and spread them across the table. Barnum pointed at two of the pages, one of them Sansone's. "You can still kick him off," he said.

Seeley looked past Barnum to the jury box, into the arresting, deep blue eyes of Sansone, then shook his head and picked instead the pediatrician and the two who said their hobby was foreign travel, guessing that, perhaps more cosmopolitan than the others, they would be less responsive to the patriotic bias he had built into his case—protecting American research ingenuity against a foreign poacher. When Palmieri agreed, he wrote the three names on a fresh sheet of paper.

Thorpe was already at sidebar, waiting to hand his three candidates up to the judge. Farnsworth took the two sheets, compared them and removed four of the Post-its she had placed on a chart that indicated the numbered seats in the jury box.

"You see this sometimes," she said. "You both want to remove the same person." The retired career counselor whose hobby was foreign travel. She returned their sheets to them. "Why don't you try again."

Seeley considered what Thorpe's reasons might have been for excluding the career counselor, and again wrote in her name. He folded the sheet and handed it to the judge. Thorpe wrote on his piece of paper and handed it up. This time, after comparing the peremptories, Farnsworth smiled and removed two more Post-its from the chart, leaving eight.

"We have a jury," Farnsworth said. She handed the chart down to the clerk, and nodded to her to swear in the jury. After that, the judge told them what their duties would be, the procedures they would need to follow in coming to court every day, and cautioned them not to read, watch, or listen to any press coverage of the trial.

Four white faces looked out of the jury box, one Asian, two Hispanics, and one black. Five were women, three men. Their ages ranged from twenty-six to seventy-one. Among them were a retired schoolteacher; a real estate broker whose avocation was collecting antique dolls; two secretaries, one with a graduate degree in education; a hospital nurse; an AT&T cable splicer from Napa; an accountant who said she lived with her "domestic partner"; and Sansone, the kid.

Rolling his chair back and forth at counsel's table, Barnum was a worrier. "The one with the ponytail," he said. "You're sure he won't be a problem?"

"No," Seeley said. "I'm not sure."

"I'm not surprised," Barnum said. "He reminds me of you."

From inside the elevator, Thorpe looped his arm around the door, holding it open for Seeley and Barnum. Dusollier, already there, nodded at Seeley. Thorpe introduced the two strangers from the defense table, partners in a well-known Chicago intellectual property boutique. Seeley recognized the names—Witkin and Gallagher—from the depositions that he'd read while he was still in Buffalo. Under the fluorescent light, Thorpe's complexion was gray and mottled with age spots. High on each cheek was a scattering of hairs that the razor had missed, each as fine as an eyelash. Seeley studied the face for some evidence of what Thorpe might have been like as a younger man, something in the set of his jaw or a trace in his eyes that might betray a spark of wonder or curiosity, even will. But if a light ever burned in those dark, rimmed eyes, it had gone out long ago.

The elevator opened to the dimly lit lobby, and Thorpe waited for Seeley while the others walked to the double doors.

"Your reputation precedes you, Mr. Seeley—or may I call you Michael? I'm honored to be your adversary." As in the courtroom the gravelly voice was reserved, even somber.

Seeley said, "I'm sure it will be an interesting trial."

"It's a tragedy about Bob Pearsall." Thorpe rested a hand on Seeley's arm. "Did you know him?"

Seeley turned to escape Thorpe's touch and said, "Did you?"

"How well do we know anyone?" When Seeley didn't respond, Thorpe said, "We had lunch from time to time. He was in a small poker group we have, some local trial lawyers. We get together once or twice a month."

"What about his family?" Seeley was still unsure why Judy asked him, and not one of her husband's friends, to look into the police handling of his death.

"You mean the loving wife, the adoring daughter? Judy told me you've taken an interest in this."

"Only because she asked."

"Surely you've been practicing long enough to know how appearances can deceive. I've been married to the same woman for fifty-three years. My wife is my bridge partner, my life companion, and I devoutly believe that she has been faithful to me all this time. But do I really know that? Would I stake my life on it? Of course not."

The privacy of the observation startled Seeley, but it was so offhand that he wondered if it was something Thorpe had said many times before, including to strangers.

At the security barrier, one of the guards greeted Thorpe by name, but he ignored it or didn't notice. Thorpe said, "So you don't think Bob threw himself in front of a train?"

"He took pictures of birds. He read philosophy."

"Bob was a complicated man. He had his secrets."

Seeley said, "But you're not going to share them."

"If I did, they wouldn't be secrets."

Seeley thought Thorpe would smile at his own remark, but he didn't. "What kind of poker player was he?"

"That's what I'm saying. You'd expect someone like Bob to be a methodical player, counting cards, figuring the probabilities, patient, like he was with those birds. But no, he was reckless. He'd bet every hand, so, even if you were holding pretty good cards, you wouldn't know whether to fold. Of course, he lost more than he won, but that never seemed to bother him."

One the other side of the double doors, a chanting crowd with placards was gathered on the courthouse plaza. Television cameras moved around the protesters.

Seeley said, "What kind of poker player are you?"

Thorpe gave the question more thought than it needed. "Methodical. You could say I'm a methodical player."

Thorpe had been playing poker with his peremptory challenge to the retired career counselor.

"And close to the chest?"

"Yes, that, too," Thorpe said. "We should have lunch next week."

Seeley said, "The week after would be better."

"Of course, after you've put on your case. Our clients will want us to discuss settlement one last time."

Thorpe went through the double doors—briskly, Seeley observed, shedding his courtroom torpor, making his way in the direction of the thirty or forty chanting protesters. One shook a placard at him, PILLS NOT PROFITS, but Thorpe moved past the crowd to where the news cameras and microphones were. Seeley knew that Thorpe wouldn't answer the reporters' questions so much as he would use the press to send Wall Street a message prepared by St. Gall's public relations and investor relations departments.

A slight-figured young woman in jeans, turtleneck, and down vest came up to Seeley, her hand outstretched.

"Michael Seeley? I'm Gail Odum from the *Chronicle*."

The business reporter. For a disconnected moment, Seeley imagined that the stenographer's pad in her other hand was Pearsall's, and that she had found a notebook Seeley missed.

"What did Lily Warren tell you about your case?"

Seeley said, "You don't even know if I called her."

"She told me you met, but she wouldn't tell me what you spoke about."

Across the plaza, Thorpe was talking to a news crew, and several of the protesters had moved behind him to be on camera. Palmieri was a few feet away from the crowd, but Seeley couldn't see whether he was listening to Thorpe or talking to one of the protesters, a tall, rangy man with curly blond hair. When Seeley turned back to Odum, Barnum was coming toward him from the courthouse.

Seeley said to Odum, "Why would it matter to you, what we talked about?"

An automobile horn blared at the intersection, and Seeley didn't know if she heard him.

"I know that Lily and your inventor, Steinhardt, worked together at UC before they split up and went to work for competitors. Then your client sues St. Gall and she gets fired. It has to be connected to your case."

The parties' stipulation on priority nowhere mentioned Lily's presence in Steinhardt's lab at Vaxtek, and Lily, desperate to keep her visa, would not have told Odum about the incident.

"Maybe it was a coincidence." Seeley was aware of Barnum standing behind him, listening.

"Or," Odum said, "maybe there's a romantic angle." The reporter had a nice scent about her, nothing as intense as perfume—soap, maybe, or her shampoo.

Seeley said, "I'd think that would be for the gossip page, not the business section."

Odum laughed. "At the *Chronicle*, the business section *is* the gossip page."

She had a nice laugh, too, and Seeley guessed that she used it to pry out facts.

Trailed by a cameraman, the television newsman who had interviewed Thorpe was coming toward Seeley. Several yards behind, the tall curly-haired protester separated himself from the group and followed.

Seeley said to Odum, "If anything comes up that's newsworthy, and that I can give you, I will."

Odum said, "On the phone, you promised that if I got Lily to call you, you'd give me an exclusive." The smile looked genuine. "And let me decide whether it's newsworthy."

As she went away, Barnum leaned into Seeley. "You didn't tell me you talked to the Chinese girl." Seeley turned from the approaching television crew to keep the conversation private. Barnum said, "All you need to know is that St. Gall stipulated priority. You're running off in all directions. The Chinese girl. The police about Bob Pearsall. You've got a trial ready to start."

"And, if Steinhardt is going to testify, I don't want any surprises."

"What kind of surprises?"

"That's what I'm trying to find out."

There was a clatter of equipment behind Seeley. "Jeff Fox, Counselor! KBAY television news!"

Seeley turned. The sprayed, blow-dried hair and unnaturally pink face gave the reporter the appearance of a heavily retouched photograph. Below the showy tie and jacket he had on worn jeans and scuffed running shoes, but the camera, just a few feet away, wouldn't catch them.

The reporter held the microphone an inch from Seeley's mouth. "Vaxtek is a tiny company in South San Francisco. Tell us what your client's chances are of winning this case against a multinational giant like St. Gall."

"That's what the trial's for, isn't it?" Seeley watched bewilderment creep into the buffed and polished face. "So a jury can listen to the evidence and weigh the facts, and then decide who has the stronger claim."

The car horn blared again. The reporter said, "But your opponent, Emil Thorpe, just explained to our viewers why your client's case is so weak."

Thorpe's remarks had doubtless brimmed with confidence that St. Gall could not possibly lose. And when, in two weeks his client did lose, the company's public relations staff would hand him a statement that explained why the loss was really a win.

Seeley put on his widest actor's smile and looked squarely into the camera. "I'm sure Mr. Thorpe has already more than fulfilled your viewers' need for entertainment this evening." He turned away abruptly before the reporter could follow up, and found himself inches from the curly-haired activist.

In black jeans and a sleeveless sweater over what looked like a Hawaiian shirt, the man was younger and taller than he had appeared from a distance, and Seeley experienced the rare discomfort of having to look up to someone who wasn't a judge sitting on a bench.

"This trial is an outrage," the man said, smiling directly at the news camera. Only the golden puff of a goatee spoiled his scrubbed all-American good looks. "How can this man defend a patent that will make it impossible for millions of people to get a lifesaving drug?"

Before Seeley could answer, the newsman signaled his cameraman to come in closer and Barnum shouldered his way to the camera. "We've spent half a billion dollars on AV/AS," Barnum said. "That makes it our property."

The protester said, "So you get rich while people die."

"We have a responsibility to our shareholders."

"So *they* get rich while people die." The protester's smile turned into a mocking laugh.

Seeley didn't like trying a case in the media, but Barnum could say something truly damaging, and he worried that one or more jurors would forget Judge Farnsworth's closing request to stay away from the news.

Seeley edged in front of Barnum. "Unfortunately," he said to the camera, "discoveries like AV/AS don't just happen. What Mr. Barnum is saying is that they consume money, lots of it."

"What's worse," the protester asked him, "that your client loses its investment or that millions of people lose their lives?"

Seeley said, "You could also feed starving people by letting them steal wheat from the field, but if you did that, how many farmers are going to invest in seed and fertilizer for next year's crop? It's the same with research. A company's not going to invest in making the next breakthrough discovery if it knows a competitor's going to be able to rip it off just like the last one."

"Jonas Salk didn't try to get a patent on the polio vaccine. He gave it away free."

The protester reminded Seeley of the idealistic young artists he represented pro bono when he practiced in New York. "That was fifty years ago," he said, "and Jonas Salk was a saint. How many saints do you know with the cash to bring a drug like this to the market?"

The man, his smile uncertain now, said, "The government should pay for the research and give the drugs away free to anyone who needs them."

"How comfortable are you letting politicians decide what kinds of drugs get developed? If it were up to the politicians, do you think we'd have the AIDS therapies we have today?"

"And you think we should trust businessmen with that decision?"

Seeley said, "There's no reason to trust businessmen any more than politicians. But you can trust the profit motive. If these therapies are what people want and will pay for, drug companies will produce them."

"That's my point," the curly-haired man said. "Your client will produce only what people can pay for."

"But, the alternative is no AIDS treatments at all."

Seeley leaned into the protester, turning him away from the camera and speaking quietly so that the microphone wouldn't pick up his words. "If you and your people gave this some thought, you'd leave off attacking our patent and, when we win our case, you'll put pressure on my client to sell AV/AS at prices that people in places like Africa an afford. That way, you get our drug and you get to save lives, too."

At the bottom of the plaza, Gail Odum, pencil in hand and notebook open, was talking to one of the protesters, a broad-shouldered woman with jet-black hair that flowed well below her shoulders. At something one of them said, the two suddenly broke into laughter, Odum touching the woman's arm. Did Odum and Lily laugh like that when they talked? Women's secrets. A woman's touch—Seeley could still feel Renata's hand flat against his chest. It came as a surprise to him how lonely he was for that.

ELEVEN

On Monday at 7:40 a.m., while Judge Farnsworth proceeded through her motion calendar, Seeley reviewed the notes for his opening statement. The benches on both sides of the gallery were filled. Palmieri had pointed out to Seeley the lawyers sent by their investment bank clients to evaluate every nuance of the trial for its possible impact on stock prices. Seven years ago, when a federal court ruled that the patent on Prozac was invalid, Eli Lilly shares plummeted more than thirty percent. These lawyers were here to anticipate any such effect on the shares of Vaxtek or St. Gall.

The press was in the back, Gail Odum from the *Chronicle* dressed today in a severe gray suit. The offhand attire of the six or seven figures talking by the gallery rail identified them as part of the protest group, but Seeley didn't see the tall curly-haired protester he had debated with outside for the evening news. Leonard was in the front row, sunny in a light-colored suit. Warshaw wasn't there, but Seeley hadn't expected him to come.

Seeley was thinking about Dr. Robert Gore and his invention of

Gore-Tex when Barnum slid an electric-red binder onto counsel's table.

"Very bright," Seeley said.

"Look inside." Barnum took his chair at the side of the table.

Palmieri watched as Seeley opened the binder. At the top of the first page, in large type, was the name of juror number seven, Bernard Adelson, the retired schoolteacher, and beneath it and on the three pages that followed, every fact a trial lawyer might want to know about the juror, his family, his medical history, his and his family's every habit and whim. The remaining pages, arranged alphabetically, did the same for the other jurors. Seeley felt an impulse to turn to the back of the binder, where the information on Gary Sansone, the kid, would be, but closed it instead.

"We can't use this."

"This is valuable material," Barnum said. "Joel hired a firm to collect it."

"Jurors don't get paid forty dollars a day to have Warshaw's investigators poke into their private lives." Seeley's words were louder than he realized, because the judge glanced up from her papers and shot him a cross look.

"Did you investigate me?"

"Of course, we did," Barnum said.

And still, Seeley thought, you hired me. He handed the binder to Barnum. "Shred everything in here."

Seeley had been thinking about Robert Gore because the invention of Gore-Tex was one of those flashes of creative genius that made a patent unassailable in court. Gore had been attempting to transform hard Teflon rods into a more pliable material by following the conventional wisdom and stretching the rods slowly. But no matter how much he slowed the process, the brittle rods continued to break. Then Gore somehow got the inspiration to do exactly the opposite, and discovered that by stretching the rods as rapidly as possible he could extend them to ten times their length without breaking, turning them into a soft, flexible material that, when bonded to cloth, produced a fabric perfect for rainwear. If only Steinhardt could convey to the jury that same brilliant eccentricity of discovery, AV/AS, too, might be invulnerable to attack.

The judge's gavel rapped. She had completed the morning's motion calendar. "We'll take a five-minute recess, and then proceed to opening statements in *Vaxtek v. St. Gall.*" At his small desk next to the jury box, the bailiff, a young Asian in blazer and gray slacks, rose at her signal to bring in the jurors.

Seeley waited for the coughs, murmurs, and shuffling of feet to subside, then walked to the wooden lectern. For the first time that morning, he looked directly at the jurors, one after the other, pausing no more than a moment to engage each pair of eyes. He moved from left to right along the back row, then right to left along the front. He glanced up at the bench. "May it please the court."

A juror in the front row, the nurse, raised her hand. Farnsworth looked at her seating chart. "Yes, Ms. Ortiz?"

Ms. Ortiz gestured at the bailiff. "The pen he gave me doesn't write."

That brought laughter from the courtroom and from the judge, who came down the stairs from the bench and handed the woman her own silver pen. She wagged a finger at her. "Now remember, Ms. Ortiz, I want that back when the trial's over." Her smile took in all the jurors. When she was back in her chair she nodded at Seeley.

"Good morning," Seeley said. "My name is Michael Seeley. I represent Vaxtek, Incorporated, the patent owner and plaintiff in this lawsuit. Vaxtek is a small biotech company with 220 employees whose headquarters *and* research labs *and* production facility"—here Seeley smiled—"whose entire business is located in South San Francisco, just eleven miles from this courtroom. Vaxtek is suing Laboratories St. Gall, the third largest pharmaceutical company in the world, with 110,000 employees and annual sales of $60 billion, for stealing Vaxtek's pioneering invention, AV/AS, the most effective treatment any scientist has yet developed, or any company has yet produced, to prevent the onset of AIDS. Although the defendant is a Swiss company, with headquarters in St. Gall, Switzerland, and facilities around the globe, Vaxtek is seeking justice here, in this courtroom in San Francisco."

This was Seeley's theory of the case, Pearsall's path to victory: the injustice of letting an overgrown schoolyard bully from outside the neighborhood steal lunch from the frail, brainy kid with glasses; the injustice that every juror would correct if he could. Research into jury behavior showed that, by the end of opening statements, nine of ten jurors have irrevocably decided how they will vote in a case, but Seeley believed that they decided earlier than that. He wanted the jurors to understand at once that he was here to guide them not so much to truth, as to justice. The schoolyard bully had to be punished.

"As Judge Farnsworth explained when she picked you for this jury, this is a patent infringement case. To protect its invention of AV/AS, Vaxtek is relying on a patent granted to it by the United States Patent Office, much as you would rely on the title to your car or the deed to your home to stop someone from stealing your property. Like you, Vaxtek worked hard to acquire this property."

The kid, Sansone, had on a sport coat today, and a poorly knotted woolen tie. If Seeley read him correctly, Sansone had decided that he was going to be, if not the jury's foreman, then at least its guiding force.

"Now, the U.S. Patent Office doesn't just hand out patents to anyone who shows up and asks for one. It has almost five thousand examiners, every one of them an expert in his or her field, and these examiners analyze each patent application they receive to determine whether the applicant's invention is sufficiently new to justify the grant of a patent. One of these examiners, Dr. Harriet Siler, studied Vaxtek's discovery of AV/AS, and only after carefully comparing AV/AS to all of the earlier discoveries in the field, did Dr. Siler, whose doctorate is in microbiology, conclude that AV/AS was indeed novel and entitled to the patent we are talking about in this trial. As Judge Farnsworth will instruct you at the end of the trial, unless St. Gall can prove that Dr. Siler made an error, you must vote to uphold the patent."

There was no need for Seeley to explain—Thorpe would certainly do so—that examiners, like Siler, who issue these patents lack the resources available to private lawyers like Boyd McKee who are well paid by their clients to extract from these government employees the broadest possible patents they can.

"Legally, then, Vaxtek has no obligation to prove that its invention meets this standard of novelty. The U.S. Patent Office has already decided that. But because AV/AS is so crucial to Vaxtek's survival as a company, we are going to put on several witnesses who will demonstrate to you why the Patent Office made no mistake, and why this invention is entitled to the fullest protection that American patent law can provide against theft."

Seeley gave the jurors a preview of the expert witnesses who would testify for Vaxtek, briefly describing the testimony of each. His nerves quickened when he reached Steinhardt. The scientist had returned from Paris on Saturday, a day early, and exploded when Barnum told him that he would not be testifying first. Steinhardt telephoned Seeley, demanding that he meet him at his home at once, and slammed down the receiver when Seeley said he was too busy with trial preparation to do so. It wasn't until Sunday afternoon, while Seeley was preparing his first witness, Nicolas Cordier, that Steinhardt called again.

"I have decided that if I am not to testify first, I will not testify at all. Without me, there would be no AV/AS."

This was kid stuff, Seeley thought, and Steinhardt a whining brat. Just to see what Steinhardt's reaction would be, he said, "I can subpoena you as a hostile witness."

"What purpose could that possibly serve?"

Seeley thought of the question Pearsall had written under his sketch of the scientist. "We can find out what you're hiding."

"What makes you think I'm hiding something?" There was less rancor in the tone than before.

The first bluff had worked, so Seeley tried a second. "I talked with Lily Warren."

After a long silence, Steinhardt said, "I have no secrets, and I will demonstrate that when I testify." This time he did not slam the receiver when he hung up.

Seeley quickly scanned the jury, then glanced at his watch. He had consumed less than the half hour he'd allotted to summarizing Vax-tek's case. He gave himself twenty minutes, no more, to anticipate and undermine St. Gall's case, and five minutes to summarize and close.

"Mr. Thorpe, who is St. Gall's lawyer"—he nodded in the direction of counsel's table where Thorpe sat surrounded by his team, and was pleased to see the jury follow the direction of his gaze—"is going to put on witnesses who will try to tell you that Vaxtek's invention does not rise to the level of novelty that the U.S. Congress, in passing the Patent Act, requires before a patent can issue to an invention. Mr. Thorpe's witnesses are also going to tell you that St. Gall's product is different from AV/AS and, for that reason, doesn't infringe Vaxtek's patent. But we will put on witnesses who will show you that despite superficial differences, St. Gall's product is in fact identical in every relevant respect to Vaxtek's."

Seeley checked the courtroom. Judge Farnsworth, in a starched white collar with a bright, knotted scarf, but otherwise neutered by the black robes, was following closely. Barnum's hands were clasped across his belly. He looked pleased. Palmieri, head down, was working at the keyboard of his laptop, activity that could distract a jury. Seeley would need to talk to him about that.

"I noticed," Seeley grinned, "that when I mentioned microbiol-ogy some moments ago, a couple of you flinched. You may be asking yourself"—here Seeley lightened his tone and inclined toward the jury box, as if to bring the jurors into his confidence—"if Vaxtek's sci-entific advance is so significant, how am I going to understand it? Well, I know that if Father Comisky, who tried to teach me high-school biology at St. Boniface Academy thirty years ago, knew I was talking to you about these scientific concepts, he'd turn over in his grave. But I promise you, you're going to hear more from our witnesses about common sense than abstract science, and the science they explain to you will be as clear and colorful as Father Comisky himself would have made it."

Sansone, whose seat in the jury box was toward the center of the back row, had been watching Seeley intently for several minutes. Alone among the jurors, he didn't smile at the reference to Father Comisky.

It was time to wrap up. "As you listen to the testimony of St. Gall's

expert witnesses, you may from time to time feel that you are losing sight of the forest for the trees. St. Gall's witnesses are going to
testify over and over again—because, really, this is all they have—that
Vaxtek's invention is too obvious to deserve a patent. They will testify
that AV/AS was so obvious that any reasonably competent scientist
could have invented it." Here was Seeley's curve ball, the one that
always worked. "Now"—he resisted the impulse to raise a finger for
emphasis—"when Mr. Thorpe's witnesses, these experts, make this
claim, I want you to ask yourself a single question. If AV/AS was so
obvious that any competent scientist could have discovered it, why
didn't St. Gall, with its 110,000 employees and dozens of laboratories
around the world, do it first?"

Seeley took in all their eyes with a glance—for the first time, even
the kid seemed impressed—then left the lectern.

At counsel's table, Barnum was beaming. Palmieri was smiling, too,
but not as broadly. Behind the gallery rail, Leonard's eyes were glazed
with admiration, a look that, even as a boy, Seeley thought would suf-
focate him.

A gray stooped profile, Thorpe moved slowly across the well of the
courtroom to the lectern. When he spoke, it was so softly that the jurors in the second row—all but the kid—had to lean forward to hear
him. Twice the court reporter asked him to repeat himself. Thorpe
could have been sleepwalking, enveloped in a languor so profound
that it threatened to silence him completely.

Seeley strained to hear as Thorpe unfolded the theory of St. Gall's
defense. "Do you think that a company of St. Gall's size and reputation would undertake to produce an important pharmaceutical without first satisfying itself that the product infringed no valid patent?"
Turning Seeley's theme of David against Goliath on its head, Thorpe
was making St. Gall's size a mark of virtue. Big business should be
trusted.

"Companies like St. Gall flee from patent infringement the way you
would flee from a charging bull. St. Gall has in its files opinion letters
from three leading law firms, each stating that AV/AS was an obvious,
even trivial advance and, even if a jury were mistakenly to find the
patent to be valid, that St. Gall's product does not infringe this patent.

My client obtained analyses from the most expert university scientists around the world confirming that its product does not infringe. Do you imagine that a company of St. Gall's size and reputation would have done any less?"

As Seeley anticipated, Thorpe then teased out from his theory that big is good a second conclusion to reinforce the first. Thorpe looked directly at the jurors, but his voice remained subdued.

"If your life, or the life of someone you truly loved, depended on it, whose judgment would you follow: that of a lone, underpaid and overworked bureaucrat in the U.S. Patent Office, or the judgment concurred in by the world's leading researchers in the relevant field— the scientific experts that physicians themselves consult when they need answers to the hardest life-and-death questions—a judgment reached in each case independently and dispassionately."

Seeley smiled to himself. As dispassionate as you can be when you are being paid handsomely for that judgment. On his legal pad, Seeley wrote a note to hit this fact hard when his time came to cross-examine St. Gall's expert witnesses.

Thorpe jammed his hands into the pockets of his suit jacket, silently studying the jurors one by one. Then he let his voice drop into the quietest whisper yet and concluded his opening statement.

"He's lost it," Barnum said, his breath damp against Seeley's ear. "How can he expect a jury to believe in his case if he doesn't believe in it himself?"

"Puzzling," was all that Palmieri said, snapping his laptop shut.

But Seeley knew that Thorpe's fecklessness was a ruse. This was the same man who last week dashed across the courthouse plaza to proclaim to the television cameras the certainty of his client's victory. But, if he was acting, what was the point? Was the purpose of the charade to get a jury that would not sympathize with a multinational drug company to identify with him instead? Pity me; pity my client. Had Thorpe, with decades of practice in San Francisco, misjudged the jury, or had Seeley?

TWELVE

On the witness stand, Dr. Nicolas Cordier was a portrait of rectitude: thin, almost cadaverous, he sat erect against the back of the leather chair, one long leg crossed elegantly over the other, hands loosely clasped on a knee. He could have been waiting for his introduction as the keynote speaker at a medical society meeting and not for his first appearance as an expert witness in a patent infringement trial. The plain navy suit, white button-down shirt, and old-fashioned plaid tie went with the gray hair cut short at the sides, longer on top. As Seeley walked to the lectern to begin his direct examination, Cordier brushed a recalcitrant lock back from his forehead.

Sunday's preparation had been trying. "What do you want me to say?" Cordier asked as Seeley put practice questions to him. "The truth." Seeley had seen this before. A witness, rigorously honest in all aspects of his life, is suddenly daunted by the novel prospect of testifying in court. The physician shrugged. "Of course, the truth, but how do you wish me to"—he grappled for the word—"phrase this truth?" Seeley asked whether he had told the truth in his deposition. "Yes, of course." Seeley had pushed the black binder containing Cordier's deposition across the table. "Then review this and make sure you stick to what you said."

Now, at the courtroom lectern, taking Cordier through his qualifications as an expert witness—medical training in Toulouse, a pediatrics residency in Algiers, research at the Institut Pasteur in Paris, and seven years working in Africa for the United Nations AIDS agency—Seeley again worried about how the physician would tell the story of AIDS in Africa. Slow down, he wanted to say, think about your answers, or Thorpe will crush you.

At the edge of Seeley's vision, Fischler was conferring with Thorpe. Fischler rose. "May I approach sidebar, Your Honor?"

This was unexpected. Ordinarily Thorpe, as first chair, would be responsible for the leadoff witness. Thorpe remained at counsel's table, as gray and motionless as a gargoyle staring out at the proceedings.

The judge rolled her chair to the corner of the bench away from the jury. "So soon, Ms. Fischler?" There was amusement in her voice. "We haven't even heard a word of testimony."

"Defendant is prepared to stipulate to Dr. Cordier's expertise in pediatric AIDS, Your Honor, but not in the demographics of AIDS. We're concerned that's where Mr. Seeley is going to take him."

Farnsworth turned to Seeley.

"Defendant has Dr. Cordier's report and they've deposed him at length," Seeley said. "They knew months ago what his testimony would be."

"Until this morning," Fischler said, "we didn't know he was going to be their lead witness." She had wrestled her hair into a prim schoolteacher's bun for the trial, but still seemed discomposed. "This changes everything. His testimony's going to have a greater impact."

That was why Fischler was in charge of Cordier. It was she who had deposed the physician. She had prepared herself for him, just as Thorpe had prepared for Steinhardt. Seeley was pleased at the unexpected windfall of his decision to put Cordier on first.

Judge Farnsworth said, "Mr. Seeley is right. You should have raised this before opening statements this morning. Now you're wasting the jury's time." Any humor was gone from her voice. The judge was also telling the two lawyers that she didn't like being away from her jury for sidebar conferences. "On the other hand, Mr. Seeley, Ms. Fischler is entitled to know what you're trying to prove with Dr. Cordier's testimony."

"Dr. Cordier's testimony will bear directly on the novelty of AV/AS."

Farnsworth studied him for a moment. "I'm not sure I know how you plan to do that, but I'm confident Ms. Fischler will have an objection at the appropriate time if it turns out to be a problem." She nodded for him to continue.

Seeley returned to the lectern and a quick back-and-forth with the witness established that Cordier practiced pediatrics at a clinic in Maseru, the capital of Lesotho, and that his practice consisted exclusively of treating HIV-positive children.

"And do these children respond well to treatment?"

"If we are able to get them antiretroviral therapy—yes, then their chances of survival are excellent."

"And if you are not able to get them this therapy?"

"They will die of AIDS."

"How many will die, say in Lesotho?"

"Today in Lesotho, we estimate that there are 22,000 children—infants, teenagers—who are HIV positive. Less than one in twenty of them will receive treatment."

Seeley glanced over at the jury box. No one seemed to be having difficulty following Cordier's accented English.

"So you're saying, of these 22,000 children, roughly 21,000 will die?"

"That is correct."

All of this was hearsay, and ungrounded in the witness's expertise, but Seeley was confident that Thorpe, with countless jury trials behind him, would not let Fischler object and risk the jury's ill will. "And, in your experience, are these numbers unique to Lesotho?"

Fischler started to rise, but Thorpe's hand moved over hers.

"Unique? Yes, but only in how small the numbers are. There are approximately 230,000 HIV-positive children in South Africa, about 300,000 in Nigeria. In all of Africa, we estimate close to three million children are HIV positive."

"And the survival rate without treatment is the same?"

"If we can treat them, perhaps 150,000 can be saved. But this is such a small number, no? The others, almost all of the three million, will die."

Fischler was on her feet. "Objection, Your Honor. Relevance."

Instinct told Seeley that he was at the edge of the judge's patience. "I can assure the court that Dr. Cordier's testimony will connect up."

Farnsworth motioned the two lawyers to sidebar. "I still don't see how this relates to the novelty of AV/AS, Mr. Seeley."

"Long-felt need, Judge."

When a pressing problem, particularly of public health, has persisted for years, and finally one company comes up with a solution, that fact counts as evidence that the solution wasn't particularly obvious.

Fischler said, "I don't see how talking about numbers of victims makes that point."

"I'm sure," Judge Farnsworth said, watching Seeley over her half-frames, "that if Mr. Seeley doesn't very quickly connect up Dr. Cordier's testimony to his theory, you will renew your objection."

When Seeley returned to him, Cordier seemed confused by the conversation between the judge and lawyers outside his hearing and the jury's. Television in Maseru, if the physician had the time to watch, probably had few courtroom dramas.

"In your clinic in Maseru, Dr. Cordier, why are you only able to get treatment to less than one in twenty of the children who need it?"

"There are three reasons—"

Anticipating that this was going to sound rehearsed to the jury, Seeley broke in. "Let's take them one at a time."

"Expense, of course. We have succeeded in getting the price for antiretroviral treatments down to two hundred dollars a year, but many patients develop a resistance to these first-line cocktails, and we need second-line treatments like Atanazavir that can cost three to six thousand dollars a year. Remember, these are people who may earn less than a dollar a day. Foundations like the Gates Foundation help out. Also, many drug companies are lowering their prices, or licensing generics free—"

"So expense may soon disappear as a problem?" He and Cordier had spent time on this part of the testimony. It was important to Seeley that the jury not think that patents or high prices were the source of the problem. "If expense is not the major obstacle, what is?"

"Delivery. We don't have the facilities or the people or the equipment to make treatment available to every child who needs it. In climates like Lesotho, the most widely used booster drug, ritonavir, needs to be refrigerated. But who has a refrigerator?"

"You testified that there are three obstacles."

Cordier closed his eyes and slumped into the wooden chair. For a moment, Seeley thought that, fatigued from his trip and Sunday's long preparation, the physician had fallen asleep. When, at last he opened his eyes, Seeley saw that the cause was not sleeplessness or overwork, but the exhausting futility of the conditions that he observed every day.

"It is the people themselves," Cordier said. "They are distracted from their medical needs by poverty, by lack of education, but, most of all, by a struggle for daily survival that is so desperate, so consuming, that HIV treatment seems a luxury to them. I had a young patient, a fourteen-year-old girl, both of whose parents died of AIDS . . ."

Seeley could picture Thorpe, at counsel's table behind him, restraining his second chair. Other than Cordier's voice, with its soft inflections, the courtroom was entirely still.

"This girl, barely a teenager, turned to prostitution to support her younger brothers and sisters. Of course, now she, too, is HIV positive, as her own child will be, when—and it is inevitable—she becomes pregnant. We have offered her treatment—one of our nurses was able to seek her out—but the poor girl forgets to come in to the clinic, or she is too busy with her . . . career."

"Your Honor—" It was Fischler, exasperated.

"Mr. Seeley?"

"I'm about to tie this up." He turned back to Cordier. "Is it generally recognized by the treatment community that there is a solution to this endless cycle you have described?"

"A treatment like AV/AS is a solution."

"Why is that?"

"Well"—he seemed surprised by the question—"of course, like a vaccine, it only needs to be administered once, so we don't have to rely on patients coming to the clinic on schedule. For one time only, we can even go out into the rural areas to administer it. Of course, whoever manufactures the treatment must make it available at an acceptable price."

Seeley was expecting the caution about prices. Throughout their preparation for his testimony, Cordier was adamant about having the opportunity to make the point.

Judge Farnsworth was nodding agreeably. If she hadn't earlier seen the direction of the testimony and how it would connect to the test of long-felt need, she saw it now.

"This perception in the AIDS treatment community of the need for a vaccine, how long, Dr. Cordier, has this perception existed?"

"The AIDS virus was identified early in 1984, and the search for a vaccine—as well as for effective therapies—began almost immediately."

"And, in all this time, have any vaccines or any treatments like AV/AS been introduced?"

"Several of them have been offered in early drug trials, but only one has been successful."

"One?"

"Yes. AV/AS. A trial for the efficacy and safety of AV/AS was conducted in part at my clinic."

"And do you recall what company provided that treatment?"

"Why, of course, St. Gall."

There was a gasp from the jury box, but Seeley didn't turn.

Cordier said, "They stole the treatment from Vaxtek, no?"

Before Fischler could object, Seeley said, "I have no further questions."

Leonard said, "I thought the cross-examination would be longer." They were in a taxi on their way from the courthouse to an early dinner. Palmieri was in charge of tomorrow morning's witness, but Gabriela Vega, the Heilbrun, Hardy associate who was preparing Seeley's afternoon witness, had less experience than Palmieri, and Seeley wanted to be there to help if needed. But Leonard insisted. This would be their last chance to talk before he went to Washington on

Wednesday for meetings at the FDA, and he promised that the Tadich Grill, only a short walk from Heilbrun, Hardy's offices, wouldn't be busy at this hour.

Seeley said, "She kept the cross short because the jury liked Cordier. She wouldn't do her client any good trying to trip him up."

Even so, Seeley thought Fischler had been more solicitous than she needed to be, and had scored only once, when she got the physician to concede that, unlike the vaccines for measles or polio, a single AV/AS inoculation might not be enough to prevent the onset of AIDS. But the setback was small. Cordier had established a strong legal foundation for their case and, even more important, a powerful emotional one.

"Why didn't the old guy question him?"

"Thorpe's controlling every move in this case." Seeley explained to Leonard how the change in their order of witnesses had put the defense team off balance. "Fischler doesn't ask a question she hasn't reviewed with him."

"You ought to think about moving your practice to San Francisco." When Seeley didn't answer, Leonard cocked his head toward the side window. "You have to admit it beats Buffalo."

"The weather is pleasant," Seeley said. After that, they didn't talk until they reached the restaurant.

Tadich was quiet, as Leonard promised. The woodwork was studded with ancient brass fittings and darkened by a century's layers of varnish, but the high white ceilings looked freshly painted. A few customers were at the mahogany counter that ran down the center of the long room, and others were at tables. Quartered lemons in porcelain bowls and massive chunks of crusty sourdough were set within arm's reach. The sounds of silver and china being arranged on linen echoed gently through the dining room. Knives chopped and pans clattered in the open kitchen at the back, and a vague but agreeable fragrance of buttery sauces wafted through the place. Suffusing it all was the easy self-assurance of an old and popular restaurant in the hour before the dinner rush.

A white-coated waiter recognized Leonard and took them to a table in one of the private, wood-paneled booths.

"You made quite an impression on Renata."

Seeley looked at the menu. For some reason, at the mention of Renata, he thought of Lily, surprised to discover how close below the surface of his thoughts she was. He found himself comparing Renata's catlike aggressiveness to Lily's laconic sensuality.

"She hasn't stopped talking about you since you got here."

Leonard was going to try to sell him something.

"I was hoping you could stop down and see her, maybe take her to dinner while I'm away. I'm not coming back until late next week."

Was it Renata's flirtatiousness or Leonard's misshapen hopes for the family circle that made Seeley hesitate at the prospect of dinner with his sister-in-law?

"I'm in the middle of a trial, Len. I have witnesses to prepare."

The waiter returned to take their order. As if to re-create the lunch with Lily, Seeley ordered the fried oysters. Leonard shot him a bemused look, patted his waistline, and ordered broiled sole.

Before Leonard could return to Renata, Seeley said, "What do you know about Alan Steinhardt's lab notebooks?"

"What do you mean?"

"Did he keep two sets of books?"

"Of course not."

Seeley watched for the small bulge in Leonard's cheek where, as a boy, he pressed his tongue when he lied, but there was nothing. "It wouldn't be the first time an inventor cooked the books to get an earlier invention date."

Leonard said, "Alan's miles above doing anything like that. He knew St. Gall's lawyers would be all over his notebooks, and they were. If anything was wrong, do you think St. Gall would have stipulated priority?"

The perfectly drawn charts and well-crafted paragraphs in the notebooks Seeley examined were as neat and precise as the scientist's custom-tailored lab coat. "How did the notebooks look to you?"

"They were fine."

"You told me the other day you didn't have time to review your scientists' notes."

Leonard picked up his beer coaster and played with it. "Are you cross-examining me?"

When Seeley didn't answer, Leonard shook his head and grinned. "We're not going to lose this case. We have Michael Seeley representing us." He went on talking about his trip to Washington, his dealings with the FDA, and how busy he was. "I promise, I'm telling you the truth about the notebooks."

The ambience of the suave San Francisco restaurant was nothing like that of the dark and fetid Germania Social Club, but it was the Germania, to which his father would drag Leonard and him when their mother was off on one of her church outings, that drifted into Seeley's thoughts. While his father drank with his friends, he and Leonard would crawl under one of the rough trestle tables and build fortresses out of coasters and empty beer bottles. It startled Seeley to realize that there had in fact been pleasant interludes in a childhood that he was accustomed to thinking of exclusively in shades of black and gray.

The waiter brought their dinners and Leonard busied himself with the food. "No one broils fish the way they do here."

The starched linen tablecloth and heavy silver were steps above Barbara's Fish Trap, but the oysters, even topped with thick strips of smoky bacon, didn't come close to Seeley's memory.

"It would mean a lot to me if you could stop in and see Renata." Leonard mopped his plate with a crust of sourdough and shot Seeley a kid brother's look. "You're not afraid of her, are you?"

Leonard had always gotten on well with women. Where Seeley's reflex as a boy was to fight back, Leonard navigated the brutalized household through manipulation, using first Seeley, then their mother as a shield. While Seeley was acquiring the habit of solitude—he could be completely alone even in the middle of football practice—Leonard was practicing the social skills that drew people to him. Maybe this was why women had always liked Leonard. He was attuned to their thoughts and moods in a way Seeley knew he would never be.

"I don't know why you need me to babysit your wife."

For the first time since they left the courthouse, Leonard lost his bounce. "Renata drinks when I'm away. Sometimes I'll call, and I can hear it in her voice. It's eleven or twelve at night and she's slurring her words. Five, six hours later she's prepping for surgery. I worry about her."

"I'd think you'd worry about her patients."

Leonard shrugged. "You're a single man. Marriage is complicated." He chewed at the bread, then remembered something. "I'm sorry." He watched to see if Seeley wanted to talk. "I'm sorry about your divorce. I never met Clare."

Seeley was thinking not of his former wife, but of Gabriela Vega and Lionel Kaplan, the witness she was preparing for tomorrow afternoon. Other work, too, waited at the office. He caught a passing waiter's attention and signaled for the check.

"It's funny," Leonard said, "talking with you about women. We never did that."

"There's a lot of things we never talked about." Seeley put two twenties on top of the check, and stood up to leave. "If I get some free time, I'll try to call her."

It was already dark by the time Seeley got to his office, and Tina had left for the day. The light was on, and a slender man, compactly built, was in Seeley's chair, his feet up on the desk. A zipper ran up the side of the black ankle boots. One of Pearsall's illustrated steno pads was on the desk in front of him and there was a smell of tobacco in the room. The man swung his feet off and reached across the desk with a business card.

Seeley looked at the card. Lieutenant Herbert Phan, San Mateo Police Department, along with an address and telephone number. On the reverse, the information was in Spanish.

Seeley nodded at Pearsall's notebook. "That's an unlawful search."

"We're all looking for the truth about Robert Pearsall's death, aren't we? His secretary said I could wait for you here."

Tina wouldn't have let him in. Phan had probably impressed the thirty-seventh-floor receptionist with his badge and made his way up to the thirty-eighth floor by himself. The lieutenant nodded at the client chair across from him. "Have a seat."

"You're sitting in it," Seeley said, remembering at the last moment to smile.

Phan's own smile parted a narrow, neatly trimmed mustache. He drummed his fingers on the armrests. The thick wrists and muscular fingers of a laborer were a contrast to the trimly tailored outfit and carefully barbered graying hair. Phan rose, came around the desk, and took the client's chair.

"What can I do for you, Lieutenant?" Seeley remained standing, so that Phan had to look up at him.

"Ah, yes, lawyers bill by the hour." The voice was nasal, flat. "You called us about Robert Pearsall. We thought maybe you knew something that you might want to contribute."

"Robert Pearsall didn't kill himself."

"What do you know about that?"

For the first time, Seeley heard an inflection of interest in the detective's voice, but it didn't surprise him. The police have no duty to disclose the scope of their investigation to anyone. They'll tell the grieving widow that her husband's death was suicide even though in fact they think it may be murder.

When Seeley didn't answer, Phan said, "It doesn't happen every day, but a white man of late middle age walking in front of a train happens often enough that it's statistically predictable." The lieutenant didn't sound convinced.

"How do your statistics explain his being a successful lawyer, in good health with no financial difficulties?"

"Our job is to screen out possibilities until we're left with probabilities. You still haven't told us what you think."

"Maybe someone knocked him out and dragged him to the railroad tracks."

"Who would have a reason to do that?"

There was no emotion or even movement in Phan's dark eyes. This was how police investigators talked to civilians, as if they knew their most shameful secrets. In Seeley's experience, they never did.

Phan took a small leather notebook from his inside jacket pocket and flipped through the pages. "His adversary in this case he was working on"—he rested a thick forefinger on a page—"St. Gall. Would they have a reason to kill him?"

"This is an important case, but a drug company doesn't kill a lawyer to win a lawsuit."

"Maybe Pearsall stuck his nose in somewhere it didn't belong."

"And you think that's my problem, too."

Phan pushed back from the desk. Even in the harsh fluorescent light, his skin was as smooth as caramel. "Over the years, Mr. Seeley, we've found that anytime an outsider like you starts asking questions about the way we conduct our investigations, he's got something bothering him."

"And that's the reason for the visit."

Phan rested his palm along a tight jaw. "Do you have any enemies?"

"None in California, that I know of."

"But now you've taken over Robert Pearsall's case."

Phan was settling in for a long interview, and Seeley was impatient to join Gabriela Vega in the conference room. He also needed to tell Judy Pearsall that the police were considering possibilities other than suicide. He took Pearsall's notebook from the desk. "I've got work to do. Turn out the lights when you leave."

"We'd like to know if anyone warned Mr. Pearsall before he died." When Seeley moved to the door, Phan said, "Have you received any warnings, Mr. Seeley? Any unusual incidents?"

"Your receptionist told me you're a busy man, Lieutenant." Seeley nodded toward the switch by the door. "As I said, please turn out the lights."

THIRTEEN

It was twenty minutes after Judge Farnsworth's regular starting time, and Palmieri's witness, Yelena Chaikovsky, was not in the courtroom. At regular intervals the Stanford economist telephoned Palmieri to say that she was caught in a traffic jam; that she had been stopped by the highway patrol for speeding; and that she was again stuck in traffic.

Palmieri said, "She'll be here in less than half an hour, Your Honor." He and Seeley were in front of the bench with Thorpe and Fischler. The jury box was still empty.

"This is why lawyers put their witnesses up in a local hotel." The judge's eyes were tired and her makeup looked as if it had been applied hurriedly.

Seeley had instructed Tina to make hotel reservations for all the witnesses, but Chaikovsky apparently told Palmieri that she slept better in her own bed.

"Do you have another witness you can put on, Mr. Seeley?"

"He's in the city, Judge, but he won't be here until one."

"This comes out of your twenty-four hours, Counselor." When Farnsworth nodded for the lawyers to leave, Fischler pivoted sharply, preening. Thorpe followed, stepping briskly, as he regularly did when he was out of the jury's sight.

At counsel's table, Barnum was livid, his thick hands clenched and white at the knuckles. Seeley steered Palmieri away. "Call Chaikovsky and tell her you'll be waiting at the bottom of the plaza. I'll send Ed out to park her car."

Barnum's voice, when Seeley took his seat next to him, was a hoarse whisper, the kind that carries. "I want you to do the direct."

"Lower the volume, Ed. She's Palmieri's witness. He defended her deposition. He's a good lawyer. They won't be able to touch her on cross."

"We wouldn't have this mess if you'd put Steinhardt first."

"We're building a foundation. When Steinhardt goes on the stand tomorrow, he'll look like a hero." The jurors were filing into the jury box. "If you want to keep the trial moving, go wait with Palmieri in front of the courthouse."

Barnum's eyes filled with misery.

Seeley said, "I don't want them wasting their time looking for a place to park."

Yelena Chaikovsky arrived twenty minutes later, without apologies and radiating the professional aura that too many lawyers look for in their expert witnesses. Her plump cheeks shone with well-being and the eyes behind her tortoiseshell glasses were keen. The salt-and-pepper hair and the dark flannel jacket and skirt communicated an encompassing competence. But there was a smugness about her that concerned Seeley.

Palmieri was taking Chaikovsky through her résumé—the endowed chair in the Stanford economics department, her joint appointments in the university's medical and business schools—when Fischler rose. "The defense stipulates to the witness's expertise in health economics, Your Honor. There's no need to consume the court's time with her entire résumé."

Palmieri glanced at Seeley. He was taking time with the witness's credentials not so much to qualify her as an expert for purposes of the rules of evidence as to let the jury know the depth of her expertise. That was why Fischler was trying to stop him. Seeley answered by shaking his head. Let the jury see that the witness had justification for being so self-satisfied.

"Your Honor," Palmieri said, "if the jurors are to be able to accurately weigh Professor Chaikovsky's testimony, they need to know the background and experience on which it is based."

Farnsworth, an experienced trial lawyer, knew what the skirmish was about. "As I reminded you earlier, Counselor, the clock is running. If this is how you want to spend your time, the court will not interfere."

Palmieri took the next five minutes to review the witness's academic degrees, her years at the U.S. Public Health Service, and an extended tour of duty working with epidemiologists at the World Health Organization's regional office in Copenhagen. A glance at the jury confirmed for Seeley that the time was well spent.

Palmieri led the Stanford professor quickly through the history of efforts to discover an AIDS vaccine, beginning in 1984. "And, yet, after twenty-three years, and all this money, and all these scientists hard at work, is it true that no one has come as close to an effective vaccine for AIDS as Dr. Steinhardt has with AV/AS?"

"That is correct."

There was a movement behind Seeley, and Barnum took his chair at the table. It had taken him all this time to park Chaikovsky's car, and he muttered something that Seeley didn't make out as he took his seat.

"But is it true that, given enough time—and enough dollars and effort—a vaccine for any disease will ultimately be discovered?"

"Unfortunately, the answer is no. For example, there is still no fully effective vaccine for tuberculosis."

The point of Palmieri's questions was to set up the economist's testimony on AV/AS's prospects for commercial success. Like Cordier's testimony yesterday on the long-felt need for AV/AS, so Chaikovsky's testimony that the treatment would be a great commercial success would help persuade the jury that Steinhardt's discovery had not been obvious to other workers in the field—for, if it had been obvious, and there was money to be made, why hadn't they discovered it first?

Palmieri turned from the witness to the judge. "At this point, may

I ask the court to have the lights in the courtroom dimmed, and the projector and screens brought in."

Pearsall's and Thorpe's teams had argued for weeks over the admissibility of Chaikovsky's charts showing the potential for AV/AS's commercial success and Pearsall had prevailed.

At a nod from Farnsworth, the blue-blazered bailiff switched off half the lights in the already dim courtroom and angled a screen several feet from Seeley's table so that it included the jurors and the judge in its field of view. The second screen he adjusted so that Chaikovsky and defense counsel could see it.

While the bailiff positioned the screens, Seeley thought of Palmieri's mistakes so far—the faulty pro hac motion, typing at his keyboard during Seeley's opening statement, letting his witness spend the night at home—but when the young partner came to the table for his laptop, Seeley said, "You're doing fine."

Palmieri placed the laptop on the lectern and, after he tapped a few keys, both screens lit up. Few mishaps disconcert juries more than an exhibit that fails to work, and Seeley released the breath that he had been holding.

Chaikovsky's first chart showed Vaxtek's research costs—$320 million—in bringing AV/AS to its current point of development, completion of phase-two clinical trials. The second chart showed the estimated cost to complete the clinical trials and bring the product to market. Total research and development costs were $450 million.

"How much time does Vaxtek have to earn back this investment?"

"Eight years," Chaikovsky said.

"Why did you pick eight years as the relevant period?"

"Well, a patent lasts for twenty years from the date it's applied for, and Vaxtek applied for this patent in 1997. But it has been ten years, and they're only now starting phase-three trials. I conservatively estimate that it will be another two years before they can actually sell AV/AS in the marketplace—twelve years in all since they applied for their patent—and that leaves them eight years to recoup their investment and make a profit."

In the shadows, there was talk and movement in the jury box. As

Seeley hoped, the brief period over which Vaxtek would be able to recover its costs was a surprise to the jurors.

Palmieri put the next chart on the screen. "On the basis of these numbers, Professor Chaikovsky, what rate of return will Vaxtek earn on its $450 million investment?"

"As you can see from the chart, the company's return over the eight-year period will average out to between twenty-two and twenty-six percent a year."

"In your experience, studying pharmaceutical companies and their revenues, is that rate of return one that a company would consider commercially successful?"

"In this business, making *any* positive rate of return on research and development is considered commercial success. Remember, only three out of ten prescription drugs in this country even pay back their research and development costs. So a twenty-two to twenty-six percent return is a great success."

Palmieri tapped a key and a pie chart came up, each slice of a different size and color. Numbers and dollar signs were inside each segment. Seeley had found the chart buried in an appendix to Chaikovsky's expert's report, and instructed Palmieri to include it in his slide show. If Seeley was right, the chart would be as important to the jury as any of the others; probably more important.

"Can you tell the jury what this chart represents?"

"This is the same estimate of revenues that Vaxtek will earn from sales of AV/AS over the life of its patent, but each segment represents a different country or region of the world."

"Why did you slice up the world this way?"

"Because the revenues from each region will differ."

"Because of different population size?"

"In part. But the big difference is the amount Vaxtek will be able to charge for AV/AS in each region. If you look at the red segment at the top, that's the United States, where they will be able to charge around two hundred and fifty dollars for each inoculation. But if you look at the big yellow segment at the bottom, that's sub-Saharan Africa, and the average price there is forty-five dollars, less than one-

fifth of what they can charge in the States—and that's only with sub-
sidies from governments and foundations."

From the first day of the trial, Seeley was concerned about the impact on the jury of the protesters outside, and he instructed Palmieri
to include the slide to let the jurors know that, in voting to uphold
the patent, they would not be pricing Cordier's patients in Lesotho
out of the market. Still, when he first saw Chaikovsky's chart, he was
surprised that the African price was $45 and not $15 as Leonard had
told him it would be.

"Does this mean Vaxtek will lose money on its sales in Africa?"

"No, they won't be losing money on individual sales. But . . ."

"But?"

"If forty-five dollars per inoculation is all they could charge around
the world, they'd never make back what they invested in discovering
and developing AV/AS."

Palmieri cocked his head at the screen, as if something there puzzled
him. "What would happen to prices in the United States if distribu-
tors in South Africa, say, who are buying AV/AS for forty-five dollars
a dose, start exporting it to the States. How could Vaxtek maintain the
two hundred and fifty dollar U.S. price, if it has to compete in this
country with vaccine one-fifth the price?"

Chaikovsky's smug smile widened into a grin. "That's what the
U.S. patent is for, isn't it? To keep out lower-priced drugs from other
countries."

Palmieri grinned, too. "In the courtroom, Professor, I get to ask the
questions, and you get to answer them."

The give and take was perfect, but it didn't calm Seeley's concerns
about the young partner. He could write off Palmieri's coolness in
their early encounters to the jitters of dealing with a new first chair.
But the negligence with the motion papers and his witness's lodging was harder to dismiss. So was his continued resistance to Seeley's
direction, like insisting that they keep Steinhardt as the lead witness,
even though Pearsall himself had wanted to place him lower in the
order. If Palmieri wasn't exactly working to undermine Seeley's case,
he didn't seem to be enthusiastically supporting it, either.

Chaikovsky said, "I was assuming when I made these charts that Vaxtek's patent would be upheld and that it would be able to exclude low-price competitors."

"And if the jury voted to strike down the patent? If Vaxtek couldn't keep the cheap drugs out?"

"Vaxtek would lose all of the almost half-billion dollars it invested in AV/AS."

Palmieri snapped the laptop closed. "Your witness."

Fischler fired off three brisk questions before she even reached the lectern. The man-tailored suit was intentionally aggressive, Seeley thought, but the oxford button-down and patterned silk tie were what a law student might wear to her first moot court argument.

"These charts you fabricated, Professor Chaikovsky, are they based on assumptions?"

The witness winced. "It's pronounced *Chi-kof-ski*. Like the composer."

The break in rhythm momentarily ruffled Fischler. She had loosened her severe librarian's bun today and the ponytail bobbed. "Are your charts based on assumptions, Professor?"

"The charts are based mainly on data, but, yes, like any diagram, they depend on certain hypotheses."

"And these hypotheses of yours, are they the same as assumptions?"

"You could say so, yes."

"It doesn't matter what I say, Professor, the jury wants to know what you say."

"Yes, for these purposes, a hypothesis is the same as an assumption."

Fischler addressed the witness, but faced the jury. "Is it correct that one assumption behind your charts is that Vaxtek will face no competition in its sales of AV/AS?"

An alarm went off in Seeley's mind. He looked over at Palmieri, whose fingers floated over his keyboard.

"Yes, they make that assumption."

Fischler's eyes were still on the jury, not the witness. "And why did you make that assumption, Professor?"

"Because the effect of a patent is to exclude competition—"

"Professor, are you aware of any patented drugs that face competition from other patented drugs?"

The bailiff had not raised the lights, and in the pale shadows, the smugness drained out of the witness's expression.

Seeley couldn't believe that Palmieri had failed to prepare his witness for the question.

A detectable tremor in her voice, Chaikovsky said, "Yes, of course."

"Can you give me an example?"

"Well, there are several patented cholesterol-lowering drugs, called statins, on the market." She glanced at Palmieri, who nodded gently, and after a moment she, too, understood that Fischler's sole aim was to rattle her. "The difference is that there is no pharmaceutical comparable to AV/AS that doesn't infringe Vaxtek's patent, and that means AV/AS will not have any competition."

Fischler's line of questioning had been a bluff. Other companies were working on AIDS vaccines but, without industrial espionage, there was no way St. Gall and its lawyers could know what they were working on, or how far they had progressed. Palmieri would need to time his objection carefully.

"Do you know how many other pharmaceutical companies are investigating an AIDS vaccine? Two? A dozen?"

"I can't give you an exact number," the economist said.

"So in your charts, and in your testimony, you just assumed that there were none."

"Keep her honest," Seeley said to Palmieri. To himself, he acknowledged that, at the moment, the best they could do was to disrupt Fischler's pace.

Palmieri rose. "Objection, Your Honor. Outside the scope of direct."

"This is an expert who's on the stand, Your Honor. We have latitude to examine the basis of her testimony."

"Overruled." Then, more gently, to Fischler: "I'm sure you will find a way, Counselor, to phrase your question so that it stays within bounds."

"So, Professor, for all you know, a dozen other companies might have done the same research as Vaxtek and were just a little late getting to the Patent Office."

"Objection." Palmieri was on his feet again. "This violates the parties' stipulation on priority."

"Counselor?" Judge Farnsworth seemed amused by the sparring.

Fischler said, "The stipulation is as to priority of invention, Your Honor, not the race to the Patent Office."

"If you have another objection, Mr. Palmieri, I'll be glad to entertain it." This time her voice was almost musical.

"The question is outside the scope of the direct examination."

"That's right, Counselor, it is. Ms. Fischler, this may be the time to turn to another line of questioning."

"I have just one last question of the witness, Your Honor." She looked hard at Chaikovsky. "Would you please tell the court, Professor, how much you are being paid for your testimony here today?"

Palmieri started up. The question was as cheap as the old yes-or-no chestnut about whether the witness had stopped beating his wife. Barnum hunched forward. Seeley looked over at Thorpe who was watching him. Thorpe smiled and shrugged. Seeley placed a hand over Palmieri's. "Let her handle this one herself." Amateurish as the question was, Seeley was sure that Chaikovsky had been asked it before.

"You've asked two questions, Ms. Fischler, so let's see if I can disentangle them." She was the professor lecturing a not very bright student. "First, I am not being paid for my testimony but for my time. Second, I am being paid at the same rate, $650 an hour, that I am paid whether the work involves courtroom testimony or corporate consulting."

Barnum sat back in his chair. Palmieri's taut posture relaxed.

"I have no more questions, Your Honor."

"Redirect, Counselor?"

Seeley whispered to him.

Palmieri said, "None, Your Honor."

Their case had taken a hit from Fischler's bluff, and redirect would only magnify it. Seeley would have to repair the damage with his witness this afternoon.

———

There is an unwritten rule among lawyers never to discuss a client's business in public places—on the sidewalk, in an elevator—even in a taxi with a driver who by all appearances understood few words of English, but whose eyes darted in the rearview mirror between Seeley and Palmieri. More often than not in these situations, Seeley found himself asking about family.

"Did you grow up out here?"

Palmieri shook his head. "Spencer, Iowa. One of the one hundred best places to live in America. My mom's still there."

"Any other family?"

"Two older sisters. One's in St. Louis, the other's still in Spencer."

Seeley nodded. "What about your father?" This was always where his curiosity ultimately came to rest. What about your father?

"He died in Vietnam. All I know about him is from my mother's stories, some pictures in an album, and a Distinguished Service Cross."

"A hero."

"A victim." Palmieri checked the rearview mirror where the driver's eyes were still watching them. "But don't get the wrong idea. I had a great time as a kid. There were uncles and aunts on both sides, lots of support. Just no father."

"But you left Spencer."

"We're still close," Palmieri said as the taxi pulled to the curb on Battery Street. "We talk every week. I go back for the family blowout at the lake every summer. But Spencer doesn't have many opportunities for big cases." Getting out of the taxi, the glow was still on him from the morning's success with his witness. "Or for gay men. San Francisco's got both."

Tina had left sandwiches and coffee for them in the conference room. Palmieri removed his suit jacket and draped it over the back of a chair. Even after four hours of direct examination and of sitting on Fischler's shoulder for every minute of her cross, his pink-and-white striped shirt was crisp, the burgundy tie neatly knotted.

Palmieri glanced at Seeley, waiting for him to start, and, when he didn't, said, "I think Chaikovsky's examination went well."

"I'm sure the jury thought it was worth the wait."

Palmieri caught the point at once. "I didn't know she was going to get caught in traffic."

Seeley waited.

Palmieri ran a finger between his neck and shirt as if the collar had suddenly grown too tight. "You think I'm trying to wreck the case just because I didn't get to run it."

"No, I don't," Seeley said. "But I think you're letting yourself get"— he paused to pick the word carefully—"distracted."

"How so?" The question came out pinched, as if Palmieri were biting back on his anger.

"The man you were talking to outside the courthouse last Friday, after we picked the jury." Seeley didn't know whether Palmieri had been talking to the protester or just watching Thorpe's waltz with the press, but he was going to find out. "Tall, curly blond hair."

"Phil Driscoll. He's a friend of my partner's. They dated once. What does that have to do with anything?"

"Do you talk to other people in the group?"

"Of course I do. These are my friends."

"And you talk about the case?"

"Do you talk about cases with your wife? Your friends?"

"I'm not married." Seeley was less puzzled by Palmieri's growing rage than he was by the obvious effort to contain it. If he let himself explode, what might he say that he would regret?

"They think I sold out when I agreed to work for Vaxtek."

"And what do you tell them?"

Palmieri said, "What anyone who knows the facts would tell them—AV/AS is the best we're going to have for a long time and, if there hadn't been a patent waiting at the end of the rainbow, Vaxtek wouldn't have spent half a billion dollars on it."

"I told your friend Driscoll pretty much the same when he stopped me outside the courtroom."

"Young gay men today think they're immortal. They don't know what it was like ten, fifteen years ago, when the entire gay population in the city was under a death sentence. They don't know what it's like when the therapy you're taking just to survive blows out your kidneys or your liver. Pop a pill, they think. Have sex and pop a pill."

Palmieri's words were coming easier now, but Seeley noticed a small circle of perspiration when he lifted an arm to gesture. It wasn't rage he was feeling, Seeley thought. Palmieri was under pressure. This wasn't the time to catalogue his mishaps for him or to question his attitude unless Seeley wanted to lose his second chair in the middle of trial.

Seeley said, "What about you?"

"Do you mean, am I HIV positive?"

Seeley nodded. For no good reason it felt as if the entire case was going to turn on the young lawyer's answer.

"No, I'm not. My partner, either." Palmieri's forehead glistened with perspiration.

"I'm glad for you. Both of you." Palmieri's struggle was tiring Seeley. "But in the future, I'd be careful about letting Barnum see you hanging out with the protesters. Barnum's a jerk, and it's none of my business where he sends his cases but, I promise you, your partners won't be happy if he stops sending Vaxtek work to your firm." Of all Seeley's offenses at his New York firm—taking on unpopular causes and too many pro bono clients—none hurt him more with his partners than losing the firm's paying clients.

"Bob Pearsall always protected me from the partners."

Seeley let the implicit rebuke pass. These were Pearsall's partners, not his. There was nothing he could do to protect Palmieri.

"If you want to know, Bob was the reason I signed on to this case. His word was all I needed that it was the right thing to do." Palmieri took a sandwich from the plate on the conference table. "Are we finished?"

"No. I'd still like to know why you let Professor Chaikovsky sleep in her own bed."

Palmieri started to push back from the table, but Seeley winked at him and the shoulders that had snapped to attention when Seeley first asked the question finally relaxed.

Dr. Lionel Kaplan had never testified before, but he was the one witness Seeley knew he would keep when he pared his witness list to fit

Judge Farnsworth's shortened schedule. The Harvard scientist's heavy-lidded eyes and broad expressive mouth, ready at a moment to break into a gleeful smile or pondering frown, made it easy to imagine him, many years ago, as the smartest, funniest, most passionate kid in class. Asked at his deposition what his hourly rate was for testifying, Kaplan must have stunned Thorpe when he answered that he had requested only that Vaxtek reimburse his travel expenses. Depositions are where lawyers try out their mistakes, and Thorpe was not going to ask that question again in front of a jury.

As Seeley approached the lectern, Kaplan pushed his utilitarian horn-rims up the bridge of his nose.

"Dr. Kaplan, before you describe to the jury the several obstacles that stood in the way of discovering AV/AS, could you describe to us how vaccines work generally—a vaccine we might be more familiar with, like the polio vaccine or the vaccine for measles?"

With a slight tilt of his head, Seeley reminded the scientist to look at the jurors as he spoke.

Kaplan smiled broadly and ran his fingers through coarse, barely combed hair. "The beauty of a vaccine is that it uses the body's own defenses to fight off infection. It makes a weak person strong."

"And how do you get a vaccine to do that?"

"The starting point for the great majority of vaccines is to take a laboratory sample of the virus, like polio, that you want to create immunity against, and then you weaken or even kill the virus so it can no longer cause the disease. Then"—Kaplan jammed his index finger into the palm of the other hand—"you inject this weakened version into a healthy patient. It's too weak to make him sick, but it's strong enough to stimulate his body to produce antibodies. Once these antibodies are in the bloodstream, they attach themselves to the weakened virus we injected and neutralize it. Effectively, the injected virus triggers its own executioner."

"What happens after the antibodies neutralize the virus in the vaccine?"

"That's the genius of vaccines: the antibodies stay in the bloodstream so that if our patient later encounters the real, live polio virus, the antibodies are already there to bind with the virus and neutralize it."

"Is HIV a virus?"

"That's what the letters stand for. Human immunodeficiency virus."

"Does immunization work the same way with HIV as it does with the polio virus?"

Kaplan threw up his hands. "If only it were that simple! In the early days we all assumed this was how an AIDS vaccine was going to work. What we didn't know—and what sadly we know now—is that HIV is a chronically replicating antivirus, uncontrollable by the host's immune response."

To this point, heads had nodded in the jury box as the jurors followed along. But now, as Seeley expected, he saw some anxious side glances. This was the point at which Gabriela Vega, helping Kaplan prepare his testimony, cautioned the witness to avoid technical terms. Seeley's first instinct, sitting with them in the Heilbrun, Hardy conference room, was to agree. But then he decided that it wouldn't hurt to remind the jury, and particularly Sansone, that it took more than high-school biology to create AV/AS.

Kaplan said, "The problem is that the HIV envelope glycoprotein displays emphatic antigenic variations, is heavily glycosylated, and is poorly immunogenic."

The mood in the jury box instantly turned from confusion to frustration. For all of Kaplan's undeniable charm, Seeley was going to have to be more careful.

Seeley forced a laugh into his voice. "Could you translate that into a language the jury and I can understand?"

Kaplan's eyebrows shot upward. He laughed and clapped his thighs. "Of course. I apologize." He rested his hands on the rail, and spoke directly to the jury. "Four unique hurdles stand in the way of developing an AIDS vaccine."

In her cross-examination of Chaikovsky that morning, Fischler left the jury with the thought that science had progressed to a point at which Steinhardt's achievement was obvious, even trivial, to anyone working in the field. Now, Kaplan was going to dispel that thought.

"Before you describe these obstacles to the jury, Dr. Kaplan, could you tell us how you came to know about them?"

The smile that played tentatively on the scientist's lips became a self-deprecating grin. "I've been working on the problem of an AIDS vaccine for eighteen years. Our experience is that we overcome one or two of these obstacles, but when we try to attack the next one, we find that the first one's come back."

"You said 'we'?"

"My research team."

"How large is this team?"

"Over the course of our work, it's been as small as six researchers, all of them PhD graduate students or postdocs, and as large as fifteen."

"And where has this research taken place?"

"At Harvard Medical School, and at the Dana-Farber Cancer Institute's Center for AIDS Research."

"Why at two institutions?"

Again, Kaplan shrugged. "This is a big job."

When they were preparing Kaplan for his testimony last night, Seeley asked him how a researcher like Steinhardt, working alone at a small drug company, could get to the finish line ahead of teams of scientists at major, federally funded laboratories. "You have to remember," Kaplan had told him, "Steinhardt was already publishing papers on this approach when he was at UC." There wasn't a hint of envy or regret in Kaplan's voice. "And," Kaplan had said, "some researchers work better alone than others." "Or," Seeley had said, "they're less inclined to share the credit." Kaplan had lifted his eyebrows and tilted his head but said nothing.

"So, Dr. Kaplan, could you tell the jury what these four obstacles are."

"Remember," Kaplan said, talking to the jurors as if it were one of his Harvard seminars, "I told you that vaccines work by stimulating the body's immune system to fight off the virus infection? Well, HIV is unique among viruses in that its target is the victim's immune system. It's in the nature of HIV that it destroys the very mechanism that we need to fight off infection. How can you use the immune system to repel a virus if the virus attacks the system itself?"

Kaplan's little tutorial had the jury's close attention and the judge's, too. Thorpe wouldn't think to break the communion between the expert and his audience. Nor would Thorpe have more than two or three questions on cross, none of them harmful. For the first time that day, Seeley relaxed. The case was going well. Cordier's testimony had also been strong, Chaikovsky's only slightly less so, and Kaplan's comments last evening in the conference room had reassured him about Steinhardt's style of research.

"You testified that there are four hurdles, Dr. Kaplan. What are the other three?"

"Recall I said that for polio and the other vaccines, vaccinologists use a weakened form of the virus to stimulate the host's antibodies."

"Go on."

"We can't do that with HIV. We can't use a weakened virus, or even a dead one. Because of the virus's effect on the immune system, it would be too dangerous to the person being inoculated. It could be a death sentence."

"So what can you use?"

"The best you can do is break down HIV into its individual proteins, and use one of them."

"What are the other two obstacles?" It was a short, smooth ride from here.

"For an antibody—any antibody—to work, for it to neutralize the virus and prevent it from invading cells, it has to bind to the virus particle. The problem is that the surface of an HIV particle is so dense and complicated that it's virtually impossible for the antibody to reach the binding site."

"Like a crumpled piece of paper?"

"No." Kaplan shook his head impatiently. "Picture a tiny sphere. An HIV particle, or virion, is only one ten-thousandth of a millimeter wide—the width of a human hair is one-tenth of a millimeter—and it has a surface like a loose piece of cloth covered with dozens of mushrooms. The mushrooms are constantly in motion, always flopping around." Kaplan waggled his fingers at the jury. "How can an antibody find a binding site if it's hidden under the mushroom caps? But it must bind to a specific site. Hit or miss isn't good enough for it to work."

"And, the last obstacle?"

"Mutation. With polio, measles, mumps, the virus you're attacking stays the same from one day to the next, and from one host to another. But HIV is different. It's constantly mutating—and not only over time, and not only from one host to another. On a given day, HIV can take on countless different forms in just a single individual."

"So you're saying that HIV is a moving target?"

"A moving target and a changing one. As many as a million totally unique virions can be created each day in a single infected host. This means that even if you could somehow manage to get an antibody to neutralize one virion, there are others it won't neutralize. You're pretty much back where you started."

"These four hurdles—did Dr. Alan Steinhardt, who created AV/AS, manage to get over or around each of them?"

"Yes," Kaplan said. "Yes, he did."

"Thank you, Dr. Kaplan. I have no more questions."

The abrupt halt had the effect Seeley wanted, and an uneasy silence hung in the courtroom. Judge and jurors were asking themselves Seeley's unspoken question: What did Steinhardt do to overcome these obstacles? Kaplan had dispelled any doubt about the scientific significance of Steinhardt's achievement and, tomorrow morning, the jurors would greet Steinhardt as a savior when he explained how he surmounted the hurdles in the way of AV/AS. The trick would be to have him on and off the stand before the jurors discovered how personally repellent he was.

Thorpe rose, but didn't move from the defense table. "Professor Kaplan, your colorful testimony has left all of us in suspense: What was it the discoverer of AV/AS did to break through these four obstacles?"

Seeley was on his feet. "Objection. The question is outside the scope of the direct examination."

"Your Honor, the question goes to the validity of this patent. Surely the jury has a right to know the nature of this supposed advance."

Seeley was not going to let Thorpe deflate his plans. "Judge, the jurors have not only the right but the duty to understand the nature of the invention. However, they deserve to learn this from the man who made the discovery, and this man will testify tomorrow morning."

Farnsworth looked at the jury, as if asking what it was they wanted, knowing that however she ruled on Seeley's objection, it could not possibly constitute reversible error, requiring the appeals court to overturn the jury's verdict.

Still watching the jury, Farnsworth said, "The objection is sustained."

Trial was over for the day.

FOURTEEN

Cypress Cove, where Lily Warren lived, was a cluster of clapboard town houses built into a hillside overlooking downtown Half Moon Bay and, beyond it, the Pacific. The flowering vines that climbed over the second-floor balconies gave the place a Mediterranean feel, except for the bite in the air and the fog just now beginning to roll in off the water. A faint mineral smell of seaweed, kelp, and wrack wafted past Seeley as he stood at Lily's door, a bouquet of spring flowers in his hand.

Seeley had thought to break the date, but then Steinhardt refused to meet with him to review tomorrow morning's testimony, leaving the evening free. "I'm not some actor who has to rehearse a part," the scientist said. Seeley wished that he were. Not only could the scientist's arrogant narcissism undo all that he and Palmieri had accomplished with Cordier, Chaikovsky, and Kaplan, but Seeley still didn't know what secrets lay behind the neat grids of Steinhardt's laboratory notebooks.

Lily's flustered half curtsy when Seeley handed her the flowers made him wonder how often she entertained. She led him up a narrow stairway and went off to find a vase. The furniture had the matched look of what someone might acquire on a rushed visit to a rental outlet, but a brightly colored pillow here and there, a couple of bulky art books on the coffee table, and some framed black-and-white photographs on the living-room wall redeemed the monotony. Just inside the glassed-off balcony, a dining table was set with good china and silver and a single gardenia in a crystal flute. Exotic aromas came from the small open kitchen where Lily fussed with the flowers.

She came into the living room carrying a tray with an imported brand of sparkling water, a frosty canister of ice, and two tall tumblers. Her eyes smiled at him. "I have wine or beer if you'd like. But I thought you might prefer this."

Seeley remembered how at lunch she had caught his lingering glance at the line of beer bottles along the restaurant wall, and he wondered how much about him she had already deduced. Everything, he decided.

She took the corner of the couch across from him and filled the two glasses. In her own home, her posture still as erect as a dancer's, she seemed less confident, more vulnerable, than at lunch.

"I'm sorry, but there's no dim sum. I had to work at the lab all day so I picked up some takeout at a Thai place on the way home."

"I didn't come for the dim sum."

"It's my favorite restaurant. I promise, you'll like it."

She crossed a leg, and an unseen slit in the floor-length skirt momentarily revealed a long graceful leg, then magically concealed it again.

"Did you have any trouble finding me?"

"Why do you live all the way out here?"

"The suburbs? You think a single woman would be happier in the city."

"No, I—"

"It's convenient. The lab's just fifteen minutes away. Some days I have to be there eighteen, nineteen hours . . ." She stopped, her thoughts elsewhere. "And, when I get lonely, the ocean's a wonderful companion."

Seeley wondered whether it was the ocean or the thought of home, six thousand miles away, that consoled her. As when she told him of her affair with Steinhardt, Lily's openness surprised him.

"Do you ever think about going back?"

"I think about China all the time, but not about going back." Again, the expressive eyes smiled. "Every Chinese graduate student who comes to the States says that after she gets her degree she's going back. But when the time comes, not even half of them do."

"China's going to be a great scientific power."

"But not for a long time and, even then, the important things won't change, especially if you're a woman. You work for months, years, every day of the week, praying for results. Then the day comes when everything you've done, every one of your intuitions turns out to be right. You've made a major discovery."

"And you can't claim it as your own."

She shrugged, but Seeley felt the heat. "Calls are made. Papers arrive. You're assigned to a different lab. Some party bureaucrat who never in his life spent an hour at a laboratory bench gets to put his name on your discovery."

"It sounds like corporate America," Seeley said. "Or Switzerland."

She instantly saw where his thoughts were going, and a rueful smile warned him off: No, not tonight; I don't want to talk about St. Gall or Alan Steinhardt. "I'm famished," she said. "Let's eat."

Seeley excused himself to wash up. The guest bathroom, on the other side of the stairway, looked barely used. Another fragrant gardenia was in a narrow vase above the sink. The hand towels could have been starched, they were that stiff, and Seeley wiped his damp hands on his trousers. In a straw basket beneath the towel rack were four or five women's magazines—*Vogue*, *French Vogue*, *Cosmopolitan*, and, on top, *Glamour*. Next to the photograph of a pouty-lipped starlet, the cover promised articles on "Seven Tips for Overcoming Shyness" and "Ten Special Treats to Give Your Man in Bed." Seeley asked himself what he had expected. Well-thumbed copies of *Immunology*?

When he returned, Lily was setting down a platter on which glistening shallots, crinkly dark mushrooms, and chive flowers surrounded a whole crispy fish. She described the other dishes to him: steamed wontons filled with ground spiced pork, stir-fried noodles with chives, and shrimp-and-olive fried rice.

"Another thing," Lily said, as if there had been no break in their conversation, "in your country anyone can eat like a party official or a big-time industrialist even if he isn't one."

The food was good. It might have been the variety, or the complex flavors, or the hour, but they ate more slowly than they had at lunch, talking less and with more comfortable pauses. The tuning fork still hummed, but at a lower pitch.

"What was it like for you growing up in China?" The question, Seeley knew, could spoil the mood but, as in the taxi with Palmieri, it was the question he asked of anyone who interested him; for him, it was the single great mystery.

Lily clapped her hands as a child might. "Oh," she said, "I had a wonderful childhood."

"What were your parents like?"

"I never really got to know them. My father's a physicist and my mother's a chemist, but when I was growing up they were either in prison or on a farm hoeing beans and being politically reeducated. I came to America before they got their lives back."

She spoke of this so lightly that Seeley was certain that he misunderstood.

"My grandparents—my mother's parents—raised me. They were wonderful people and they spoiled me terribly."

She described trips with her grandfather to a local zoo populated with a weird assortment of animals, and of toiling side by side in her grandmother's small vegetable garden, offering the stories as gifts that implicitly asked for Seeley's memories in exchange. To Seeley's astonishment, he found himself talking about adventures of his own: bicycle excursions to places like the Ellicott Square Building that he'd only read about in the newspaper or seen on television; the long solitary hours he spent in Buffalo's wondrous art museum. He had grown so accustomed to thinking of his childhood as a single, unremittingly dark passage that, as when he remembered building beer-bottle castles with Leonard at the Germania, the memories were like bright windows opening.

Seeley said, "Besides being able to eat like a party official, what else do you like about America?"

"The independence." She pronounced the word carefully, as she had "relationship" the other day, as if the very word was a treasure to be handled gently. "Young Chinese women come here, they find good work and, for the first time in their lives, they have financial independence. Sexual independence, too. That's another reason they don't go back."

Which *Glamour* article had she turned to first, Seeley wondered, the one about overcoming shyness or the one about ten bedtime treats?

"It must be hard," he said, "balancing relationships with independence." It was his last attempt to get her to talk about Steinhardt.

"You're a good listener," Lily said.

"I liked the stories about you and your grandparents."

"No, I mean your remembering what I said about relationships at lunch. Not many people listen that closely."

"I would have thought that's mostly what scientists do. Observe. Listen."

She poured tea from a teapot and the fragrance of jasmine blossomed over the table.

"The ones I meet, all they want to talk about are their toys. I can tell you anything you want to know about every concept car and useless electronic gadget ever made."

"You ought to enlarge your circle."

"I'm trying."

She rose to gather the dishes. When Seeley started to help, she said she was sure he had been a very dutiful husband—how did she know that he had been married?—but that he should go out on the balcony and watch the fog come in.

On the other side of the sliding doors, the night air was damp, and the ocean and the town were already lost in fog. Seeley listened for the foghorn that at lunch had sounded every fifteen minutes, but didn't hear it. The silence must have transfixed him, because at some point, without his realizing it, Lily had come onto the balcony. She slipped next to him at the rail, and Seeley was aware of a fragrance, like the gardenias in the apartment, but paler.

"It's so quiet," he said.

"Not really. Concentrate. Listen to the ocean."

After a long minute in which Seeley tried to block out the street sounds, she said, "What did you hear?"

"Waves splashing against rocks."

She put her arm around his shoulder to cup a hand at his ear, making it a shell. "Listen."

"Nothing." Seeley shook his head.

"It takes time. With practice, you can actually hear the ocean itself, the animal life, the plants, everything."

At that moment, Seeley wished that he could stay on the balcony with Lily at his side forever. Any hope that he had of discovering Steinhardt's secret lifted off from the balcony rail and soared like a gull out over the Pacific.

Lily said, "The fog will be like this all the way back to the city. It won't clear until just before dawn."

"I bet you knew that when you asked me to dinner."

"I'm a scientist. Of course I knew."

She took his hand—her fingers were as cool, as he'd imagined they would be—and led him back to the living room, indicating the place next to her on the couch. When she drew her legs up beneath her, the magic slit in her skirt parted once more, just barely, but this time remained open.

"Would you like more tea? Anything?"

Seeley said no. "What was your name? In China."

She smiled but shook her head. "You'd never guess."

"Something beautiful, I'd imagine."

"Or mysterious."

Her hand slipped to his wrist and, unbuttoning the shirt sleeve, she let her fingertips graze his arm. The other hand rested casually on her thigh.

Watching the dark thoughtful eyes, Seeley placed a hand against Lily's cheek. She brushed it with her lips and opening his shirt, leaned into him, pressing her ear to his chest so that she could listen to his heartbeat. Eyes closed, Seeley traced in his mind the imagined arc of the seagull until it was no more than a speck against the night sky.

Seeley felt Lily draw away, and when he opened his eyes she was above him, her features in the dim light—the perfect curve of an eyebrow, the slope of a porcelain cheek—like fragments of a puzzle. She unbuttoned the top buttons of her blouse and pulled his head against her own heart. "Listen! This is how the ocean sounds." After a time, long fingers gently pulled him upward. She touched her lips to his, and Seeley tasted some flavorful trace—tamarind? ginger?—before taking her head in his hands and kissing her.

His lips barely touching hers, Seeley said, "You didn't tell me your name."

"You're very persistent." Her fingers rested on his arm, as if she were waiting for something to happen.

"So are you."

She ran her other hand through his hair. "Mi Huā."

"Which means?"

"I knew you'd ask."

"Which is why you wouldn't tell me."

"Would you like to stay the night?"

"That would be nice," Seeley said.

"Secret Flower."

Ah.

FIFTEEN

Trials are theater, a fact that Seeley considered once again, while waiting for Judge Farnsworth to make her entrance. Palmieri was busy at his laptop and Barnum faced the empty jury box, his back to counsel's table. In the bright tiled washroom, Steinhardt preened before the mirror for a full five minutes, patting his already slicked-back hair, running a small ivory comb through the neatly trimmed beard, adjusting and readjusting his tie before finally unknotting and retying it. Coming into the courtroom, he wanted to know where the press was. Was there someone from *The New York Times*?

"They're in the row on your left," Seeley said, "but, when you get on the stand, don't look at them. Look only at the jury or at me."

Leonard was two rows back, gesturing that he needed to talk to Seeley. Seeley saw the jury filing in through the back door, and shook his head, no.

The clerk cried for all to rise, and from the same door as the jury, Judge Farnsworth swiftly ascended the bench. Even before she settled into her high-backed chair, she signaled Seeley to put on his witness.

Seeley's original plan was for Steinhardt to describe how AV/AS overcame the four hurdles that Kaplan described yesterday, having him on and off the stand in no more than half an hour. The longer his testimony went, the greater was the risk that he would antagonize the jury; and the wider it went, the greater was the risk that he would say things that Thorpe could use to destroy him on cross-examination. But Steinhardt insisted that he be able to tell the whole story, beginning with his early work at UCSF, and in a conference call Barnum ordered Seeley to go along.

Now, observing Steinhardt on the witness stand, shoulders back, gaze fixed on the row of journalists in the gallery as he answered Seeley's questions, Seeley regretted giving in to Barnum. He took Steinhardt briskly through his years at UCSF, introducing into evidence the lab notebooks that he'd kept there, directing the scientist to specific entries to quicken the pace and to give Thorpe little elbow room on cross. When Seeley introduced into evidence the two leather-bound notebooks from Steinhardt's work at Vaxtek, he slowed the pace only when the witness approached the completion of his experiments.

"And the entry in your laboratory notebook dated September twelfth, 1997, was that also made under your direct supervision?"

An eyebrow arched, Steinhardt's sign of displeasure. "I made the entry myself. You can see from the handwriting."

"And the signature below yours, of a Daniel Turnley. Who is that?"

"One of the scientists who works for me. As at UCSF—as at any creditable research laboratory—all notebook entries must be witnessed."

"And, through October third of 1997, when the experiments were completed, there is at least one entry for each day. Is it usual for you to work like that, to be in the lab every day, without a break?"

"When a scientist is on the brink of discovering a new vaccine, he doesn't take the weekend off for golf."

That got an appreciative murmur from the jury box, and it occurred to Seeley that he may have worried too much about the impact of Steinhardt's self-importance.

"But there are three different witness signatures over this period, September twelfth through October third. Why is that?"

"My staff have families." Steinhardt cocked his head in a gesture intended to mimic sympathy, but that to Seeley only looked disingenuous. "I don't require them to put in the hours that I do."

Seeley glanced at the jury and felt a spasm of resentment. Against expectations, Steinhardt was going over well. Only the kid and the juror next to him, the AT&T cable splicer, were impassive. The jurors' acceptance of Steinhardt was good for Vaxtek's case, but the thought that they were being taken in by this pious charlatan angered Seeley.

"And did an event of significance occur in your laboratory on October third?"

Steinhardt ran a manicured finger over the notebook page as if he was reviewing it.

There was a cough from plaintiff counsel's table.

"An event of overwhelming significance." Steinhardt nodded gravely. "Yes."

There was a second cough, more insistent, and when Seeley turned, Palmieri was frantically signaling with his eyes for him to stop.

"Please review that entry again," Seeley said, stalling. He went back to counsel's table.

Line after line filled Palmieri's computer screen, and Seeley immediately recognized Steinhardt's résumé.

"Mr. Seeley." It was Judge Farnsworth. "Are you finished with your witness?"

On the screen was the section of Steinhardt's résumé that listed his presentations to scientific groups. "No, Judge. I'm just checking a fact." Seeley would have to keep Steinhardt occupied with harmless questions until Palmieri explained what was on his mind.

"Returning for a moment to your work at the University of California, Dr. Steinhardt, could you tell the court about your work practices there? The size of your team?"

Steinhardt, puzzled, launched into a description of what he called not his team but his staff at UCSF.

Barnum grabbed Seeley's arm. His whisper was harsh as gravel. "What the hell are you doing?" Seeley shrugged him away, not taking his eyes from Palmieri's computer screen.

Palmieri pointed to a line in the résumé. On September 17, 1997,

Steinhardt presented a paper in Berlin. He pointed to the next line. On the twenty-fifth, he delivered a paper in Geneva. And on October 3, 1997, the very day that in his laboratory in South San Francisco, California, Alan Steinhardt stood on the brink of discovering AV/AS, he was delivering the keynote address at a conference on immunology to the faculty of medicine of the University of Bologna.

Seeley's clients lied to him all the time. Witnesses lied, too. But, so far as Seeley knew, he had always caught the lie in time and refused to let the witness testify. A lawyer could argue that Steinhardt had not yet lied on the stand. Seeley hadn't asked whether he'd in fact made the entries on the dates indicated, only whether they were made under his supervision. Seeley glanced over to where his brother was sitting in the gallery. Leonard knew that something was wrong. When Seeley looked at Palmieri, he was surprised to see something like triumph playing in the young partner's expression.

A beautiful woman reveals, then instantly conceals, a long white leg. Steinhardt knots his necktie to perfection, but keeps two sets of books. In one set, Steinhardt recorded his experiments as he made them. The other set meticulously copied these entries but gave them earlier dates, well ahead of St. Gall's experiments, to establish Steinhardt as the first inventor of AV/AS. This was Lily's secret, and it was still intact as she slept and Seeley drove back to San Francisco in the five a.m. fog. She had given Steinhardt St. Gall's dates of invention. That was why she was in Steinhardt's lab that night.

Steinhardt had completed his answer to Seeley's last question and the courtroom was silent. Seeley needed time. Ethical obligations required him to tell his client—Barnum—why he had to take Steinhardt off the stand.

"Mr. Seeley?"

"May we request a fifteen-minute recess, Judge?"

"Your witness has been on for less than half an hour."

"There's some urgency, Judge—"

"You can have your recess when you are finished with your witness. If you're finished now, you can have your recess now. Otherwise, you will please continue."

Across the courtroom, Fischler was talking intently to Thorpe. If, during the months of pretrial discovery, the St. Gall team had caught the discrepancy between Steinhardt's notebook and his travel dates—how could they miss it?—Thorpe would destroy Steinhardt on cross-examination.

Seeley calculated. He had two witnesses who were going to testify that St. Gall infringed the AV/AS patent and, with some intensive preparation, he could have them describe how AV/AS worked. But he remembered his promise to the jury that Steinhardt would explain the invention; this was why the scientist was on the stand. Leaving the black leather notebook on the table, Seeley returned to the lectern.

"Dr. Steinhardt, are you familiar with the expert's report that Dr. Lionel Kaplan prepared for this lawsuit?" Seeley worked to keep the anger out of his voice.

"I read it. Yes."

"And do you remember that the report describes four obstacles to the development of an AIDS vaccine?"

"Of course I do. Everyone—"

"Do you agree with Dr. Kaplan's assessment of these obstacles in his report?"

The scientist's narrow face darkened. He didn't like being cut off. "Yes," he said. "I do."

"Could you remind the jury of these obstacles?"

Steinhardt fumed as he described the obstacles in clipped sentences. That was fine with Seeley if it kept his answers short.

"Could you describe how AV/AS overcomes these obstacles?"

Steinhardt straightened in the chair and the small chest expanded. This was, finally, his moment. He crossed a leg. "I would be glad to. The idea for taking this approach occurred to me—"

"Please confine yourself to the specific question, Doctor. Just tell the jury how AV/AS overcomes the obstacles that Dr. Kaplan describes in his report."

Judge Farnsworth leaned forward on the bench, her eyes moving between lawyer and witness. She knew that Seeley was scrambling, that something had gone wrong with his case. Two or three jurors picked up on the judge's interest. But Seeley was not going to let Steinhardt implicate him in perjury by taking credit for being the first to discover AV/AS.

Steinhardt adjusted his tie and looked over to the reporters' section of the gallery, his eyes revealing the profound confusion of a man who was not often confused. He didn't know why Seeley's questions had taken this turn, and this meant that Seeley would need to direct each of his answers.

"How does AV/AS resolve the problem that HIV mutates so rapidly?"

"There is no perfect solution, but I concluded—"

"Not what you concluded, Doctor, just how the vaccine works."

"The vaccine employs a second-best solution." Steinhardt's tone was injured, petulant. "Since it is impossible to neutralize the virus completely, the vaccine works instead to contain it."

"How does that solve the mutation problem?"

"There is in all forms of HIV a genetically conserved region, a portion of the virion—the virus particle—that does not mutate."

Seeley felt as if he was binding the witness with rope. "If the conserved region of the virion can be neutralized, is that the same as if the entire virion has been neutralized?"

"Effectively, yes. If we can get"—Steinhardt saw Seeley's warning look, and gave the first sign that he understood what Seeley was doing—"if it is possible to get an antibody to bind to just one isolate— one part of the conserved region—that can be enough to block the virus's ability to infect a cell."

"But there is an obstacle here, too?"

"The forest of mushrooms. With the mushrooms flopping around, and the envelope surrounding the core of the virion constantly slipping and sliding, the conserved region is the hardest part to reach. It doesn't mutate, but what good can you do if you can't reach it?"

"And how does AV/AS reach the conserved region?" Here was the elegant arc of the invention, and for a brief moment Seeley regretted depriving this miscreant, this would-be perjurer, of his shower of glory.

"To reach the conserved region," Steinhardt again drew himself up in the witness chair, "AV/AS employs a human antibody, specifically a monoclonal antibody, that does not exist in nature but has been synthesized in the laboratory expressly for this purpose. This antibody can specifically target a receptor in the conserved region of the virus envelope, bind to it, neutralize it, and prevent it from infecting cells."

"Would you say that AV/AS works like an arrow, piercing through this mushroom forest until it reaches its target?"

"Yes, Mr. Seeley"—the familiar arrogance replaced the confusion in his voice—"it works like an arrow, and when it reaches the targeted part of the virus it disables it."

Seeley imagined the picture in Steinhardt's mind of that arrow piercing his lawyer's heart.

"Thank you, Dr. Steinhardt." The rhythm of the questions had so far subdued Seeley's rage, but now it rose like a gorge in his throat, making it difficult to speak. "We have no more questions, Judge." He didn't trust his voice. "May we have a recess?"

Pushing through the courtroom's double doors, Seeley evaded Barnum's reach and, grabbing the man's elbow instead, steered the general counsel to the alcove at the end of the long corridor. Leonard trailed, trading looks with Barnum. Leonard had lied when he told Seeley there was only one set of lab notebooks. Seeley dropped Barnum's arm. "Where's Steinhardt?"

Leonard said, "I've got a plane to catch, Mike. I have to be in Washington tonight." He looked back down the corridor. "He went to the men's room."

"You can wait until I finish with your general counsel." To Barnum, Seeley said, "Your scientist wasn't in his lab when his notebooks say he was, and Thorpe knows that. He's going to chew him up on cross."

"Maybe Alan got some of his dates mixed up. Thorpe's not going to call him on it."

Leonard, his back to them, was studying the black-and-white photographs of old-time San Francisco that hung on the alcove wall. The styled, too-blond hair was like a taunt to Seeley, the sum of his brother's contrived innocence. Golden boy.

"The only way the dates got mixed up is if there were two sets of books. Steinhardt wasn't the first inventor."

"You're forgetting that St. Gall already stipulated priority. Thorpe won't be able—"

Behind them, the double doors of a courtroom opened and the broad black face of a bailiff emerged. The man smiled at them gently and placed a finger to his lips before disappearing behind the doors.

"Bob Pearsall knew about the second set of books, didn't he?"

Steinhardt arrived at Barnum's side. "What are you talking about?"

"Your résumé puts you in Berlin, Geneva, and Bologna on the dates your notebooks have you in your laboratory."

Steinhardt drew his lips into a grim line and dropped his head. On the stand, he must have suspected Seeley's discovery of the amateurish deceit. "You have to understand—"

Seeley said, "I don't want to hear anything from you. The less you say from now on, the less harm you're going to do to your employer's case. Right now, I don't give the case much of a chance."

Leonard wandered down the corridor, still looking at photographs. How deep is his shame, Seeley wondered. If he knew his brother, Steinhardt's lies had barely made a dent.

Steinhardt glanced at Barnum, but got no response, then turned to Seeley. "What should I say if Thorpe asks me about the notebooks? The dates?"

"First," Seeley said, "make sure you understand his question. If you don't understand it, ask him to repeat it."

"And, then?"

"Tell him the truth."

An unhealthy reek came off the scientist; his breath had turned rank.

"Look at this as your Miranda warning, doctor. People go to jail for perjury." Seeley gestured at Barnum to take Steinhardt back to the courtroom. "I'll catch up with you in a minute. Remember what I told you. Pause before you answer, no matter how innocent the question sounds. Give me the chance to object if I need to."

Leonard was back in the alcove, examining a San Francisco harbor scene as intently as if he might find the words there that could win over his brother. Seeley spoke to Leonard's back. Neither wanted to see the other's face. "You knew about the second set of notebooks when you came to see me in Buffalo."

"Would you have taken the case if I'd told you?"

"That's why you needed me. Pearsall found out about the notebooks, and wouldn't go along. You figured that even if I discovered Steinhardt's fraud, I'd stick with the case out of loyalty to you."

"Pearsall didn't know. If he knew, Barnum would've told me." Leonard turned to face him. "You've got to give us cover on this, Mike."

"If this comes out in Thorpe's cross-examination, there's nothing I can do."

"It won't come out."

His brother was deceiving himself. "You should be proud of yourself, Len. All these years, and you haven't changed at all."

Leonard immediately understood what his brother meant. The events of thirty-two years ago remained fresh for him, too.

"You're forgetting," Leonard said, "I was the one who stole the gun from his dresser. I was going to throw it in the sewer."

"And when you lost your nerve, you got me to cover for you."

"You haven't changed, either." Leonard's smile was tentative, his eyes worried. "You'll find a way to fix it."

The leather-clad doors of the neighboring courtroom burst open in a din of voices and a crush of people swept by. Seeley recognized a Silicon Valley CEO whose picture was in that morning's *Chronicle* over an article about a stock option scandal. The crowd disappeared and the corridor returned to silence.

It was more than fifteen minutes since Farnsworth called the recess, and Seeley knew she would continue the trial without him. It didn't matter. Palmieri could take over and Seeley could walk away from the trial right now. Wasn't this why he had gone into solo practice—to take the cases he wanted, and leave the ones he didn't? Even remembering why he took the case—David against Goliath—failed to move him.

Leonard said, "What happened wasn't my fault." He had turned back to the pictures on the wall.

"Of course it was. You screwed up and you were weak, so I took the blame for you."

Leonard continued speaking to the wall. "He was a bastard, but you didn't have to knock him down. Hold his own gun on him."

What so infuriated Seeley was that Leonard had no idea what a pitiful coward he was. He knew what had happened while he hid in the bedroom only because their mother had told him. But the possibility that he was complicit never occurred to him.

"Go catch your plane."

Leonard didn't move. Seeley studied the back of his brother's plump neck, and for an instant had the sensation of the damage he could do with a baseball bat.

Leonard turned, his features as contorted by pain as if Seeley had in fact struck him.

Seeley stuffed down his fury. "You had something to tell me. Before, in the courtroom."

Sensing forgiveness, Leonard brightened, quickly recovering, the way he did as a boy. "Renata arranged a field pass for you. You can pick it up at the will-call gate."

The Stanford football game. My brother creates misery and this is what he thinks about.

"You won't tell her, Mike? The problem with Steinhardt?"

Seeley said nothing, but walked back to the courtroom. He was grateful to Palmieri for heading off Steinhardt's perjury. But the timing disturbed him. Palmieri had reviewed Steinhardt's notebook entries a week ago, and had seen the scientist's résumé long before that. Why had he remained silent about the conflict in dates until Seeley was in the middle of his direct examination, when the disruption would do the most harm? Or was Seeley just passing the blame for not catching the discrepancy himself?

Thorpe's cross-examination of Steinhardt was already under way when Seeley came in. The courtroom felt like a crime scene. Palmieri slid a legal pad across the table. On it was a hastily scribbled outline of Thorpe's questions and Steinhardt's answers so far. Thorpe had for some reason started with Steinhardt's work in his UC lab. But, even if the scientist kept two sets of notebooks there, too, they had no bearing on the discovery of AV/AS, which came much later. Unless Thorpe's plan was to show that duplicity was Steinhardt's standard practice.

Steinhardt's easy condescension of an hour ago was gone. Although he followed Seeley's instructions to pause after each question, to give Seeley time to object, and to face the jury when he answered, the answers faltered. The rigid set of his narrow shoulders was a poor imitation of the earlier self-assured bearing. This was, Steinhardt had to know, just a warm-up. Thorpe could at any moment turn to the discrepancy between the scientist's travel schedule and his notebook.

As he followed Thorpe's questions, Seeley outlined on a legal pad a strategy that, on redirect, might at once deflect Thorpe's exposure of the second set of notebooks and yet keep Steinhardt clear of perjury. Leonard's pleas echoed in his thoughts: Fix this up, Mike. Don't tell Renata. This was as close as he and his brother got to fellowship.

Thorpe shuffled from the lectern to the defense table and whispered something to Dusollier. The Swiss lawyer nodded and lifted a folder from a pile on the table. Thorpe opened the folder, studying the contents at arm's length, as if there was something there that he found offensive.

"Earlier in your testimony, Dr. Steinhardt"—Thorpe spoke from the table and Steinhardt leaned forward to hear—"you referred to AV/AS as a vaccine. Is that correct?"

The court reporter asked Thorpe to repeat the question, and this time Steinhardt answered at once. "Yes, that's correct."

Barnum leaned across the table and wrote at the bottom of the legal pad: "Where's this going?"

Seeley knew where Thorpe was headed, but didn't understand why.

Steinhardt looked at Seeley again, and this time Seeley nodded. AV/AS was not a true vaccine, but Steinhardt's concession on the point would not help Thorpe's case. He could argue that it weakened Vaxtek's claim of long-felt need for the therapy, but that would make no difference to the jury.

"Does AV/AS in fact work that way, as a vaccine, like the polio vaccine or measles vaccine? Does it use the body's immune system to neutralize a virus?"

Then Seeley saw Thorpe's strategy: he was trying to goad Steinhardt into overstating the scope of his discovery, to put on display for the jury the same arrogant scientist that Seeley was trying to hide. But Thorpe had miscalculated. Steinhardt had already been humiliated once today, by his own lawyer, and he was not going to let St. Gall's lawyer do the same. When he looked at Seeley for guidance, Seeley discreetly shook his head.

"No, it does not," Steinhardt said. "As effective as AV/AS is in neutralizing infection, it is not a true vaccine, like the polio vaccine, that inoculates against it."

"So, then, this *vaccine*"—Thorpe was waving the folder now—"AV/AS is not the Holy Grail that everyone's been looking for?"

Steinhardt didn't wait this time, but answered at once. "I'm not a theologian, sir." The attempt at humor wrenched Steinhardt's face; humor and its expressions were unfamiliar to him and Seeley felt a moment's sadness for the scientist.

Thorpe sighed and leaned back on the table. "I was using the term colloquially, Doctor. Let me rephrase the question. Is AV/AS the AIDS vaccine that has been the object of scientific research since 1984?" If he couldn't portray Steinhardt as arrogant, Thorpe was going to show him as evasive. But why was he pressing so hard?

Steinhardt said, "Science doesn't work that way. With a disease as deadly as AIDS, there is a multiplicity of research goals. AV/AS achieved one of them."

"But AV/AS does not trigger human immunity to the disease."

Seeley was on his feet. "Asked and answered."

Farnsworth looked from Seeley to Thorpe. The questioning puzzled her, too. "The witness may answer."

"No," Steinhardt said. "Sadly, it does not."

Thorpe turned to the jury. "I have no more questions of the witness."

Seeley caught his breath. Thorpe was not going to ask Steinhardt about the inconsistency between his travel dates and the dated entries in his lab notebook. It was inconceivable to him that Thorpe and his team of lawyers had failed to ask the question that any competent solo practitioner would have asked: Was the inventor in his lab at the time he said he made his discovery? And then Seeley reminded himself that until this morning he, too, had failed to compare Steinhardt's lab dates with his travel schedule.

"Redirect, Mr. Seeley?"

Seeley reckoned quickly. Two or three questions could repair the small damage from Thorpe's questions about the efficacy of AV/AS as a vaccine. But they might also open the door for more questions from Thorpe and—Seeley believed his witness still had it in him—perjury by Steinhardt. However, Steinhardt's new humility reduced the risk of arrogance or perjury from another question.

"Just one question, Judge. Dr. Steinhardt, we have in the course of this trial been referring to AV/AS. Could you tell the jury what those letters stand for?"

"AV, of course refers to AIDS vaccine. That's standard reference."

"And AS?"

Steinhardt actually managed a shrug, and looked down as he spoke. "Alan Steinhardt."

The approving nods in the jury box confirmed that Seeley had been right to ask the question.

When Thorpe declined to question further, Farnsworth said, "Then we'll take our lunch recess now." She looked at the clock high up on the wall on the defense side of the courtroom. "We'll resume at one p.m. sharp."

Pounding on Seeley's back, Barnum leaned into his ear. "I knew Thorpe wouldn't catch the problem with the dates."

Seeley looked at him hard. "This is no time to celebrate."

Barnum smirked as if to say, the two of you are suckers. Thorpe and you.

What Seeley was thinking was that the line in Pearsall's sketchbook hadn't asked what Steinhardt was hiding, but what *else* he was hiding.

SIXTEEN

The low brown dog strained toward Seeley's car, barking angrily, stopping only when the woman trying to give Seeley directions yanked sharply at its leash. The Stanford game had already started, but Seeley missed the first freeway exit for the university, and the next one took him onto a residential section of the campus. The large homes on deep, shaded lots belonged, he supposed, to a pampered faculty. While the woman quieted the dog, the attractive girl with her gave Seeley directions to the stadium. "After the dormitories," she said, "just follow the noise."

The girl's directions took Seeley past parking lots, playing fields, and low sandstone buildings under red tile roofs. Students in shorts and T-shirts tossed Frisbees or punched volleyballs. Tufted palm fronds were green against the cloudless sky.

Seeley grew up playing football in the northeast, and he couldn't dislodge from his visceral passion for the game the memory of freezing mud and raw numbed fingers. Still, when ahead of him a huge, throaty roar went up—a touchdown? a crucial pass completed?—his nerves quickened. He found a place at the edge of a dirt lot already crowded with cars, collected his field pass at a booth on the other side of the stadium, and had to restrain himself from running down the ramp to the game.

Men in chinos, white turtlenecks, and cardinal red windbreakers moved up and down the sidelines, black-shirted television crews maneuvering between them. Seeley showed his pass to a security guard and made his way to the yellow-bordered rectangle, twenty yards on each side of the fifty-yard line, reserved for the team. Looking surprisingly young and vulnerable in jerseys pumped up with protective gear, some players watched from the bench, others milled about, and a few huddled with coaches. Renata, trim in jeans and a white polo shirt, was talking with two men in Stanford windbreakers, but broke away when she saw him.

She touched a hand to Seeley's back by the way of greeting, and when he glanced at the scoreboard, said, "Don't get your hopes up. We're a heartbreaker."

There was no score yet, but Seeley knew what she meant. In the end, in college football, strong teams beat smart ones. He said, "I only root for underdogs."

"Leonard called last night. He said you're doing a great job on the case."

Seeley imagined his brother worrying that he was going to tell Renata about their confrontation over Steinhardt's second set of books.

One of the men who had been talking to Renata approached, but before he could speak, she told him to go to the locker room to see if her X-rays were ready.

"Second play of the game," she said to Seeley, "one of our wide receivers gets hit and cracks his femur."

From his playing days, Seeley remembered the yellow-chalked rectangle as a world apart. Bodies constantly brush past as offense, defense, and special teams come on and off; from moment to moment there is the concussive, sledgehammer force of the game that no spectator in the stands can hear or feel. The hoots and calls from the crowd were a disembodied wall of noise, and a smell like ozone crackled all about. The giant scoreboard clock moved erratically toward triple zero, but

inside the rectangle it was timeless. The immediacy of the next play
sucked every atom out of the dense air.

Renata put a hand on Seeley's arm and nodded downfield. On
the sideline was the lumpish figure of Joel Warshaw, football jammed
under his arm, hands cupped around his mouth, shouting advice to
the team.

"He's in the top tier of Buck Club donors," Renata said. "That gets
him a field pass whenever he wants. I've never seen him miss a home
game."

Seeley watched the entrepreneur. At every down, he moved with
the play, running along the sidelines, screaming at the players, stopping only to talk with other men, dressed like him in chinos and Stanford sweatshirts and caps. Several times he passed by the chalked-in
rectangle but didn't appear to notice Seeley or Renata.

Renata's other assistant rushed up with the suitcase-sized surgeon's
kit and in the next moment was following her onto the field.

Seeley thought about the trial. No matter how many times he told
himself that his examination of Steinhardt had violated no legal or
ethical rules, he came up short. He should have caught the discrepancy in dates earlier and refused to let Steinhardt testify. It was no
consolation that the American justice system left it to his adversary
through cross-examination to root out untruth, nor was it a comfort
that his remaining witnesses had been as honest and seamless in their
testimony as the first three, and that St. Gall's attacks had left few
bruises on his case.

Renata's assistant returned from the locker room with a legal-sized
black envelope under his arm.

"The doc's amazing," he said to Seeley. "How do you know her?"

"We're related," Seeley said.

When Renata came off the field, she took the envelope the assistant
gave her to a bench to study the film. Seeley looked away, and in the
next moment a mass of bodies tumbled toward him like the onrush
of a wave. Less than a yard from him, a healthy farm boy's face, pink
except for the black smudge of grease high on each cheek, looked up
at him from under the pile. The quarterback had taken some elbows

going down and there was a glimmer of pain in the intelligent eyes, but what took Seeley back to his own college play was the humor he also saw there: What am I doing here, with all these big guys on top of me?

Renata came to Seeley's side.

"Hey, Doc," the boy said.

The players peeled themselves off the boy and he managed a smile.

"You okay, Ron?"

"Never better." He lifted himself into a crouch, steadied himself for a moment, then rose and limped off to the huddle that was forming.

Seeley said, "How's your receiver?"

"His season's over." She slid the X-ray back into the envelope. "When Leonard said you were doing a great job in the trial, I figured something was wrong."

She knew Leonard almost as well as he did.

"Nothing important," Seeley said.

Washington scored a touchdown and the extra point, then it was halftime, and Renata went off to the locker room with the team.

Warshaw came to the edge of the rectangle and gestured to Seeley. The air had turned cool, but sweat streamed down his unlined face, and his voice when he spoke was several decibels louder than necessary, as if he was still exhorting the players. "What do you think of my team?"

"Which team is that?" Seeley knew that Warshaw wouldn't be listening for an answer.

"How's my trial going?"

"Your top scientist was ready to commit perjury." Even after the near-disaster of Steinhardt's testimony, Seeley was confident he could win the case. He had promised victory to clients before, but he'd be damned if he would do so for Joel Warshaw.

Warshaw was looking out at the field, where the Stanford band was gathering for its halftime performance. "Do you know how many wins we had last year?" He held up a plump index finger with a dimple where a knuckle would be. "One." With the other hand, he rolled the football along the side of his thigh. "But do you know what we did to USC last month? USC's the favorite by forty-one points, and what do these rocket scientists do—beat them 24–23!"

"Steinhardt just made this a harder case than it was before."

For the first time, Warshaw looked directly at Seeley. Perspiration had created a damp V at the neck of his cardinal sweatshirt. "That's why I hired you. Your brother and Ed Barnum told me you specialize in hard cases. I want you to do anything you have to—*anything*—to win this case."

"Is that what you tell your team?"

Warshaw looked away, his gaze taking in the stadium. "They've got fifty thousand people watching. They have to play fair. You don't."

Seeley remembered his exchange with Warshaw outside the auction tent. Here was a man who thought that slicing an infant in half was a solution, not a threat.

"You know," Warshaw said, tossing the football from one hand to the other, "if you lose, it's going to wipe out your brother."

Before Seeley could ask what he meant, Warshaw was on his way down the sideline, throwing the football to another man in chinos and Stanford sweatshirt.

In the third quarter, Stanford scored its first touchdown, but Washington was making fewer on-field mistakes and, if Seeley's instincts were right, was gathering physical momentum just as Stanford was losing it. The sun was going down and Renata pulled on a windbreaker. She'd gone onto the field two more times with her crew, and when she wasn't on the field, she was busy with one player or another or with the coaches. Seeley noticed that, unlike the first half, her jaw was tight and her hands balled into fists.

Early in the final quarter, Washington made another touchdown, and then Renata was on the field again, this time attending to the downed quarterback. His helmet was off and he had propped himself up on his elbows. Renata's hand was on his leg, her assistants and the trainer looking on. For a moment she turned from the youth to look across the field to the sidelines, and her gaze, when it found Seeley, was so filled with longing that he had to turn away. When he looked again, Renata had the quarterback's hands in hers and, like playmates on a seesaw, the armored giant rose as Renata, slight but determined, pulled back.

When she returned to the sidelines, Renata said, "Why do I get stuck on these guys? Leonard says I should stick with the winners."

That was the kind of thought that Leonard would call a philosophy. Seeley said, "Winning isn't all it's cracked up to be."

In the last minute, Washington scored another touchdown and won the game.

Renata said, "I could use a glass of wine."

Renata was in the shower at the other end of the house. In the dining room, Seeley opened the bottle of Bordeaux that she had set out earlier with two glasses. When he went into the kitchen to fill a glass with water from the tap, a salver on the countertop was piled with crab legs cracked open to reveal pink-and-white meat.

Seeley asked himself what he was doing in his brother's house alone with his brother's wife. He dismissed the obvious reason—Lily was the only woman he wanted a relationship with right now—but could think of no others.

The sensual figures in Renata's painting gave out no more secrets about the artist than they did on Seeley's first visit. Logs and kindling waited in the fireplace, and striking a match against the rough brickwork, it occurred to Seeley that he was re-creating that last visit and, in doing so, invoking his brother's disquieting presence. He thought of how just the other day he could have clubbed Leonard in the corridor outside the courtroom.

Since he stopped drinking a year ago, Seeley had fallen into the habit of counting other people's drinks. No one, he concluded, drank as much as he did, and no one he'd met since coming to California drank the way Renata did. It occurred to him that this was why he had come home with her. Like probing an old but still-sensitive wound, he was revisiting the one great romance of his life, alcohol, to see if a spark of feeling remained. He had no desire to drink; he just missed the companionship of his old friend. Sometimes the notions that came into his head astonished Seeley. My mind, he thought, should have a warning label glued to it: FOR ENTERTAINMENT USE ONLY.

Renata came in, a glass of wine in her hand. She had put on a blouse, skirt, and heels, and either the wine or the shower had given her pale skin a gentle flush.

She glanced at the fire as she took the chair across from him. "There's a cracked crab in the kitchen if you're hungry."

"I saw."

She noticed the water in his glass. "No wine? We have beer, too. Gin, vodka."

"I've already had more than my share." He tilted the glass in a mock toast. "To Stanford's next win."

"What was it like being a college football player? I bet the girls never left you alone."

"Between part-time jobs and football and baseball practice, there wasn't much time for girls." Seeley didn't like talking about that time in his life. "What about you?"

"My parents didn't approve of the crowd I hung out with in high school. I always seemed to wind up with the guys who were on suspension. So they sent me to a small Methodist school in Ohio. All the preachers sent their sons there." She laughed. "My freshman year, *Playboy* rated it one of the top-ten party schools in the country."

Renata talked more about her time in college, the flickering firelight softening the delicate planes of her face. After a while, when the silences grew longer, she drained her glass and crossed the room to refill it. When she returned, she took a place on the couch next to Seeley, crossing her legs beneath her. "When you came here for dinner the other night, did you have any idea how hard I was shaking?" She touched the back of his hand.

The touch saddened him; Seeley felt cheated, but of what, he couldn't say. A fantasy escaped from a corner of his memory that Renata's whispered message to him at her wedding was that she had chosen the wrong brother.

A log snapped in the fireplace and there was a hiss and the sharp fragrance of resin.

Seeley said, "I need to be going."

"What are you afraid of?" Her voice trembled.

"This isn't right."

"Because of Leonard?"

"Yes." It was a lie, but there was nothing else he could say.

"So, now we know." Her voice was bitter.

"What's that?"

"The question I asked you at dinner. You're someone who'd rather be admired than loved."

"You're my brother's wife, Renata."

"And I'm a flirt. You don't think I'd go through with it, do you?"

"I guess we'll never know."

She lifted the wineglass from the table, put it to her lips, and emptied it. "You think I drink too much."

"It's none of my business how much you drink."

"You judge people."

"Somebody has to."

"Who gets to judge you?"

"Believe me, I'm hardest on myself."

"Do you have any idea how important your approval is to Leonard?"

"Look, Renata, I have to go. I'm in the middle of trial."

"From the day I met him, all Leonard could talk about was his big brother. 'Mike did this' or 'Mike did that.' Mr. Perfect."

No tears with this woman, Seeley observed, only fury burning in her too-clear eyes.

"Leonard could never live up to your standards. Now that I've seen what you're like, I don't think anyone can."

Seeley rose to go.

"Do you want to know why he begged you to come out here?"

Seeley had the feeling that he hadn't even begun to penetrate the layers of Leonard's motives.

"So you could see how well he's done. What a success he's been."

"Warshaw told me it's going to wipe you out if I lose the case."

"He's right. Every dime we have is in Vaxtek. We sold everything, all our stocks and bonds. We took a second mortgage on the house.

Leonard said it was our one chance to make some real money, Silicon Valley money. He told Joel that Michael Seeley doesn't lose cases."

"That doesn't sound like Leonard."

"Then you don't know your brother."

"The problem is, I do."

"You are going to win, aren't you?"

Unlike Warshaw, she waited for reassurance from him that, yes, he would win the case.

"Good night, Renata."

The railroad crossing where the 4:30 a.m. commuter train out of San Jose struck and killed Robert Pearsall was twenty minutes from Leonard's house, a drive that took Seeley through a neighborhood of small, neat homes, and then a succession of shabby strip malls, warehouses, and auto body shops. The run-down industrial area was as dark and deserted at 8:30 on a Saturday night as it doubtless was in the early morning that Pearsall died here. Other than parked pickups and panel trucks, the street was empty, and the only sound was the hum of distant freeway traffic.

Seeley left his car on the gravel-strewn hardpan next to the track, where the dense shrubs would hide it from the street, and walked to the railbed. It was, he knew, useless to think that by pacing the tracks he could somehow reconstruct Pearsall's thoughts in the last minutes of his life, or re-create the events and images of his death. But Seeley never defended a criminal case without first visiting the crime scene, and he would do no less for Pearsall.

Seeley did not accept that Pearsall took his own life, but neither did he believe that the lawyer's discovery of Steinhardt's fraudulent notebook entries was responsible for his death. As important as AV/AS was to Warshaw, no client kills his lawyer for uncovering a hole in his case. Seeley had only been taunting Leonard when he asked whether he pushed Pearsall in front of the train. Still, Leonard's gamble on Vaxtek stock surprised him. Leonard was someone who squirreled away nickels and dimes in a pickle jar. He didn't make financial wagers.

Without realizing it, Seeley had walked more than fifty yards along the track. When he looked out to the street through a gap in the rough screen of hedge, he noticed a dark sedan parked among the panel trucks and pickups that he was certain hadn't been there before. No one was visible in the sedan, and although the rattling sound nearby could have been a car engine cooling, it could also be dry leaves blowing across the street.

There was a rustling in the shrubbery across the tracks and, when Seeley turned, a hulking presence emerged from the foliage. Moonlight glinted off the silvery white bone of a modest rack of antlers, and the instant the buck saw him, it froze. The two of them remained absolutely still, studying each other. Ears twitching, depthless eyes alert, the buck heard the locomotive before Seeley did, and by the time the train was upon him, the only evidence of the buck's appearance was the receding white bun of a tail bounding between two dark warehouses.

The moon-size headlamp of the locomotive passed in an instant, followed by a racket of driven steel and the hellish reek of fire, oil, and pulverizing metal. The force of the rocketing cars was like an arm's blow across Seeley's chest.

As if crystallized from the blast of sweet night air that trailed the train's passage, a thought dropped into Seeley's head. The thought—it sent a shiver through him—was that the motive for Robert Pearsall's murder lay not in Warshaw's perspiring progress up and down a football field, measuring every yard of his team's advance and retreat, but in the entrepreneur's observation at a charity auction that the two bleeding warriors should split their bid. It was a spark of intuition, nothing more. But if it was true, then everything Seeley had accomplished in the trial so far was now irrevocably going to recoil back at him.

The juniper fragrance of gin blossomed on Seeley's tongue, and he craved a drink—gin, vodka, scotch, anything so long as it was alcohol. The dark sedan, when he went into the street to look for it, was gone.

SEVENTEEN

Seeley slept little and spent most of the night and early morning sorting, arranging, and rearranging facts, rejecting some, adding others—each one felt like the touch of a dentist's drill—to the gradually expanding picture. If he was right, Leonard's purchase of Vaxtek stock had not been profligate at all, but was the sort of shrewd, cowardly calculation that he expected of his brother. Alan Steinhardt's secrets were trivial when compared to Emil Thorpe's. How many other facts still escaped his grasp? What did Chris Palmieri know?

Rain poured steadily outside the hotel window as Seeley dressed. He borrowed an umbrella from the desk clerk, but passed up the hotel taxi line to walk the mile to Battery Street and the office. Abandoned on an early Sunday morning, the streets and sidewalks of the financial district underlined in thick charcoal strokes the isolation that Seeley now felt from his client and his case. Rain silvered the gray buildings and streamed onto the sidewalks. What client, Seeley thought. What case?

A war room in the middle of trial would ordinarily be a shambles of notebooks, half-used legal pads, and the remains of Chinese takeout, but Tina had done a good job keeping papers filed and notebooks reshelved. When Seeley came into the conference room, Palmieri was already there, his back to the rain-streaked glass, studying the black deposition binder for Thomas Koosmann, the Washington University epidemiologist who would be Thorpe's first witness tomorrow morning. In chinos, loafers, and polo shirt, his face flushed with health, Palmieri looked like he had come directly from a workout at his gym. A sweater was draped over his slender shoulders.

Seeley glanced quickly through the papers that Palmieri slid across the polished tabletop. There was a summary of Koosmann's deposition, proposed questions for cross-examination, and a memo from a junior associate at Heilbrun, Hardy collecting gossip from lawyers around the country about the epidemiologist's tics and foibles as a witness. Seeley pushed them to the side.

"How do you think we're doing, Chris?"

"Pretty well. We've taken a few hits, but the jury looks like it's with us."

"Do you think we're doing *too* well?"

The question should have surprised Palmieri, but for a long moment it didn't, and this indicated to Seeley that his second chair already knew what he himself had just begun to piece together.

Finally Palmieri said, "What do you mean?"

"Why didn't you tell Chaikovsky that she had no choice—that she had to stay at a hotel in the city?"

Palmieri reddened. He had a habit, when defending himself, of closing his eyes and pushing back from the table, and he started doing this now, but caught himself. "I didn't think it was important. She told me she always got up early and there wouldn't be any problem making it to court in time."

"Why did you wait until the last minute, when Steinhardt was about to perjure himself, before you showed me the discrepancy between his lab notes and his travel dates?"

Palmieri shot out of the chair, his eyes fierce. "You've been after me since that mistake with your pro hac papers."

If there wasn't a conference table between them, Seeley was sure the young partner would have lunged at him.

"If you think I'm not carrying my weight, then run the damn case by yourself. That's pretty much what you've been doing anyway."

A gust of wind drove a sheet of rain in crazed patterns across the glass. Instinct told Seeley not only that Palmieri knew that Vaxtek and St. Gall had made a deal, but also that the young partner had reacted to it just as Seeley had: he had no choice but to sabotage his own client's case.

"I'm sorry, Chris." He waited for Palmieri to take his chair again. "My point wasn't to criticize you."

"Whatever your point was, you certainly did a good job disguising it."

Seeley knew that if he couldn't tell Palmieri about his suspicions, he could tell no one. He had weighed the alternatives for, it seemed, most of last night. There was the risk, a real one, that Palmieri was himself a part of the puzzle, just one that Seeley had not yet connected to the rest. But the fact remained that if completing the trial was the only way Seeley could reverse what had happened, he could not do so without Palmieri's help.

Watching Palmieri for his reaction, Seeley said, "I think this is a collusive lawsuit. I think Vaxtek and St. Gall set this case up between them to get a court to hold that the AV/AS patent is valid, and then to split the profits."

The young lawyer's expression revealed nothing. Seeley had given him too much time to prepare himself.

Palmieri said, "And you think I'm part of this collusion."

"No," Seeley said, "just the opposite. I think you're trying to sabotage their deal. You're trying to wreck Vaxtek's case so the jury will vote against the patent."

Palmieri pushed back from the table, and this time closed his eyes. "Why would they need to collude?"

Palmieri didn't trust him and, for that reason, wouldn't admit that he knew about the collusion or that he had done anything to obstruct it. Otherwise, Seeley thought, he just would have told him that he was wrong, and that he wasn't trying to undermine the deal between the two companies.

"Let's say . . ." To his surprise, Seeley found that his heart was racing.

He took a breath and started over. "Let's say that a small pharmaceutical company develops a blockbuster drug and gets a patent on it. Time passes. The company's chairman receives a visit from an executive at another pharma company, but this one's a giant, a multinational."

Seeley remembered Leonard's story about his encounter with St. Gall's head of research at a scientific conference. *We're going to crush you.*

"We can copy AV/AS, the executive tells Warshaw, and you can sue us for patent infringement. We would put on a strong defense and, with our resources, we'd overpower you. In all probability we'd convince a jury that your patent's invalid. But how would that benefit us? AV/AS would no longer be protected by a patent, and anyone would be free to manufacture it. After you spent all this money to develop AV/AS, and we made our lawyers rich, where would that leave the two of us? We'd be scrambling to compete with the generic houses to sell AV/AS at Wal-Mart prices."

Palmieri was listening, but his expression told Seeley nothing.

"All of this is informal," Seeley said. "The St. Gall executive says, 'On the other hand, wouldn't it be interesting if . . .' and Warshaw says, 'Very interesting if . . .' and by the time they're done, they've agreed— nothing in writing of course—that Vaxtek will sue St. Gall for patent infringement, as it planned to do, and that St. Gall will attack the patent's validity. But, as its part of the deal, St. Gall will mount the weakest possible attack on the patent, guaranteeing that the jury will uphold the patent. Vaxtek will win the lawsuit and St. Gall will lose."

"What's does St. Gall get out of the deal?"

"Vaxtek gives them a license to manufacture and sell AV/AS and agrees not to license the patent to anyone else. The two companies divide the world market between them. I figure Vaxtek gets North and South America and St. Gall gets Europe, Africa, and Asia."

"They could get the same result by settling the case without a trial."

Palmieri knew better than that, and Seeley wondered why he was still resisting.

"No," Seeley said. "They need a formal judgment from a court that the patent is valid. That's the only way they can be sure they'll have the AV/AS market entirely to themselves. Some other company could challenge the patent, but when was the last time you heard of a competitor doing that? Once a court decides that a patent is valid, no one is going to go to the expense of trying to prove that it's invalid. But, for this to work, they have to have a court decision that the patent is valid."

That was what Warshaw had said about the two crazed bidders at the charity auction. If they were smart, they'd stop the auction and split the prize. This is what Warshaw did with St. Gall. If keeping his patent meant making a deal with his adversary, he would do that. That the scheme would price AV/AS beyond the reach of AIDS victims who needed it most meant no more to him than did implicating his lawyer in a fraudulent lawsuit.

"The federal circuit could reverse the decision on appeal."

Palmieri had to know that this objection, too, was weak.

"There won't be an appeal," Seeley said. "And St. Gall won't move for a new trial or for the judge to overrule the jury's verdict. It's all part of the deal."

"This is just a theory," Palmieri said. "It's all hypothetical."

Do you want facts, Seeley thought, a glimpse of the treacheries that kept me up all last night? He said, "Did it seem unusual to you how gentle Thorpe and Fischler were with our witnesses on cross? I kidded myself that it was because we prepared the witnesses so well. Why didn't they go after the discrepancies in Steinhardt's dates? They had to know about them."

"If they knew our case was that weak they could have flattened us."

"That's exactly my point. They did know, and they could have flattened us. But if they did that, if our patent was declared invalid, the price of AV/AS would fall through the floor." Why was his bright second chair being so willfully obtuse? "They'd rather have half a loaf than none." Another slice of Warshaw's wisdom. "And, remember," Seeley said, "each company had a hammerlock on the other. St. Gall may have known about Steinhardt's double bookkeeping, but Vaxtek had its security officer's report on a St. Gall employee being in Steinhardt's lab alone, at night."

It occurred to Seeley that, in a puzzle that fit with all the precision of a nightmare, he hadn't thought about Lily's role. Or Leonard's. "Some people," he said as much to himself as to Palmieri, "are going to make a fortune if they bought Vaxtek stock, betting on the outcome of this case."

"It's strange," Palmieri said, "you spinning out a conspiracy theory."

"Why strange?"

"Bob Pearsall dies, and of all the lawyers Vaxtek could hire to take over the case, they choose you—the brother of the company's head of research. No offense"—his voice was taut and close to breaking—"but if I were speculating about collusion, you'd be right at the center of it."

This was why Palmieri was resisting. He was terrified. Someone had killed Pearsall because of what he knew, and now Palmieri was afraid for himself. Michael Seeley—Leonard Seeley's brother—was the last person he would confide in. It was Seeley who had been obtuse, not Palmieri.

"You're wrong about me," Seeley said.

"How would I know that?"

"Farnsworth hears motions tomorrow morning at seven-thirty. I'm going to ask for a mistrial."

"You're going to do this in open court—in front of Barnum and Thorpe?"

"I'll do it ex parte. Just the judge and me in chambers."

"She'll never see you alone in the middle of a trial."

"She's going to have to."

"Even if she does, what makes you think she'll believe you? Where's your proof?"

"Farnsworth's been around a lot of trials. She'll understand."

"And if she doesn't give you a mistrial, she's going to watch everything you do. Every question you ask Thorpe's witnesses. Or don't ask."

Cross-examination, when it works, does so in only one direction—to weaken an adversary's case. Seeley didn't need Palmieri to remind him that it would be impossible to try to reverse the course of the trial through cross-examination of Thorpe's witnesses. This was why he had to get Farnsworth to declare a mistrial.

"You mean she'll be watching to see if I try to sabotage my client's case on cross the way you tried to do on direct?"

"I never said I did that. You did."

Seeley slumped back in his chair and picked up the Koosmann papers. Deciding what questions to ask the epidemiologist was going to consume even more time than he ordinarily gave to preparing for cross-examination. Palmieri was right. If Farnsworth didn't believe him about the collusion, and refused to declare a mistrial, she would be watching his every step in the courtroom. But so, too, would the lawyers who helped set up the collusive lawsuit, Barnum and Thorpe.

"Let's get to work," he said.

EIGHTEEN

On Monday, Judge Farnsworth proceeded through her 7:30 a.m. motion calendar, giving none of the lawyers waiting inside the gallery rail more than two minutes to argue their positions, and taking no more than a minute to give them her decision before dismissing them and moving on to the next pair of adversaries. The double doors opened and Thorpe came in, trailed by Fischler. The courtroom was darker than usual, and when Seeley looked up one of the lights in the coffered ceiling was out. For a moment, his eyes met the judge's. Even Farnsworth would be unable to dispose of his motion with her hangman's speed.

Farnsworth handed down the last pile of motion papers to the carrot-haired court reporter and was gathering her calendar to return to chambers when Seeley came through the gate. "In the *Vaxtek* case, Judge, we have a motion to file."

Farnsworth remained standing. "You're not on the calendar, Mr. Seeley. Do we have papers from you?" She looked over Seeley's shoulder to where Thorpe was approaching. "Mr. Thorpe?"

"This is a surprise to me, too, Your Honor." He stepped in close to Seeley so that their arms touched.

"It is a matter of some urgency," Seeley said. "We didn't become aware of it until over the weekend."

"Have you communicated with Mr. Thorpe?"

"We ask to speak with you ex parte." In an ongoing lawsuit, a judge will meet with a lawyer outside the presence of his opponent only in the most extreme circumstances. "The motion involves a serious question of professional ethics."

"That's an unusual request, Counselor. Mr. Thorpe, like you, is an officer of the court—and, I would add, a respected member of this bar."

Seeley heard the reprimand—she had not forgotten that he was from out of state—but he ignored it. Thorpe drew closer to his side, crowding him.

Seeley said, "This is about more than two parties, Judge. It implicates the integrity of this court." He glanced sideways at Thorpe. His adversary's body was tensed, but the dark pouchy eyes gave away no secrets.

"Mr. Thorpe, you've been uncharacteristically silent. Will your client consent to my meeting ex parte with Mr. Seeley?" She leaned over the bench. "Just so you know, I'm not putting any pressure on you or your client to do so."

"I can't say whether my client objects or not, Your Honor, without knowing what's on counsel's mind."

Seeley would have said the same. He turned to see whether Barnum had arrived, and made a quick decision, regretting the implicit deception in what he was about to say. "There is a question about the veracity of testimony that was given last week. I'm sure Mr. Thorpe will understand our disinclination to explain this with our adversary present." Steinhardt's brush with perjury last week could get Seeley into Farnsworth's chambers. It could also deflect any suspicion Thorpe might have that Seeley had discovered the collusion.

"Mr. Thorpe?"

"My client has no objection to an ex parte conference on this issue."

Of course Thorpe had no objection. He already knew about Steinhardt's fraud and, as part of the parties' collusion, had carefully skirted it in his cross-examination.

The court reporter, who was taking down the exchange, looked up to the bench. Farnsworth said, "My meeting with Mr. Seeley will be on the record—"

"That's fine," Seeley said, "but we request that it be sealed." Not to seal the record would defeat the purpose of the meeting; anyone could see the transcript.

"Sealed is no problem," Thorpe said.

"The meeting will be on the record and sealed." Farnsworth nodded at the reporter to join her in chambers. "It will also be brief. I want both sides ready to proceed with trial in fifteen minutes."

Seeley waited for the judge to descend the few steps from the bench, then followed her and the court reporter through the paneled door, down the narrow corridor to chambers. He passed the fluorescent-lit jury room where some of the jurors were already gathered, their take-out coffee cups and breakfast pastries on the conference table.

Inside chambers, Farnsworth's arms folded across her chest signaled impatience, but Seeley had already revealed too much to get this far, and she wasn't going to dismiss him easily. He moved in so that, tall as she was, the judge had to look up at him. The reporter set the steno machine on the coffee table and, perching herself on the edge of the couch, waited for one of them to speak.

"Emil Thorpe was generous to you out there," Farnsworth said. "He could have embarrassed you in front of the press. Instead, you're going to get a private lecture from me."

She moved back a step. "The rules here are the same as in New York. If you think a witness perjured himself, you talk to your client about it, not the judge."

"Vaxtek's general counsel doesn't think there's a problem."

"But you do." She arched an eyebrow. "Have you talked to your client's CEO? To its board of directors?"

Sure, Seeley thought. That was how Pearsall got himself killed. "I'm certain they would only rubber-stamp their general counsel."

Over the judge's shoulder, at the edge of the bay, a pair of towering construction cranes moved jerkily toward each other, then backed away, two stick insects mating.

"Which witness are we talking about?"

In the courtroom, with the court reporter taking down every word, Seeley had been careful not to use the word "perjury," and he would not do so now. But whether the question was about perjury or just the witness's veracity was a lawyer's distinction at best.

"I believe that Alan Steinhardt kept two sets of lab notebooks, and that the fake set was introduced as an exhibit."

"What proof do you have?"

"There's a conflict between the dates in one of the notebooks and Steinhardt's travel schedule. The notebook puts him in Vaxtek's lab in South San Francisco discovering AV/AS on days that he was out of the country."

"And you don't think the defense would have caught this during discovery?"

This was the tenuous bridge that Seeley hoped would carry him from the pretext of perjury to the fact of the parties' collusion, but Farnsworth could crush it in an instant.

He said, "St. Gall could have discovered it. They probably did discover it. But they would not be inclined to raise the point at trial."

Farnsworth walked to a chair by the long window and gestured for Seeley to take the one across from it. She sat and crossed her legs. "What do you mean, St. Gall wouldn't raise it at trial?"

Judge Farnsworth knew what he meant. The court reporter's fingers waited, half an inch above the keyboard.

The words caught on Seeley's tongue, then freed themselves. "I believe this is a collusive lawsuit, Judge. I believe that Vaxtek and St. Gall have staged this case to get a ruling that the patent is valid."

Farnsworth colored deeply, and Seeley saw at once that he had miscalculated.

"This is way out of bounds, Counselor. Do you want the reporter to read back the representation you made in the courtroom that this meeting was going to be about perjury?"

Seeley didn't know what the anger was about—his misrepresentation in court or the charge of collusion now—and he struggled to respond.

Farnsworth said, "Emil Thorpe needs to be here."

The naïveté behind the statement stunned him. It was as if he had done no more than point out a small infraction of courtroom etiquette, a matter for the lawyers to adjust discreetly between themselves. Then Seeley realized that Farnsworth had no reason to make the connection that he had drawn at once: Pearsall was dead because he had discovered the collusion and confronted the parties on it. These are not only people who collude; these are people who kill.

"My courtroom, as you may have discovered, is not a comfortable place for lawyers who think the rules weren't made for them."

"I'm talking about a fraud on your court."

Farnsworth's eyes grew careful, and for the first time it appeared that she understood the magnitude of his charge. "Are you telling me that you want to withdraw as counsel?"

Seeley shook his head. That was probably what Pearsall had tried to do.

"For the record," Farnsworth said to the reporter, "counsel shook his head no." She turned back to him. "What would you have me do?"

"Declare a mistrial."

"That's out of the question. What evidence do you have that the lawsuit is collusive?"

A sleepless night piecing together the puzzle and an hour cross-examining Palmieri over his part in it was all that Seeley had. The judge was right, and the red-and-tan law reports that filled her wall mocked him. We have cases, facts, and law, the volumes said. What do you have? How many times had Seeley ventured out like this, without a shred of evidence to support him, with nothing but the certainty that he was right and that he could impose that conviction on anyone he needed to.

He said, "If the parties aren't colluding, why didn't Thorpe ask Steinhardt about the discrepancy in his dates?"

"There could be any number of reasons. Maybe he doesn't know about the discrepancy, or maybe he does, but he has some other strategy. I am sure that if he were here, he would tell us."

Again, Seeley ignored the reprimand. "There's a difference between knowing something and being able to prove it according to the rules of evidence."

"I'm not asking for evidence," Farnsworth said. "I just want you to give me a single fact that backs up your claim."

"AIDS victims are going to die because two drug companies colluded to get a worthless patent declared valid."

"Did you do anything to find out about this before you took the case?" She was on her feet. "I'm not going to declare a mistrial just because a lawyer conveniently had an attack of conscience."

When Seeley rose to face her, the judge rested a hand on the court reporter's shoulder to signal her to stop.

"You know, Mr. Seeley, you're a real piece of work. You come into my chambers and demand—not request, *demand*—that I declare a mistrial for no better reason than you suspect that there's collusion here."

"I can assure you—"

"No. Our meeting is over."

Seeley had a desperate thought, dismissed it, and then the words came out anyway. "You'll have to declare a mistrial if in closing argument I tell the jury that the lawsuit is collusive."

Farnsworth's face was suddenly inches from his. "If you mention one word of this to my jury, I will revoke your admission to my court and hold you in contempt before you can finish your first sentence." To the court reporter, she said, "Back on the record. You can note that the ex parte meeting ended at"—she glanced at her watch—"eight fifty-seven a.m."

Farnsworth started toward the door, but then stopped. "I don't want you talking to the jury through the media, either. When we get into court, I'm going to issue a gag order barring the parties and their lawyers from talking to the press. The order will bind both sides. But," with her eyes she signaled the court reporter to go off the record, "you will understand that the order is aimed directly at you. If I see a word of this in the papers or on the news, I'll know whose name to put on the contempt citation."

Seeley said, "I'm sure there won't be any need for that."

"You know, Counselor, if your suspicions are anywhere close to the truth—and I'm not saying that I think they are—you're going to be walking a tightrope out there."

One, she could have added, without a net.

Farnsworth glanced at her watch. "We've already kept the jury waiting half an hour. That comes off your time."

Click, click, click.

NINETEEN

Palmieri and Barnum were waiting when Seeley returned to the courtroom. At the defense table, Thorpe broke off talking to Fischler and watched Seeley walk to counsel's table. Dusollier was busy riffling through a folder jammed with papers. The two patent lawyers from Chicago were gone; they had been ornamentation, Seeley decided, window-dressing for a high-powered defense that St. Gall never had any intention to launch.

Barnum's features were thick with worry. He nodded toward the paneled door from which Seeley had come. "What was that about? You and the judge in there alone?"

"Let's try to concentrate on the witnesses, Ed." If Barnum knew that it was impossible for Vaxtek to lose the case, why was he so anxious over Seeley's every move? "We have four more trial days."

"What did you talk to her about?"

Where was the judge? Seeley thought that she and the court reporter had been behind him when he left chambers.

"We talked about Steinhardt's notebooks." It wasn't entirely a lie.

"Judges don't meet ex parte in the middle of a trial."

Seeley started to answer but Palmieri interrupted, the first time Seeley saw him address Barnum directly. "Do you want the press and the stock analysts back there to know that your company's star scientist kept two sets of books? Do you want your adversary to know? Taking it to chambers was the smartest thing your lawyer could do for you."

The crease at the corners of Barnum's mouth deepened. The case was escaping his grasp. "What did she say about the notebooks?"

"If I were you," Seeley said just for malice, "I'd keep my bar card handy in case the ethics committee calls."

The paneled door opened and the bailiff called for everyone to rise. Farnsworth climbed swiftly to the bench. She gazed out at the gallery, her brow furrowed as if she were looking for someone.

"I am addressing this to the members of the press who are with us here," she said. "I am aware of your interest in this case, and I believe that it is a good thing. Intellectual property is becoming as important in our lives as taxes and crime, and the public should learn as much about these cases as about criminal cases. You are an important channel for doing that. However, going forward, you will have to do this without communications from the parties or their lawyers."

There was a murmur from the press corner of the gallery.

The judge lowered her gaze to the well of the courtroom. "Unless counsel can give me a good reason not to, I am hereby entering an order barring the parties from having any contact with the media about this case."

Barnum drew so close that Seeley could smell the breakfast bacon on his breath. "What the hell did you say to her in there?"

Seeley shook his head as if to dismiss a buzzing fly.

"Mr. Seeley? Mr. Thorpe?"

Seeley rose. He wondered whether Thorpe had guessed the true reason for his ex parte visit. "No objection, Judge."

Thorpe rose. "None, Your Honor."

"This order binds not only counsel, but the parties." She consulted a pad. "Mr. Barnum, Mr. Dusollier, this means you put a muzzle on your public relations people. Do you understand that?"

Seeley touched Barnum's elbow for him to rise. "Yes, Your Honor."

Dusollier, too, agreed, but Seeley heard more than the usual dose of condescension in his voice.

"And, so that there is no question about the reach of this order"—here the judge looked directly at Seeley—"the order encompasses not only direct communications to the press by counsel or the parties, but through friends, associates, or any other third parties." She turned to the bailiff. "Let's not keep our jury waiting any longer."

The kid, Gary Sansone, was the second through the door. He had untied his ponytail and the blond hair hung almost to his shoulders. The wondering look he shot at Seeley left no doubt that he had seen Seeley in the corridor on his way to chambers. An important turn had occurred in the trial, but he didn't know what it was. Seeley hoped that, in leaving the kid on the jury, he had done the right thing, even if for the wrong reason.

Farnsworth moved to the jury side of the bench and leaned over the rail, her custom when talking to the jurors. After apologizing for the delay, she said, "You will remember, when you were first impaneled, that I asked you not to read any newspaper articles, or to watch or listen to television or radio coverage of the trial." She paused to let them nod. "I just want to remind you of that precaution now. It is crucial that you decide this case strictly on what you hear in this courtroom. Were you to do otherwise—were you to act, even in part, on something you saw on the TV news, for example—it would be necessary for me to declare a mistrial. I could sequester you, have you put up in a hotel away from your loved ones, but I'd rather not do that. Do you all understand what I am asking of you?"

This time the nods of assent were more vigorous, but Farnsworth hesitated, doubtful. Then she gave them a friendly smile and swiveled back to the center of the bench. "Counsel will remember from our final pretrial meeting that the judges of the district have their monthly conference today, so we will continue until one thirty and then break for the day. Let's get under way. Mr. Thorpe?"

Thorpe's order of proof was the mirror image of Seeley's. Thomas Koosmann, the Washington University, epidemiologist, was first. His role was to rebut Cordier's testimony about the long-felt need for an AIDS vaccine. Behind aviator-style glasses, Koosmann looked younger to Seeley than the fifty-two years indicated in his résumé, or perhaps it was the boyish way that he blinked before answering a question. That, and a thin, pointed face made him appear slightly furtive, even vulpine, as Thorpe took him first through his résumé and then into his testimony. Where Cordier described the desperate situation in sub-Saharan Africa to illustrate the demand for an AIDS vaccine, Koosmann focused on the United States and Western Europe, testifying that widespread access to effective therapies and the slowing number of deaths had alleviated any pressure there to develop a vaccine.

"So," Thorpe said at the end of Koosmann's direct testimony, "would it be fair to conclude from your testimony that in the very markets where drug companies make the most profits—the United States and Europe—there is the least demand for a vaccine, and that the demand for a vaccine is the greatest in those regions, primarily Africa, where there is virtually no opportunity for these companies to profit at all?"

"Yes, that is correct."

"So it is no surprise that the most aggressive research by for-profit companies is being directed to objects other than vaccines?"

"That is correct."

"No more questions, Your Honor." Thorpe shuffled away from the lectern, each step a sigh.

Watching the performance, Seeley saw how cleverly Thorpe had arranged his maze of smoke and mirrors. When it came time for the jurors to weigh the evidence, it was not what Koosmann said on the stand, but his coy hesitations and weaselly demeanor that they would compare to the heroic Cordier's forthright manner. Koosmann's effective dismissal of African AIDS victims would repel them. But if Thorpe were ever charged with collusion, no member of an ethics committee reviewing the transcript of Koosmann's testimony would think that Thorpe had done anything less than St. Gall's counsel should have done in refuting Cordier's testimony.

Thorpe's examination of Koosmann had purposely left open several holes through which Seeley could have skewered the witness, and Seeley's reflex as a trial lawyer was to do so. Instead, he took no more than a short jab at Koosmann here and there, and otherwise let his testimony stand. If Thorpe wanted the AV/AS patent upheld, Seeley now wanted it struck down. You are me, Emil, and I am you.

When Seeley returned to counsel's table, and the judge ordered a break, Barnum said, "Is there something wrong with you? That was no cross."

Heads turned at the defense table. "Let's just take it one step at a time, Ed." Seeley put a hand over Barnum's. "I need to talk to Chris."

Palmieri followed Seeley out of the courtroom to the picture-lined alcove at the end of the corridor. Five days ago, Seeley stood here grasping an imaginary baseball bat, fighting the impulse to slam his brother from behind.

Seeley said, "I've decided to do Gupta's cross myself."

"But we agreed that I—"

"I know we did, Chris, but I need to do Gupta."

Palmieri backed away, averting his eyes. "You're going to dance around him, the way you did with Koosmann. You're not going to touch him."

"I'll do whatever I think is right."

"You don't even know for a fact that the parties are colluding."

He started away and Seeley grabbed him by the wrist. "There are only a few things I'm certain of, Chris, but this is one of them." Palmieri shook himself loose and Seeley followed him back to the courtroom.

Dr. Manesh Gupta, chairman of the Immunology Department at Duke University's School of Medicine, was a pouter pigeon. Short, plump, chest puffed out in a dark three-piece suit, his arrogance approached Steinhardt's. Like Koosmann, his testimony would look good on paper, but his attitude would destroy him with the jury.

"Yes," Gupta said for the third time when Fischler asked whether, in light of the research done by others, the discovery of AV/AS was obvious. This time he added, "Any competent first-year graduate student could have done this work."

When Fischler finished, Seeley took the notebook Palmieri handed him and brought it to the witness stand. "Dr. Gupta," he said, handing him the notebook, "I'd like you to look at the expert declaration you provided in this case, which has been marked as defendant's exhibit E. Is this your declaration, Doctor?"

The immunologist answered that it was.

"Looking at page nine, Dr. Gupta, do you see references to three publications from scientific journals?"

"Yes. There are two by Reeves, Kumar, and Constantine, and one by Goldblum et al."

"Did you rely on these references in concluding that AV/AS was an obvious discovery?"

"Yes, I did."

"Were these articles difficult to find, Doctor?"

"No, not for any moderately competent researcher. Someone seriously working in the field wouldn't have to look for them at all. He · would have a subscription to the journals."

"And is it your opinion that any ordinarily skilled researcher who read these three articles would find it obvious to make AV/AS?"

The dark head bobbed. "That is correct."

This was the moment for Seeley to drive home the dagger's blade, as patent litigators have done since experts first began to testify: If, speaking as an expert, this discovery was so obvious to you, why didn't you make it yourself? Instead, Seeley said, "In your opinion, Dr. Gupta, does Dr. Alan Steinhardt possess at least the knowledge and experience of a moderately competent researcher?"

Savagery sparkled in the witness's eyes. "Yes, at least." The patronizing tone left no question about Gupta's estimate of the gap between Steinhardt's talents and his own.

"In terms of reputation, where would you place Dr. Steinhardt among the ranks of immunologists like yourself?"

"I'd say that he's generally reputed to be among the top twenty researchers."

"How about the top ten?"

Gupta paused, as if to think. "Yes, perhaps the top ten."

"Thank you, Dr. Gupta."

"Redirect, Ms. Fischler?"

There was a hurried conference at the defense table before Fischler said, "No, Your Honor."

"Then we will recess for the day." To the jury, the judge said, "I look forward to seeing you bright and early tomorrow morning."

Barnum's fists were on the tabletop, plump knuckles white. "Why didn't you ask him, if AV/AS was so obvious, why he didn't invent it himself?"

"It's a cheap trick—"

"And it works—"

"Read Gupta's deposition. Fischler already prepared him on it. He would have testified that the government grants that fund his lab don't support the kind of work Steinhardt was doing. He was pursuing a completely different line of research."

Barnum started to answer, but Seeley was already rising. "Thorpe's waiting for me." It seemed like months since he agreed to the lunch meeting with his adversary. "I'll see you tomorrow morning."

Through his cross-examination of Koosmann and Gupta, Seeley had been aware of the judge watching him. Once, when he slipped over an obvious point of attack on Koosmann's testimony, she shook her head unhappily, as she might at a rookie. She understood what he was doing but, short of granting the mistrial Seeley had asked for, there was nothing she could do.

Gail Odum was at the gallery rail by the gate, and she managed a fleeting smile when Seeley walked by. She had witnessed his colloquy with the judge earlier and it took no great journalistic insight to connect his visit to Farnsworth's chambers to the judge's order barring contact with the press. Odum knew that there was a story here, and Seeley wondered whose ache was deeper: hers to hear the story or his to tell it.

"Do you know Schroeder's? A wonderful old place." As usual, Thorpe's shuffle disappeared as soon as he was out of sight of the jury, and he had no trouble keeping up with Seeley. Market Street where it crossed McAllister churned with life. Young men in wheelchairs zipped across the broad sidewalk, practicing wheelies. Others in elegant exercise outfits and just-out-of-the-box running shoes talked and smoked in clusters at corners and in the doorways of shuttered storefronts.

"It's an old-style German place," Thorpe said. "A bit of a tourist trap, but if the Koenigsberger Klopse is a special, be sure to order it."

So reticent in the courtroom, Thorpe now couldn't stop talking. "San Francisco used to be a real trial lawyer's town. There weren't more than ten of us who had a real trial practice back in the fifties. Jake Ehrlich, Mel Belli. Of course, I was just a kid coming up. Federal or state court, civil or criminal, it didn't matter. What mattered was the art of trial practice. Today, anyone with a law degree thinks he's a trial lawyer. There's a lot the old-timers could teach them."

As they approached the financial district, steel-and-glass office towers crowded the bantam office buildings of another age, and Thorpe, still spilling with stories, pointed out the Monadnock Building where his small firm had its offices. The Art Deco façade shimmered like a mirage in the mirrored sheathing of the office tower opposite it.

Schroeder's was on Front Street, around the corner from Tadich, its fresh blue-and-white façade and gothic heraldry evoking old Bavaria. Inside, pillars lost themselves in the murky heights of the dining room. Waiters scuttled about in the amber light below and there was a faint malty scent about the place. Thorpe ordered his Koenigsberger Klopse and a dry martini. It startled Seeley how just the word "martini" shot adrenaline into his heart. He asked for a steak sandwich, rare, and a glass of water.

When Thorpe started in again about the legendary Jake Ehrlich, Seeley said, "I'm sure this is fascinating, but I could be back in my office preparing for your next witness."

Thorpe's laugh sounded genuine, but the eyes, wary as ever, told Seeley that there was a point to the story, and that he should listen closely.

"Back then," Thorpe said, "the really great trial lawyers like Jake had a single ideal: represent your client as shrewdly and strenuously as you humanly can. They played fair, but that was their ideal. They didn't get mixed up with *causes*. A lawyer today, representing people who care about the environment or abortion or access to medicine, nine times out of ten, he'll sacrifice his client if he thinks it will serve the cause."

It astonished Seeley that this profoundly immoral man should rebuke him for what he was doing, but the message was unambiguous. Thorpe knew that Seeley had discovered the collusion.

"Jake and the others lived rewarding lives—and long ones." Thorpe studied his manicured fingers spread out on the table. The nails, bluish at the edges, glowed against the dark, scarred wood. This time, when Thorpe looked up, he was smiling.

Seeley said, "And this is why your courtroom work for St. Gall has been so aggressive."

If Thorpe caught the irony, he didn't reveal it. "You know how this kind of litigation works, Michael—or do you? For a drug company like St. Gall, every one of its patents represents millions of dollars in R&D, hundreds of millions for the blockbusters. So any time a court rules that a patent is invalid—not just a St. Gall patent, but a Vaxtek patent, too—it makes for . . . let us say, a precedent, a legal climate, that is unfavorable to my client's patents."

Thorpe waited for the white-aproned waiter to place the cocktail glass in front of him before continuing.

"Today a jury in a San Francisco courtroom holds your client's patent invalid and, who knows, tomorrow, maybe in Boston, or London, or Amsterdam, it will be my client's turn to have its patent struck down."

Thorpe couldn't expect him to believe that this was how St. Gall plotted its litigation strategy. On this premise, no pharmaceutical company would ever sue for patent infringement.

"If that was your client's strategy, you wouldn't have stipulated priority."

"As you know"—Thorpe sipped at his martini, but kept his eyes on Seeley—"we have a small problem with a witness on the question of priority."

"How's that?"

"I know about your lunch with Dr. Warren. That was inappropriate, of course, for you to talk to an adverse witness without going through me."

"She wasn't an adverse witness when I talked to her." How did Thorpe know about the meeting? "You'd already dropped her from your list."

"Well, I suppose we had." Thorpe looked around the room. Most of the lunch crowd was gone. "What do you think of this place?"

"Very . . . old world."

Thorpe tilted his head and gave Seeley a silly grin that didn't fit the haggard features. "Old San Francisco."

The waiter arrived with the food. Thorpe's Koenigsberger Klopse were two large meat dumplings under a layer of cream sauce mixed with capers. A small mountain of red cabbage crowded one side of the plate, a pile of fried potatoes the other. Thorpe sampled a forkful of dumpling. "This is wonderful. Would you like some?"

Seeley shook his head. He'd had another sleepless night and was exhausted from the morning's cross-examination. Thorpe's winks and grins chafed at him. The dregs in the martini glass looked like salvation.

Seeley said, "I wonder if Jake Ehrlich would have done any of the harebrained things you tell me you've been doing for your client."

Thorpe's smile disappeared. "At the end of the day, Michael, you're out of your element here, and you would do well to take instruction about this case." He went back to his meal.

For all of the lawyer's chatter, Seeley realized, Thorpe had said nothing expressly to admit that Vaxtek and St. Gall were colluding, or that he had a part in it.

Thorpe took his time chewing, and when he finished, said, "You think I invited you to lunch to talk about settlement."

Ten days ago, when they made the lunch date, that had been the object.

"You know," Thorpe said, "a case can settle at any time—five minutes before the jury returns, or five months before the complaint is even filed."

"What are you getting at?"

"What I'm saying"—Thorpe was as tired of Seeley as Seeley was of him—"is that you know nothing about this case. What if—and I'm only speaking hypothetically of course—what if this case that you want us to fight like two gladiators has already settled? Say that our clients signed off on it months ago. In that event, we would be no more than actors, you and I. Actors in a charade. We'd do well, wouldn't we, to play the part we've been assigned?"

Seeley said, "Two parties can settle a case, but they can't turn an invalid patent into a valid one."

"Validity. Invalidity. This is a gray area, a swamp. Wise men stay clear of swamps." Thorpe speared a home fry. "This is a good time to be wise rather than smart."

"There's an issue of principle here."

"No, in my hypothetical case there's only an issue of money, and when the case is over all that will happen is that money will move from one party's bank account to another's—"

"But only because patented vaccines cost more than unpatented ones. What about the millions of AIDS victims in Africa who can't afford AV/AS?"

"Who's talking about AV/AS? This is just a hypothetical situation I'm describing. What you're talking about is international politics. That's way over our heads—who's going to subsidize access to the vaccine, who's going to lobby for condoms, who's going to insist on abstinence. This is way beyond the reach of two trial lawyers."

"Did you have this little heart-to-heart with Robert Pearsall before he was killed?"

For the first time since he started eating, Thorpe put down his silverware. Two tables away, a head turned. Thorpe's voice was quiet but pitiless. "You know even less about Bob Pearsall than you do about his case. He was a complicated man."

"Studying philosophy never killed anyone."

"Then you have forgotten your *Dialogues*, what Plato had to say about the trial and execution of Socrates." Thorpe took in Seeley's surprise. "You attended a Jesuit college. Of course you read the *Dialogues*."

The old lawyer surveyed the almost empty dining room. "You have also mistaken San Francisco's surface charms for its substance. This city can be a very dangerous place for lawyers who let their ideals get in the way of their pragmatism."

Seeley said, "We really deceive them, don't we? You, your buddy Jake, and me."

"Deceive who?"

"We let people think that some lawyers are good, doing their pro bono work, while others just chase after money. But that's only a distraction so that people don't consider the real harm we can do, the corruption, the profound evil that a lawyer can commit."

After that, they could have been strangers, or a father and his son, the way that they finished their meal in brooding silence.

Seeley spent the rest of the day preparing for tomorrow's witnesses. He needed a break from Palmieri, and the young partner didn't complain when Seeley sent him off to write the first draft of his closing argument. McKee was in and out of Seeley's office, educating him on technical details of the AV/AS patent that Seeley would need for his cross-examination. It was almost 11:00 when Seeley filled his briefcase with papers and turned out the lights.

As much as he enjoyed his solitary morning walks from the Huntington down to Heilbrun, Hardy's offices, it was retracing that route at night, the great dark bay at his back, that truly gave Seeley pleasure. Except for Grant and Stockton, still a blaze of neon with streams of shoppers and late-night diners, the maze of streets spidering out from the Embarcadero along and across the borders of Chinatown was deserted at this hour. The signs on the darkened storefronts mixed Chinese characters with English words and, in the shuttered tenements that rose above them, Seeley felt the presence of alien lives, sleeping, eating, watching the Chinese soap operas on cable. He felt safer on this empty street than he did across a restaurant table from Thorpe.

He thought of Lily, as he had throughout the day. If he could persuade her to tell the *Chronicle* what she knew about Steinhardt and his work on AV/AS, that could be the trigger for the mistrial that he needed. Each time, though, Seeley dismissed the thought of asking her for help. It wasn't Judge Farnsworth's order not to talk with the media, directly or through others, that concerned him; he could handle those consequences if he had to. No, he admitted to himself, what stopped him was the simple thought of picking up the phone. Asking for help was Leonard's weakness, not his.

As he crossed Joice Street, a dim alley off Sacramento, Seeley felt his skin prickle. He sensed that he was no longer alone. A sound like the rattling of dry leaves swept up the alley—his thoughts shot back to the dark sedan by the railroad tracks—but the tempo was pointed and rhythmic and had an unmistakably human source.

The rattling stopped, and an instant later a sharp blow at the back of Seeley's knees sent him crashing to the pavement. A second blow stung a shoulder, and his chin struck the asphalt. A burst of high-pitched chatter like a quarrelsome flock of birds flew up from his assailants, and at once pointed sticks expertly dug and prodded at his body. The voices were harsh and nasal, and the words—it sounded like an Asian language—were as sharp as the probing sticks. His attackers were rebuking him for some offense.

In English, one cried, "DO NOT ENTER! DO NOT ENTER!"

Seeley turned in the direction of the screeching demand and raised himself, crooking an arm to protect his eyes from the continuing blows. He was looking at a boy, no older than seventeen or eighteen, his long dark hair streaked with blond, frantically shaking a bamboo rod in the direction of a street sign where the alley began. Seeley was stunned that the blows had already driven him this far from the intersection.

"DO NOT ENTER! DO NOT ENTER!"

The traffic sign at which the boy was pointing displayed a red circle with a slash through it, warning drivers not to enter the one-way alley. The boy's cries turned to shrieks of hysteria as he gestured with the bamboo to his companions. All three were in T-shirts and baggy chinos cut off above the ankle, rubber flip-flops on their feet. At a whoop from the leader, there was a flurry of lashings, several striking Seeley across the ribs, others pummeling his sides. The pain of each blow was excruciating, but Seeley forced himself not to cry out; he would not give them that satisfaction.

"DO NOT ENTER!" the leader jeered, his laughter pure idiot hatred.

The alley was empty, as was the crossing where the sticks first brought him down. Seeley could make out figures moving along Clay Street at the other end of the alley, but they were too distant to hear him even if he did call out. Street grit scraped at his jaw; the stench of garbage rotting at the curb sickened him. From his dog's-eye view the long brick wall of a building stretched across from him. Behind him, he remembered, was an empty parking lot surrounded by a torn chain-link fence. Even if anyone was watching from the dark tenements, no one would call for help. He had to get up; lying on the street like this, he could not possibly maneuver. But when he moved to rise, the beatings quickened.

Seeley felt a tug of nausea, the taste of copper at the back of his throat. These are kids, he told himself. If they were going to rob or seriously injure him, they would have done so by now. Ignoring the pain, he pushed himself up, forced his body into a crouch, waited for his strength to gather, then lunged at the youth closest to him, the leader. He caught the boy's wrist and, twisting it against his back so that the bamboo dropped, Seeley lifted and hurled him against the chain fence. The surprise of the boy's weightlessness threw Seeley off balance. When the dazed youth came back at him—a rebound, not an act of will—Seeley circled one arm around a thin neck and with the other again pulled the boy's arm up behind his back.

While his captive gasped and whimpered, the two other youths froze, staring at Seeley, uncertain of what the rules now were. Panic replaced the empty looks and one, then the other, dropped their bamboo rods and ran off in the direction of Clay Street. So much for loyalty, Seeley thought. The leader was shivering in Seeley's grip, his entire body exhaling a spoiled, meaty smell. Breathless, Seeley said, "What's this about?"

The panting youth didn't answer.

Through the cheap T-shirt, Seeley felt the boy's heart beating frantically, like a small bird's. He said, "Your friends aren't coming back to help you." Against his will, Seeley felt sympathy for the terrified boy—why did he take pity on his tormentors?—and thrust him away. "Get out of here!"

Staggering, the boy went down the alley where the others had gone. Pain seeped into Seeley's bones as he bent down, lifted the bamboo rods, and threw them over the chain-link fence. Then he walked to the corner and retrieved his briefcase.

The traffic on Sacramento was light and none of the few pedestrians noticed as Seeley made his slow, unsteady way up the hill. He thought about the strangeness of the encounter. The boys had demanded nothing from him. Not a word they said, in English at least, indicated racism. He would have expected a street thug to be strong, a scrapper, yet the leader was a weakling and his companions were cowards; had he restrained the boy any more strenuously, Seeley was certain that he would have snapped his bones. The oddest part was how dispassionately, almost casually, the attack unfolded, even the leader's rant about the DO NOT ENTER sign. It was as if the boys were amateurs reading a script for the first time. Their panic, when Seeley struck back, was as much from ignorance as fear.

When Seeley came into the Huntington lobby, the clerk at the reception desk greeted him gaily, then stopped short. "Are you all right, Mr. Seeley?" The worried look showed more than professional concern. "Would you like us to call a doctor?"

Seeley realized that he had no idea how torn-up he looked. "No, I'm fine. Thanks."

The man's look lingered for another moment as if he were making a decision. Then he gestured for Seeley to wait as he retrieved an envelope from beneath the counter.

The cheap feel of the unmarked envelope as Seeley opened it reminded him of his attacker's thin T-shirt. Inside the envelope was a folded square of newsprint, no larger than a cocktail napkin, advertising an expensive brand of wristwatch. He turned the scrap over and at once recognized the typeface of the *San Francisco Chronicle*. The story had the terse rhythm of the police blotter and was about gangs of three to five Vietnamese youths attacking lone pedestrians, evidently without discrimination, usually at night in deserted areas, but occasionally even on crowded sidewalks during the day. Sometimes wallets, purses, and watches were taken, other times not; always the attacks were conducted with bamboo sticks the length of a fishing rod or longer.

"Who delivered this?"

"An Asian boy, a couple of hours ago."

"Have you seen him before?"

The clerk shook his head. "I remembered because none of our usual messengers are Asian. It was the first time I've seen him."

"Would you recognize him if you saw him again?"

"He wasn't here for more than a second or two." The man was still studying Seeley's injuries. "Are you sure there's no way we can be of assistance to you?"

Sure, Seeley thought, tell me who set me up to be attacked and then sent this clipping so that I'd know it was a warning, not a random act. He rubbed the flimsy newsprint between his fingers as if it were the wrapping of some absent magic lantern whose genie might yet appear.

Seeley went to his room and dialed Lily's number. There was no answer, so he left a message on her machine for her to call him when she returned.

TWENTY

Seeley was dressing slowly and painfully when the telephone rang. He felt as if last night's beating hadn't missed a square inch of his body.

"Mike?"

He started to speak, but his jaw stiffened.

"Are you okay? I got your message. Gail Odum said you were in some kind of trouble."

A newspaper reporter sees you follow a judge into chambers alone and she concludes, correctly, that you have a problem. Seeley massaged his jaw, but to no effect.

"The trial's gone off the rails. I need your help." The word left his lips with surprising ease.

"This is about Alan's notebooks?"

Of course Lily wouldn't know about the collusion between Vaxtek and St. Gall. It was a week since Seeley last saw her, when he hadn't even known of Steinhardt's double bookkeeping. "You knew he kept two sets of books, didn't you?"

"Gail didn't say anything about it coming out in court."

Seeley stretched one shoulder, then the other. A boiling shower had done nothing to ease the soreness. "Lily, in this country you can't play around with the judicial system like that. People go to jail. Lawyers get disbarred."

"But nothing happened, so no one's hurt."

"People are going to be hurt because it didn't come out." He thought of Pearsall. "People have already been hurt. That's why I called."

"I'm sorry, I was in the lab all night. I—"

"Lily, I could use your help." Again, that word. There's nothing like a beating to enlarge the vocabulary. "I need you to tell Gail Odum everything you know about Steinhardt's work on AV/AS." He had decided that if he couldn't destroy Vaxtek's case from counsel's table, he would do it in the press.

"I already told you. This is none of my business." Her voice tightened into a knot. "I can't get involved."

"Well, now you have no choice."

"I like you, Mike. I want to see you again. But the fact that we slept together doesn't give you any claim on me."

Seeley realized that, from the moment he picked up the phone, he had been waiting for her to say something about their night together. But this was all he was going to get.

Lily said, "I already told you. I can't testify."

"You don't have to testify. I just want you to tell Gail Odum how Steinhardt keeps his records."

"We've been over this—" She caught herself, apparently remembering that they had not discussed this. "How could it help your case for me to tell the *Chronicle* that Steinhardt is a fraud?"

Seeley looked at his watch on the night table. "I have to get to court. Can you come into the city?"

The phone went dead, as if she'd hung up. Then she came back on. "Sure, if it's not at your office or anywhere we'd be seen together."

"One o'clock?"

She gave him an address on Dolores Street in the Outer Mission. "It's a friend's apartment. She'll be at work."

Barnum, when he saw the bruises on Seeley's face, asked if he'd fallen off a barstool. Palmieri gave him a concerned look. Thorpe was in a banker's pinstriped suit this morning, his starched white collar as sharp as a knife against his neck. The dead black eyes examined Seeley and his twisted eyebrows rose in a pantomime of sympathy. Didn't I warn you, they seemed to say. Dusollier was not in the courtroom this morning.

The reality struck Seeley that virtually everyone of consequence in the courtroom knew that *Vaxtek, Inc. v. Laboratories St. Gall, S.A.* was a collusive lawsuit. Thorpe knew, as presumably did his second chair, Fischler. Barnum knew. For all of his objections, Palmieri knew as well. And, as the mock trial progressed and the evidence of collusion accumulated in front of her, Judge Farnsworth—whose expression showed genuine worry when she saw Seeley's battered face—now had to believe in the truth of what he had told her in chambers. Yet the charade went on, a corrupted show trial of the sort practiced in Lily's country but not, Seeley had implied to Lily, in his own. The only people who didn't yet know of the collusion were the jurors, and Farnsworth would stop at nothing to protect them from that knowledge.

Thorpe's witnesses today were testifying that even if Vaxtek's patent on AV/AS was valid, St. Gall's product did not infringe the patent. Seeley decided that if he couldn't control the jury's decision on the validity of the patent, then he could at least tar St. Gall as an infringer. He savagely went after Thorpe's witnesses—an immunologist from Johns Hopkins and a biologist from Columbia—starting his cross-examination slowly, sharpening the rhythm of his questions, forcing the witness to speed the pace of his answers, all the time moving faster, yet giving Thorpe no ground to object, until the witness's answers spilled over themselves in contradiction. The performance delighted Barnum, and at the end of the morning session, when Seeley returned to counsel's table, the general counsel vigorously clapped his injured shoulder.

Before he could press the bell at the street door of the yellow-and-white Victorian, Lily buzzed Seeley through. She was waiting for him on the second-floor landing in a white, man-tailored shirt and slender black pants; high-heeled pumps showed off her long legs. She looked as cool and carefully made-up as if she were ready for a fashion shoot, but her eyes were weary from her late night at the lab and when she showed him into the apartment her voice was as strained as it had been on the phone that morning. She studied Seeley's bruised face, probing it gently with cool fingers. "Can I get you something?"

"I have a taxi waiting. I can't stay long."

She settled into a white-cushioned rattan chair and didn't stir as Seeley explained how Vaxtek and St. Gall had conspired to control the outcome of their lawsuit. She asked questions, each a step or two ahead of Seeley. "If they killed Robert Pearsall for what he found out, what makes you think they're not going to come after you?"

"Pearsall must have confronted them. I didn't. They don't know that I know." After yesterday's lunch with Thorpe, and last night's assault, he no longer believed that, but Lily might. "Right now I'm thinking that Nicolas Cordier's patients in Lesotho are going to die because whether it's Vaxtek or St. Gall that gets the exclusive rights to Africa, they're going to price AV/AS out of their reach."

She gave him a small, pensive smile. "So this is something else I get to learn about Michael Seeley. You're an idealist. I didn't expect that."

A truck rumbled by outside and the windows of the grand old room rattled in their frames.

"I want you to tell Gail Odum about how Steinhardt backdates his notebook entries."

She shook her head. "I didn't say that I liked your idealism. Remember, where I come from it only gets you in trouble. You're trying to wreck your own client's case."

"And you're the only person who can help me."

"Gail told me the judge won't let you talk to the press. Isn't asking me to talk to her the same thing?"

"I'll give you whatever information you need. The notebook dates, Steinhardt's travel dates."

"I don't know anything about how Alan keeps his notebooks."

The acting was not as polished as it had been at Barbara's Fish Trap.

"You're not going to be deported for telling the truth about Stein-hardt."

"What if Gail asks what I was doing in Alan's lab that night?" She twisted the braided silver bracelets on her wrist. "My agreement with St. Gall is that I can't talk about that."

"You told me that you went to see Steinhardt about co-authoring a couple of articles."

"Do you think anyone will believe that? Did you believe me?"

"Did Steinhardt ever list you as a co-author when you were both at UC?"

"Alan and I had a relationship. You know that. It was over, but in some ways he can be very loyal."

The high heels. The eyebrows plucked into thin parentheses. In his mind, Seeley winced at the pain women subjected themselves to, and for what? To get the nod from a vain little prince like Alan Steinhardt.

Seeley said, "Did it occur to you that your boyfriend set you up? Letting his company's security guard find you. Making it look like in-dustrial espionage, so that Vaxtek could blackmail St. Gall because one of its researchers was in their labs alone at night. That's why St. Gall was willing to stipulate that Steinhardt was the first to invent AV/AS. They thought Vaxtek was going to expose them for having a spy on their payroll."

"And that's why, if I go to the press, St. Gall will get me fired and I'll lose my visa."

Seeley glanced at his watch. "I have to get back to the trial."

Lily got up and walked to the tall window looking out onto the street. When she came back to Seeley, she was trembling.

He held her gently by the arms. "Don't tell me you took some-thing from Steinhardt's lab."

She looked at him and dropped her head. The groan that escaped from her was an animal's cry, pained and despairing. She said, "I didn't take anything from Alan."

"I didn't think you did."

"Do you want to know what happened that night?" When she looked up tears had filled her eyes.

"Tell me."

"I brought Alan a sample from my own lab."

"You stole a sample from St. Gall?"

"That's how a lawyer would look at it. But it was my sample. It was my work. It was the approach I started working on at UC. The guy who ran my lab at St. Gall thought it was a dead end, so I played by the rules and followed their orders. That's how corporate science works. But early mornings—four or five o'clock—when no one was there, I continued doing my own work. I believed in it. I kept my own notebooks."

Seeley remembered Lily's claim to have discovered AV/AS. Everyone had dismissed her as a crackpot. "When you got your results, why didn't you show them to St. Gall?"

"I did. But you can't go to the FDA with results in a petri dish. That's all I had. I was young, a woman, and Chinese, and this wasn't the team's product, so St. Gall wasn't rushing to run trials on it. I told you, this is how corporate science works."

"So you gave it to Steinhardt."

Telling the story seemed to calm her. "It was only when Vaxtek filed its lawsuit and the head of my lab at St. Gall looked at Vaxtek's patent that he realized it was the same as my work." She stifled a laugh. "Of course it was the same. It was my discovery! So they picked up my work and threw a lot of money at trials and got to market first."

"Does St. Gall know it was your sample that Steinhardt used?"

Lily shook her head. "After Vaxtek gave them the security guard's report, about my being in Alan's lab, they wouldn't believe anything I told them. They thought the results were Alan's, not mine. They thought I stole Alan's work."

Seeley had to get back to the trial. "Did Steinhardt promise you credit for your work?"

"He said we'd be co-inventors—him for his work at Vaxtek, and me for my work at UC before I went to St. Gall."

"But when the patent issued," Seeley said, "there was only one name on it. His. St. Gall stipulated priority and dropped you as a witness. And they had the vaccine in their lab all the time."

Seeley saw at once how the trial had to end. If a story in the

Chronicle that Steinhardt had lied about the dates of his discovery would give any juror who saw it second thoughts about the validity of Vaxtek's patent, then an article that Steinhardt had in fact stolen the discovery from another researcher would effectively destroy the company's case. But only Lily could make that happen.

Seeley said, "Why did you decide to work in this field?"

The emotion of moments earlier had dissolved and the tears disappeared. Quietly, she said, "To save lives," and then after a moment, "the same reason you're trying to destroy your own client's case."

"Do you have any idea how many lives you could save by giving your story to the *Chronicle*?"

"I'm not a hero like your Dr. Cordier. I'm just a scientist."

"For God's sake, Lily, this is your invention that Steinhardt's putting his name on. How is that different from some party hack in China doing the same thing?"

"Even if I told Gail the story, why would anyone believe me?"

"Because it's true." Even as he spoke, Seeley knew that she had appraised the situation more astutely than he had. Gail Odum might believe her, and Odum's editor might let her run a story with only one source. But Vaxtek and St. Gall would drown the story in a flood of press releases and news conferences. And quietly they would arrange for Lily's deportation.

Seeley said, "You have to do this for yourself."

"I liked you a lot better when you were letting me seduce you." She traced the bruises on his face with a finger, hurting him. "I worry about you. You remind me of the dissidents at home. My parents. Beaten, exiled, sent to prison."

"This isn't China."

"There are people who create trouble for themselves wherever they are. I think you're one of them."

Seeley said, "You have to trust me."

"I trust you, Mike, but I don't trust the real world to come through the way you want it to."

"I need your help. Just talk to Gail Odum." As he spoke, Seeley watched his reflection in her eyes, and found himself listening to his own words. What he saw and heard was that he was as much a dissembler and user of people, as much an avoider of reality, as was his brother. For the briefest moment, he felt weightless, as if the earth had been pulled out from under him.

Seeley said, "We can make this work."

She pressed a finger to his lips. "Can you really promise that?"

Seeley saw the pain in her eyes. "No, I can't."

"That's better. If you really care about me—and I think you do—you'll trust me with this."

"You're right."

"About caring for me?"

"About both."

TWENTY-ONE

At four in the morning, Seeley was still awake, stretched out on his bed in shirt and trousers, too restless, but also too exhausted, to get under the covers. He left Lily fifteen hours ago. If it took her two hours, even three, to call Gail Odum, the story exposing Steinhardt and Vaxtek's fraud could appear in this morning's edition of the *Chronicle*. She and Odum had talked before; this was no stranger calling with a wild tale. Big stories made it from street to press in less than half the time.

He had left a message at the hotel front desk for the *Chronicle* to be delivered to his room as soon as it arrived, and when there was a sharp metallic rap of a key against the door, he knew it was the bellman with the paper. The man was sullen and reeked of off-hours cigarettes. Seeley handed him a twenty-dollar bill from the night table, as if it were a bribe to ensure that the story would be in the paper.

The *Chronicle* front page was as crammed with color as the Sunday comics. A political opponent charged the city's youthful mayor, recently out of rehab for alcohol abuse, with using cocaine. An article explained step by step how a middle-class Bay Area resident could pay for an otherwise unaffordable home. Conditions in an Iraqi orphanage were squalid, and circumcision was falling into disfavor among American parents. But nothing on the crowded page told the story of a Chinese researcher whose discovery of a major AIDS breakthrough had been stolen by a world-renowned scientist and patented by his employer.

Christmas and birthday gifts were rare when Seeley was growing up, but he experienced the same electric sense of anticipation as he turned over one page to the next, scanning each quickly but carefully. Is there any cocktail more potent than the expectation that your every desire is just around the corner and the simultaneous certainty that it will not be there?

There was nothing in the paper's first section or in the regional news, but Seeley's heart caught when Odum's byline jumped out from the third page of the business section. The headline seemed a jumble, and the story, when he looked more calmly, was about not Lily but the Silicon Valley executive whose trial had been under way in the federal courtroom next to Seeley's. In the photograph that accompanied the story, Seeley recognized the handcuffed defendant as the man who had moved quickly past him in the corridor last week.

Seeley paged through the rest of the business section and, his hope rapidly dwindling, the sports and entertainment pages, even the classifieds. Then he examined the entire paper again, running his index finger down the columns of each page until it was stained black. By the time he put the paper down, he realized that the sadness he felt was not so much for the missing story, as for his selfishness in pressing Lily to tell it. He was just a lawyer caught up in a miscreant case. This was her entire future.

He went into the bathroom and washed his hands, then collapsed onto the bed, falling at last into a dreamless sleep.

The rest of the day slipped by like a familiar nightmare. A microbiologist, the first of Thorpe's two remaining infringement witnesses, took the stand in the morning. As deliberately as Seeley framed his questions for the scientist—adjusting their pace, hiding traps—the futility of the effort ground down what little hope remained in him. Once, when his concentration broke, his thoughts veered to Lily and his rash surrender to her of the decision whether to go to the newspaper. His tone when he returned to the witness was so harsh that Barnum gave him a puzzled look, Palmieri a worried one. Who, Seeley asked himself, was he so angry at? Candidates filed through his thoughts like figures in a police lineup. Who was he *not* angry at?

Midway through the afternoon cross-examination of Thorpe's last infringement witness, an immunologist, Seeley's thoughts again wandered. Tomorrow would be the last day of testimony. Charles Weed, a prominent New York patent lawyer who was on Thorpe's witness list to sustain the illusion of a vigorous attack on the Vaxtek patent, would testify that he had long ago advised St. Gall that the AV/AS patent was invalid, so that the company was free to copy it. How was Thorpe going to slant Weed's testimony to advance the fraudulent lawsuit? Perhaps he wouldn't try. Closing arguments were on Friday, when Seeley would attempt an illusion of his own: arguing for the AV/AS patent's validity while trying desperately to undermine it.

The immunologist droned on, and the space between him and Seeley seemed to darken. With a start, Seeley felt himself surrounded by the same gray, turning mass that once wallpapered the bleakest of his hangovers.

No message from Lily waited for him at the Huntington, and there was no story on the evening news about a Chinese scientist blowing the whistle on the theft of her pioneer discovery. Seeley didn't bother to call down to the hotel desk for an early copy of the *Chronicle*, but when he walked through the lobby the next morning he glanced at the first page of the paper lying on the scarred wooden counter. There was nothing there or in the business section, so he went out into the bright day, striding the mile to the courthouse briskly, as if that would shake the needling demons. When he arrived, Palmieri was waiting outside.

"Another gorgeous day in paradise," Palmieri said, without the barest hint of irony. Seeley thought that if he had a gun he would shoot his second chair. No, he changed his mind, he would shoot himself.

———

Even seated on the witness stand, it was easy to see that Charles Weed was the tallest man in the room. Thorpe had qualified the witness— Princeton 1952, Harvard Law 1955, senior partner of Weed and Weed, the Manhattan firm founded by his father and uncle, and one of the few patent specialty firms not yet absorbed into a large corporate law firm—and Weed was now testifying about the opinion that he had written at St. Gall's request when the company was deciding whether to develop an AIDS vaccine. All bones and paper-dry skin in his heavy herringbone tweeds, only the patent lawyer's austere, patrician bearing hid the meanness of his narrow eyes, the hawk's beak, and lips thin as wire. Eight years ago, Seeley had retained him as an expert in a patent case and quickly discovered that behind the upright pose was a thoroughly unprincipled man. Seeley also remembered Weed's one fine physical feature, hands as long and slender as a pianist's or a magician's. They now rested gracefully on a crossed knee as he answered Thorpe's questions on direct examination.

The patent opinion that Weed had prepared for St. Gall was one of the first documents Seeley read when he was still in Buffalo, and it addressed both the validity of the AV/AS patent and St. Gall's possible infringement of it. Weed wrote out his opinions in longhand and, studying the copy Barnum sent to him, Seeley could picture the long tapered fingers moving across page after page. The Vaxtek patent was invalid, Weed wrote, and even if a jury were to find it valid, St. Gall's own product would not infringe it. So far, though, Thorpe had asked Weed only about the infringement part of his opinion, not validity, and Seeley was certain that the examination would end without Weed once stating his opinion that the patent was invalid.

"Cross-examination, Mr. Seeley?"

Seeley glanced at Palmieri, who gave him a desolate look. Thorpe had been meticulous in limiting the scope of his direct examination— as had been Weed in giving his answers—and neither gave Seeley an opening to question the witness about his opinion on the patent's validity.

"Mr. Weed, you have testified that in your opinion defendant St. Gall's product would not infringe the patent on plaintiff Vaxtek's AV/ AS, is that correct?"

"That is correct." The voice, somber and august when answering Thorpe's questions, had acquired a patronizing edge.

"And on what do you rest that opinion?"

"I rest it on my forty-nine years' experience as a patent lawyer."

Weed was playing with him. The witness knew what Seeley's question meant, but had willfully misinterpreted it. Seeley let himself be distracted for a moment by Weed's green silk tie with its pattern of horse heads and riding crops.

"Let me rephrase that for you, Mr. Weed. I didn't mean to get into your background. What I meant was, do you rest your opinion on any assumption about the validity or invalidity of the AV/AS patent?"

"Oh, well, in that case, of course, I premised my opinion on the assumption that the patent was valid."

More than any question so far in the trial, Seeley wanted to ask: And in your opinion is the AV/AS patent in fact valid? But, before the words were out, Thorpe would object that the question went beyond the scope of direct, and Farnsworth would sustain him. Weed was the trial's last witness, and Seeley's time was running out. While Seeley waited for an opening, he hammered at Weed, as he had at Thorpe's infringement witnesses, on his opinion that the St. Gall product did not infringe. The harder Seeley pressed, the more severe Weed's condescension grew. This was not an adversary's ploy; it was in the man's genes. Weed had looked down on Seeley even when it was Seeley who hired him.

Weed leaned forward to emphasize a point, exposing a snowfall of dandruff and a few wisps of hair across the shoulders of the dark tweed. At that moment a fact struck Seeley that, had he not been so absorbed by his dislike for the man, he would have seen at once: Weed knew about the collusion. The moment Thorpe told Weed that he was not going to testify on validity, this man who had in his career been through hundreds of patent trials, both as a litigator and as an expert, knew that the case was rigged. It probably wasn't his first such trumped-up case. He and Thorpe had probably laughed about it over cocktails the night before. The old bastard knew, and Seeley was his sport.

Seeley was done. "No more questions, Judge."

"Mr. Thorpe, redirect?"

Thorpe's questions on redirect moved quickly, and Seeley watched the practiced rhythm of two lawyers who instinctively knew each other's moves. When Weed was Seeley's expert, they had never worked like that. One by one, Thorpe took Weed through the three other patents that Weed had analyzed in his opinion in addition to AV/AS.

Why was Thorpe doing this? By having Weed give his opinion on the validity of these other patents, Thorpe seemed to be inviting Seeley to ask the witness about his opinion on the validity of AV/AS itself. Without waiting for the judge, Thorpe turned to plaintiff's table and, with a look that told Seeley nothing, said, "Recross, Counselor?"

Like Thorpe, Seeley marched Weed through his conclusions on the validity of the three other patents, working to establish the same rhythm his adversary had, asking himself all the time how to wedge in the same question about AV/AS. He saw no way other than forward. Drawing in a quick breath, but not losing the rhythm, he said, "Mr. Weed, did you render an opinion on the validity of the AV/AS patent?"

"Yes, I did."

Seeley knew he did. Weed's opinion had been that Vaxtek's patent was invalid. Seeley blocked out any awareness of movement at the defense table and stayed with the tempo he had established, as if by will alone he could drive past any objection from Thorpe and any consequence for abandoning the pretense that he was defending the AV/AS patent, not attacking it.

"And would you tell the jury what that opinion was?"

There was a beat in time, but no reply. Then another missed beat. In front of him, high on the ridge of Weed's cheekbones the scattering of small burst capillaries—was he a drinker, Seeley wondered, or just a cold-weather duck hunter?—grew redder. For the first time, a light went on in the witness's narrow eyes, a twinkle that only Seeley would see. At that moment, Seeley realized the catastrophic scale of his error. The two of them, Thorpe and Weed, had set him up. With one stupid mistake, he had undone all of his cautious footwork of the last three days and won the case for Vaxtek and St. Gall.

"Well," Weed said, "in my written opinion, which has been made an exhibit, I concluded that the AV/AS patent was not valid, but—"

"Thank you, Mr. Weed, I have no more—"

Thorpe was on his feet. "Let the witness finish!"

Judge Farnsworth shifted forward in her chair. "Is that an objection, Mr. Thorpe?"

"Yes, Your Honor, it is. The witness has a right to finish his answer."

Farnsworth at once saw what was happening. The trial was rolling to the conclusion the parties had planned, and there was nothing legally she could do to stop it.

"Sustained. Mr. Weed?"

Weed leaned back in the witness chair and tented his slender fingers in front of him. "As I was saying, I wrote in my opinion that the patent was invalid, but I will confess to you, Mr. Seeley—I'm under oath here—that I have written hundreds of validity opinions in my career, but I have never been more ambivalent about one of my opinions than I was about this one. Some mornings, before finally writing my opinion, I'd wake up and think, That patent's valid. The next morning, though, I'd be of a different mind." Condescension seeped from him like a toxin. "And it was the same even after I wrote the opinion and sent it off to my client: some days valid, other days not."

Seeley rapidly scanned the jury as he returned to counsel's table. Even the dullest of them understood what had just happened. A defense witness had admitted the possibility that Vaxtek's patent was valid, an admission that, however equivocal, would weigh as heavily as all of the opinions of Vaxtek's hired experts together. The kid slunk down in his chair, and fingered his ponytail; his expression—was it a smirk? a scowl?—was indecipherable.

Barnum's large hand clasped the sore shoulder, and Seeley felt the moisture of the man leaning into him. "Talk about a wild ride," he said. "I don't know how you pulled that off."

How could Seeley have forgotten that, from Barnum's perspective, Weed's concession that the AV/AS patent might be valid was a triumph.

"You took ten years off my life, asking him what he thought about the patent. How did you know he changed his mind?"

"Second sight. A trial lawyer's instinct." Which was precisely what had failed him: the instinct to skirt a trial's black holes. You never ask a witness a question when you're not certain of the answer, and the fact that Weed's deposition gave one answer was no assurance that, at trial, he would not give another.

On the bench, Farnsworth appeared unconcerned about what had just happened and sorted through the stack of papers in front of her. "I'm hearing motions on my criminal docket this afternoon." She set down the papers. "Counsel can make their closing arguments tomorrow morning and then I'll instruct our jury. You can obtain the jury instructions from my clerk. If you have changes to propose, I'll hear them first thing tomorrow morning." She straightened the papers and started to rise. "Oh, yes. The clerk will tell you how much time you each have left."

Seeley already knew. Palmieri, who had been busy at his laptop, searching for contradictions between Weed's testimony and his pre-trial deposition, had also been counting time. He pushed a legal pad across the table to Seeley. At the top of the otherwise blank page he had written: "53 minutes." Two years ago, drunk in a judge's chambers in New York City, Seeley had managed in less than a minute to come within a hair's breadth of being disbarred and destroying what was left of his career. Fifty-three minutes was more than enough time for him to finish hanging himself.

Seeley was in Pearsall's office working on the notes for his closing argument when the night operator buzzed that his brother was in the reception area. While he waited for Leonard, Seeley reflected on what had happened over the time that his brother had been gone. There was the confrontation with Renata after the football game. She had been flirting, yes, but only to see whether Seeley was the loyal, heroic brother that Leonard had endlessly praised to her. It seemed to Seeley that every other incident, from the discovery of his client's collusion to this morning's humiliation by Weed, also bore the imprint of Leonard's craven spirit. The thought for the first time occurred to him that, as consistently as he had been Leonard's protector, Leonard had all that time been his enemy.

Leonard wheeled his suitcase inside the office door. There were no arms poised for an embrace this time, but the salesman's smile was there.

"Great news, Mike. The FDA likes the data we're getting from the phase-three trials."

"Congratulations. If the jury votes for your patent, you and St. Gall get to divide the world between you."

The smile disappeared, but not because Leonard had been listening. He came closer to study Seeley's face as a physician would, taking hold of his shoulders and turning him into the light. "What happened to you?"

Seeley had forgotten about the bruises. "Why didn't you tell me you were colluding with St. Gall?"

Leonard stepped back. Behind him, the glass wall reflected the office and open doorway so that they appeared to hang outside in the night. Thirty-two years, Seeley thought, and how far have we come from two boys waiting in a shared room for their drunken father to crash through the door.

Seeley said, "You made a deal with St. Gall."

"Of course we did. This goes back to before you got into the case. Joel worked it out with the Swiss. It was a business adjustment. I didn't have anything to do with it."

"But you knew about it."

"Look, we've sunk almost half a billion dollars into AV/AS. St. Gall had a problem with one of their researchers being caught in our labs, and we had a problem with Steinhardt's notebooks. So Joel made a deal."

Seeley wondered if Leonard and the others at Vaxtek knew Lily's secret. Their most famous researcher hadn't just fabricated a few dates in his notebooks; he had stolen another scientist's discovery and claimed it as his own.

"And because you knew how the case would come out, you went into hock buying Vaxtek shares. You knew about the collusion when you came to see me in Buffalo. You dragged me into it."

"The way I see it," Leonard said, his voice becoming a whisper, "I dragged your ass out of the swamp you were sinking into." This was an old trick of Leonard's when they argued, lowering his voice to taunt him, forcing him to draw closer. "Would you have taken the case if I told you it was a sure thing?"

"I was your insurance policy," Seeley said. "You thought you could control me."

"Me?" Leonard's face went slack-jawed, incredulous. "When did Leonard Seeley ever control his brother? Did I once tell you that if you lost this case it would break me?"

No, Seeley remembered, he hadn't. And if he hadn't asked, Renata would not have told him, either.

"Come on, Mike, whoever's name is on it, AV/AS is going to save lives."

"But only at a price that the people who need it most won't be able to pay."

"I already told you," Leonard's voice had returned to normal, "we're only going to charge fifteen dollars a dose in Africa."

"But Vaxtek isn't going to sell AV/AS in Africa. St. Gall is. And according to Chaikovsky's numbers, they won't sell it for less than forty-five dollars."

Twelve-year-old Lenny peered out from the supplicating face in front of him, and a dam burst inside Seeley. One hand grabbed for Leonard's neck, flesh and collar slipping in his fingers, and the other slammed into his brother's chest, propelling him back against the window. There was a boom and the glass shuddered, flashing back reflected shards of desk, chairs, doorway, and, at the center, a face—his own—that Seeley didn't recognize.

Perspiration or tears streaked Leonard's cheeks. "What did I do wrong?"

Seeley's nerves, muscle, bone throbbed with rage.

"Who hired the Asian boys? Was that Vaxtek's idea or St. Gall's?"

"I've been away all week. If I'd known, it never would have happened."

But he knew now, and that meant Warshaw or Barnum was behind the attack.

Seeley jammed Leonard's head sideways against the glass so that one fear-struck eye observed him while the other stared thirty-eight stories down to where pedestrians waited at a bus stop. The fury inside Seeley was like alcohol. It felt to him that he was devouring one drink after another.

"You weren't away when Pearsall died. Who arranged that?"

Leonard's body went slack. He said, "You're kidding me, right?"

Leonard knew something that he didn't, and Seeley expected that in a moment he was going to feel like a fool.

Seeley said, "Pearsall discovered the collusion, he confronted Warshaw about it, and that got him killed."

Leonard said, "Who do you think set up the deal between us and St. Gall? Pearsall didn't discover a collusive lawsuit. He orchestrated it. He and Thorpe did."

"Pearsall would never do that." Even as he said it, Seeley asked himself what in fact he knew about Pearsall other than that he was a successful trial lawyer who took bird pictures, read philosophy, and played poker with Thorpe. Still inches from his brother's choked-up face, Seeley said, "You're lying."

"Why would I lie, Mike?"

"Because that's what you do, Len, you lie. That's who you are."

"This time I'm not."

A halo of condensation formed on the glass around Leonard's head. Above it was the reflection of three or four figures standing at the office doorway, looking in. Seeley let go of Leonard and turned.

"There's nothing here," he said, dismissing the onlookers. "We all have work to do. Let's get back to it."

Leonard, breathing evenly again—was it part of his brother's insanity that he recovered so quickly?—said, "What are you working on?"

"Tomorrow's closing argument."

"I'm glad I got back in time," he said. "I wouldn't miss it for anything."

TWENTY-TWO

The courtroom on Friday morning was bedlam. The bench, where Judge Farnsworth should have been disposing of motions, was empty. In the back row of the gallery, Phil Driscoll, the protester, was gesturing wildly at one of the investment bank lawyers; the lawyer, arms folded across his chest, nodded parentally. Seeley could just barely make out Gail Odum's slender figure inside the crowd of lawyers around her. Leonard, who said that he wouldn't miss Seeley's closing argument for anything, wasn't there.

She did it, Seeley thought, cheering silently. Lily did it. Hope leapt inside him.

Barnum wasn't at counsel's table, and if Seeley was right about what had happened, the general counsel would not be there for the remainder of the trial. Seeley looked across the well of the courtroom. Dusollier was missing, too. This evidently was not a day for clients to be out and about. Palmieri's arms rested expansively over the back of the chair on either side of him. His hair looked as if someone had ruffled it. His voice was excited. "Have you seen it?"

Seeley lifted the newspaper from the table. Odum's byline was on the front page, beneath the fold. The picture next to the article looked like it came from Lily's college yearbook—a serious girl in a buttoned-up blouse and an out-of-date hairdo with a bow-shaped barrette at each side of her forehead. She was unsmiling, except for a certain brightness in her eyes. Even without reading the article, Seeley's admiration for the smart, vulnerable-looking girl in the photograph made him gasp.

The first three paragraphs condensed what Lily had told Seeley: her work on AV/AS at St. Gall; her nighttime visit to Steinhardt's lab; Steinhardt's appropriation of her discovery as his own. In the remaining four paragraphs, Odum pieced together her own speculations about the odd progress of the trial proceedings and their connection to Lily's story. Vaxtek and St. Gall hadn't returned her phone calls, and she nowhere directly charged them with collusion. However, there was a quote from an anonymous lawyer that Thorpe's defense was the weakest he had ever seen in a major federal case, and readers could draw from that whatever inference they wished.

Seeley read the article a second time. When he looked up, he was aware that the courtroom had turned silent. From the bench, Judge Farnsworth was beckoning to him and Thorpe to come forward.

The judge's calm expression was impenetrable and her voice, when she asked the court reporter if she was ready, was contained. Studying Seeley and Thorpe over her half-frames, she said, "I am not going to ask if you or your clients were responsible in any way for the article in this morning's *Chronicle*. I'm told it was also on the television news. But I am going to ask the U.S. attorney to look into whether there is any connection between your clients and Dr. Warren's decision, on the eve of closing argument, to give her story to the press."

Seeley glanced sideways at Thorpe who, for once, was not crowding him at sidebar. The old lawyer's face was clotted, a deep, unhealthy crimson. Whatever the outcome of this trial, Thorpe's career as one of the handful of lawyers of choice for large, difficult cases was over. St. Gall's public relations team could put whatever spin they wanted on Odum's musings, but no Fortune 500 corporation would ever retain a trial lawyer so tainted by the scent of corruption.

The judge's polished red nails tapped at the wood trim of the bench.

"Unless either of you gentlemen has a well-grounded objection, I am going to interview the jurors in my chambers to determine whether any of them has been prejudiced by this morning's story."

Seeley was already thinking about numbers. If three of the eight jurors saw or heard Odum's story, Farnsworth would lack the six she needed to complete the trial. "We have no objection, Judge."

Thorpe said, "None, Your Honor."

Farnsworth instructed her clerk—"Bring them in one at a time, starting with juror number one"—and the court reporter—"This will be on the record, so bring your machine." To Seeley and Thorpe she said, "You gentlemen are welcome, but only you, none of your colleagues, and just to observe. I don't want anyone intimidating my jurors."

The small parade followed Farnsworth down the narrow hallway and past the jury room, moving quickly at the judge's pace. The clerk waited for them to settle themselves in chambers before returning to the jury room to collect juror number one, the AT&T cable splicer from Napa.

"Please come in, Mr. Gutierrez." The judge was all warm smiles. She patted the empty chair next to her. "No one here is going to bite you." As she explained to him the importance to the fact-finding process of insulating the jury from information acquired outside the courtroom, Gutierrez neither spoke nor even nodded. But the acuteness in the way he listened, a slight sharpening of his features, left no doubt that he was taking it all in.

"Have you heard or seen anything about this lawsuit outside the courtroom?"

"No, Your Honor." Seeley noticed that Gutierrez held his head up, jutting his chin a fraction of a degree, the way a career military man might or someone accustomed to wearing a construction hard hat.

"Do you read the newspaper in the morning, Mr. Gutierrez? Watch the television news?"

Gutierrez shook his head and, for the first time, his expression relaxed. "Your Honor, it takes me an hour-and-a-half to get here in the morning. I barely have time to brush my teeth."

"Do you listen to the radio when you drive down here?"

"No, there's not much to listen to."

"How do you keep yourself occupied, then?" If she wasn't genuinely interested in the answer, she was an accomplished actor.

"I listen to audiotapes."

"What are you listening to these days?"

"The new biography of Albert Einstein. It's pretty good. It moves right along."

"I'll have to buy the book." She rose to take the cable splicer's hand. "I want you to know how much the court—how much *I*—appreciate the work you are doing on this jury, Mr. Gutierrez. I'm certain it can't be easy."

When he went out the door, Farnsworth's glance raked the two lawyers, as if she needed to remind them that she preferred jurors to lawyers.

The second juror, one of the secretaries, came into the room, and before she could take the chair next to Farnsworth, blurted, "I know what you're going to ask me," then broke into tears. Between sobs, she explained that her roommate had come into the kitchen and spilled the *Chronicle* story before she could gather her wits to stop her. "I told her when the trial started that we couldn't talk about the case."

The woman's face was a blur of tears and dissolving makeup. She said, "Do you think the story in the paper was true?"

Farnsworth briefly tried to console her—the woman was bereft at the prospect of leaving the jury—but said, no, it would present too great a risk if an appeal were taken for her to remain on the jury. "I'm sorry, but I must dismiss you." Farnsworth nodded to the clerk, who led the woman out.

Farnsworth's dwindling jury was, Seeley knew, all that stood between the truth of Odum's story and the lies that Vaxtek's and St. Gall's public relations firms would soon enough begin circulating. He said, "You know, Judge, by tomorrow this story's going to be all over the news. If this jury doesn't hold together, it won't be possible to retry the case."

"I'm fully aware of that possibility, Counselor." The words could have been splinters of ice.

With questions and persistent prodding from the judge, jurors three
and four, the other secretary and the nurse, stuck to their stories that
they didn't know a single fact that had not been presented in court.
Juror five, the real estate broker who hadn't worn the same outfit
twice over the course of the trial, started down the same path.

Farnsworth glanced at the yellow legal pad on her lap. "What about
your husband, Mrs. Barton. Does he read the paper?"

"Only when I'm in the shower and he's making breakfast. He puts
it away as soon as I come in."

"And he didn't tell you anything about a story in the *Chronicle*?"

"No, of course not. I've told him not to."

"Well, then, what did you and your husband talk about this morning?"

"Ah . . . well . . . the 49ers. We're great fans."

"How are they doing this season?"

Mrs. Barton hesitated. "They're a fine team."

"I'm sure they are, but I don't always get a chance to look at the
sports pages. How did they do on Sunday?"

The polished woman sputtered but had no answer.

Farnsworth looked over at Thorpe whose expression signaled
nothing and then at Seeley, who gave her no encouragement.

"I'm sorry, Mrs. Barton, but I'm going to have to dismiss you from
future—"

"I only wanted to help!"

"I'm sure you did." The judge was cooling quickly, and she signaled
her clerk to bring in the next juror. "You have the appreciation of this
court for staying with the trial so far."

The kid, Gary Sansone, was the sixth juror. His hair was in a ponytail today, and he twisted it with his fingers after he took the chair
next to the judge.

Farnsworth went through the preliminaries, then said, "Did you
see this morning's *Chronicle*?"

"I don't read newspapers."

"What about television? Radio?"

"Ditto. Old-line media's a waste of time."

"Where do you get your news?"

"On the Web. CNET, Slate sometimes. I have a few favorite blogs."

"Have any of them carried stories about our trial?"

"I wouldn't know, ma'am. I haven't looked at them since we started."

How about e-mails, Seeley thought. Your buddies must know you're a juror in this trial. One of them must read the paper or watch the television news. You're the only juror who doesn't wear a wrist-watch. If you check your phone for the time, you must check text messages, too. Seeley imagined that the same thought had occurred to Judge Farnsworth.

Farnsworth said, "Then you have received no information about the parties or their dispute other than the evidence presented in court?"

"That's right, Judge." He clapped his hands on his thighs and pre-pared to leave.

Farnsworth hesitated, as if she thought that the kid's lighthearted-ness was a front, masking a deeper knowledge of the case than he wanted to let on. Finally, she said, "Well that's good. I'm glad you can remain on our jury."

She was even more cursory with the remaining two jurors—the retired schoolteacher and the accountant whose domestic partner had evidently been less talkative than the real estate broker's husband.

"Well, counselors," she said, "it looks like our jury is intact. Some-what smaller, but intact." She rose. "Before you go, the marshals tell me there are TV cameras and who knows what else all over the plaza. After we finish in there," she nodded toward the courtroom, "I want you to leave by the basement entrance in the back. Emil knows the way. There may be reporters there, too, but if either of you even nods to one of them, I'll have your license."

The din in the courtroom quieted when Seeley and Thorpe came through the paneled back door but then immediately resumed. The six remaining jurors filed in, taking their previous seats, the two empty chairs a demonstration to the gallery of the narrow precipice on which the trial now perched.

Judge Farnsworth came in quickly and before she could touch her gavel, the noise abruptly abated. Her chair squeaked as she turned to the jury. "We have become better acquainted over the past hour or so," she said, "and I am grateful for that. I am confident that you can perform your duties in this case free from external influence." The jurors, all but the kid, looked at one another, congratulating themselves. They were survivors.

"I could order that you be sequestered in a downtown hotel to ensure the integrity of your deliberations, but with the weekend coming up, and my confidence in your probity, I have decided not to do so." She paused. "I just wanted you to know the complete faith that I have in you."

She swiveled back to the center. "Mr. Seeley, I believe you have a closing argument."

When circumstances force a lawyer to argue against his client's ostensible best interest—Seeley that the AV/AS patent was invalid; Thorpe, that it was valid—the less said, the better, and the short time left for closing argument was a blessing to both lawyers. Following the notes that he had drafted from Palmieri's outline, Seeley evenly balanced his witnesses against Thorpe's, emphasizing only slightly the evidence on validity; the case for validity was stronger, he was saying, but only modestly so. If Barnum, who was still missing, read the transcript, Seeley would explain that he did not want to overstate their case to the jury. Of his theory of the case, the story that he had carefully wrought of the out-of-town bully who stole the local boy's lunch, Seeley said nothing. He finished with three minutes left in his allotted time.

Thorpe's closing statement vacillated, too, but, perhaps chastened by Odum's speculations in the *Chronicle*, the old lawyer didn't once suggest that a reasonable juror might consider the patent to be valid. Like Seeley, and as if circling a bomb that might explode, Thorpe made no reference to Steinhardt.

While Thorpe addressed the jury, Seeley observed Judge Farnsworth. She looked tired and, from the lines across her brow, worried. Once, when she looked away from the jurors to survey the courtroom, her eyes met Seeley's and, for the briefest moment, an uncomfortable intimacy passed between them. Farnsworth was a talented lawyer, and if she hadn't believed Seeley when he came to her chambers with his tale of collusion, or later when Thorpe put on his witnesses, she believed him now. Her eyes in that moment said, Forgive me, but this is my jury, what is left of it. I am going to get a verdict and there will not be a mistrial. Which is why her own closing comment to the jurors was no surprise.

"This has been a difficult trial," the judge said. She rose and walked to the jury side of the bench. Resting her hands on the wooden molding, she leaned over the edge, as she had with the lawyers at sidebar. "But you have been admirable jurors, all of you—admirable in your steadfastness and in your continued attention. I think you all deserve the afternoon off. That will give you the weekend to catch your breath and return refreshed on Monday. You will remember what we discussed about news coverage in chambers and here in open court. I will instruct you on the applicable law at eight thirty Monday morning after which this case will become your complete responsibility."

At 11:20 a.m., she adjourned for the day.

TWENTY-THREE

For Seeley, the hardest part of a trial was the waiting. He turned down an offer to spend the weekend with Palmieri and his partner at their cabin in Sonoma. Lily was going to be working at the lab until late Saturday night, but invited him to come to Half Moon Bay on Sunday. He filled the rest of Saturday aimlessly walking through surprisingly empty San Francisco neighborhoods and visiting art museums. As a boy in Buffalo, he had found consolation, even meaning, in the city's single art museum, but now the prints and paintings on the walls only left him feeling restless and on edge. At the peak of his practice in New York, he would fill the vacuum at the end of a major trial with preparations for the next one. But no big trial awaited him.

On Sunday, Lily had prepared a picnic for the beach, and when Seeley objected that it might be unwise for them to be seen together—if he saw any reporters outside the town house in Cypress Cove he would have just driven by—she insisted that the gray sky and strong winds at the shore would keep all but the hardiest picnickers away.

As Lily promised, the beach was almost empty, and the steep dunes offered fine shelter for a lunch of roast chicken, French bread, and green salad, with fresh lemonade from a thermos. Surfboarders in their black wet suits looked like water sprites against the horizon, and Seeley envied them the patience with which, straddling their boards, they waited hours, it seemed, for the right wave.

Seeley took off his shoes and rolled up his pants at the water's edge. The firm sand made him want to run, not walk. He and Lily talked about movies, art, places they had visited, but not about Odum's story. It was as if they had just completed a marathon and were too consumed by exhaustion to revisit the race. Still, Seeley's thoughts drifted back to the trial. If the jury voted that Vaxtek's patent was valid, the company's public relations people would immediately crown Steinhardt as a savior and brand Lily as a thief. Any hope that she might have for a future in science in the United States, or anywhere else, would dissolve.

Lily said, "My friends tell me I'm pretty poor company when I'm waiting for a result in the lab that's completely out of my control."

Distracted by the water and wind, as well as thoughts of the trial, it took Seeley a moment to catch her meaning. "I'm sorry," he said. "I can't get my mind off the jury. I'm sure I'm lousy company."

"Let's just say you're a little preoccupied." She squeezed his hand. "We can get together after the trial's over. I'll make dim sum this time."

On Monday morning, the Golden Gate Bridge was lost in fog and the light falling onto Pearsall's desk—Seeley still thought of it as belonging to him—was a watery gray. He tossed a handful of telephone messages taken by the weekend operator into the wastebasket along with a note from Tina that his voice mailbox was filled to capacity. From the scraps of notes that he kept over the last two weeks, he methodically filled in the neat grids of Heilbrun, Hardy's time sheets, pausing once to consider a question of legal ethics that he had never faced before: Is it ethical to bill a client for time spent trying to destroy the client's case? The question stopped him for no more than a few seconds. Vaxtek had bought his time, not his moral choices.

Until Tina came into the office and switched on the light, Seeley didn't notice that he was working in the dark. She handed him two days of trial transcripts that a paralegal had marked with yellow tags where he or Palmieri made an objection at trial so that he could identify any overruled objections that might be the basis for an appeal. He didn't tell Tina, but it was just another necessary charade. There would be no appeal. If Vaxtek won, neither party would risk having the result overturned by a higher court, and if it lost they wouldn't risk having the result affirmed. Warshaw had been exaggerating when he said that he didn't mind risk, only competition. In his sandbox, there was no room for either.

Tina said, "The rest should be ready for you this afternoon."

Palmieri called from the courthouse. The jurors had asked Judge Farnsworth to clarify two points of law in the instructions she read to them that morning. Jury instructions in patent cases usually follow a standard format, but before the trial started Farnsworth allowed the parties to propose changes to the usual formula. Seeley's proposed changes slanted the instructions in favor of the patent's validity, and he had been surprised when Thorpe didn't object. He regretted those changes now, but reminded himself that he needed just one juror who had seen or guessed about the news coverage of Lily's story to vote for a mistrial. That lone juror—Seeley's compass regularly pointed to the kid—would need to be sufficiently obstinate to resist the others and, ultimately, to withstand Judge Farnsworth's ardent seduction.

On Tuesday morning, Seeley called his office in Buffalo, but Mrs. Rosziak didn't answer. She hadn't been there yesterday, either, and this worried him. She had not missed a morning since she started working for him, and never left the office before noon. His feeling of dread—had something happened to her husband or son?—was, he knew, irrational, another affliction of his idleness.

Barnum came in after ten and took the chair across from Seeley, propping his feet on the desk. "That was a real roller-coaster ride you took us on the last couple of weeks."

"Like the county fair," Seeley said. He had no desire to pick over the details of the trial with Barnum and wondered why the general counsel had come. "Everything except the cotton candy and corn dogs."

"You sent the Chinese girl to the *Chronicle,* didn't you?"

Seeley decided that it was Barnum who had told Thorpe about his lunch with Lily. He said, "If you ever met Lily Warren, you'd know that no one gets to send her anywhere."

Barnum's smile disappeared. "You don't really believe what that reporter wrote in the *Chronicle* about Thorpe?"

"What do you believe, Ed?"

"I thought Thorpe was brilliant. I would have hired him if St. Gall hadn't already retained him."

The weekend had obviously been busy for Barnum, with meetings and conference calls with Warshaw, Thorpe, and Dusollier. Doubtless, St. Gall executives in Switzerland had also been involved. The two companies that had set out to collude in a trial were now coordinating their positions for the aftermath. If, as they had planned, the jury voted to uphold the AV/AS patent, everyone would agree that Thorpe had fought gallantly to attack it. And if the jury voted against the patent, or failed to reach a verdict . . .

Now Seeley saw the reason for Barnum's visit. The lawyers and executives had not only scripted their companies' response to the possible trial outcomes; each, including Barnum, had plotted to protect his own future. Seeley was certain that Thorpe had begun building his own protective wall the day he took the case.

Barnum said, "We thought Bob Pearsall designed a brilliant offense."

"We?"

"What do you mean?"

"You said, 'we.' You and who else?"

"Well, me . . . and Joel, of course."

Warshaw hadn't been near the trial, nor would he have read the transcript. "We" was Barnum, Thorpe, and Dusollier, and it was now clear to Seeley who would bear the blame if the jury came back with less than a victory for Vaxtek. A criminal defendant can sometimes win a reversal of his conviction by arguing that his trial lawyer was less than effective. This didn't happen in patent cases, that Seeley knew, but items leaked to the press by Vaxtek's public relations firm, hinting at Seeley's distractions during the trial, might salvage Barnum's career.

Seeley pushed the pile of transcripts across the desk to Barnum. "If you think I wasn't effective as your counsel, look at the record. I built as strong a case for the AV/AS patent as any patent owner could hope for, even when I had to save your star scientist from committing perjury."

Barnum rested shaking fingers on the papers, but Seeley didn't give him a chance to speak. "You were in the courtroom every day, except for closing argument when you were too scared to show your face. If you thought I was wrecking your company's case, it was your job to let me know. To let Warshaw know, too."

Barnum's smile was a grim scar. Seeley had left him no room to distance himself from his trial counsel.

"What was it you told me when we were in Leonard's office—you run your cases with an iron hand."

"The Chinese girl's going down, you know."

"How's that?"

"When the jury votes that the patent's valid, it's going to vindicate us and Steinhardt. You can be sure our people will be available for interviews. And, if anyone asks who this girl is, what can we say? She's an ambitious single woman from a country that leads the world in piracy and industrial espionage."

"It sounds like you and your friends had a productive weekend."

"Let me know as soon as the jury comes back."

"You'll be the first on my list, Ed."

At 12:30 Palmieri called to tell Seeley that the jury was deadlocked. Judge Farnsworth had ordered them back to the jury room, and told the jurors not to return until they reached a unanimous verdict.

Seeley waited until 3:30 before calling Mrs. Rosziak at home. She picked up at once and, before he could ask, apologized for not being in the office the last two mornings. "I was visiting Harold at Buffalo General."

Harold, her son, had been in a bar fight. Seeley wondered how gentle the police had been if they recognized Harold as the man who, just months ago, successfully sued their department for excessive use of force. "Are you okay with bail?"

"We've already posted it." He heard the fatigue in her voice. "He's coming home as soon as the doctors let him."

"Tell him not to talk to anyone. I'll take care of it as soon as I get back."

There was a hesitation at the other end. "I already got him Andy Lewandowski." Anticipating Seeley's reply, as she always did, she said, "We didn't know when you were coming back."

"No more than a week." Whether the jury reached a verdict or remained deadlocked, the trial would be over long before then, and he wanted to spend time with Lily. "Andy's a competent lawyer. Tell Harold he's in good hands." Seeley would look into it when he got back.

"Are you going to stay?"

She could have been inviting a visitor to dinner, but Seeley knew what Mrs. Rosziak was asking. It was the question he'd been avoiding all the time he was in San Francisco. For years, when he was practicing in New York City, Seeley romanticized the prospect of a return to Buffalo, to a solo practice. Now, from this distance, he could see the move for what it was. Leonard was right: he'd dug a rut for himself and begun decorating it.

As Mrs. Rosziak talked, Seeley idly paged through the steno pads that Pearsall used for sketchbooks and that he had left on the credenza almost three weeks ago.

"You know what Harold says—wherever you go, there you are."

"Thanks, Mrs. Rosziak, that's very helpful."

In the first pad was the sketch of Farnsworth, intelligent and self-confident, and in the next, the portrait of Steinhardt, boundlessly arrogant. Seeley studied the drawings of Thorpe, looking for even the faintest trace of the man's depravity, but could find none. If Leonard was telling the truth and Pearsall had in fact conspired with Thorpe to bring the collusive lawsuit, perhaps it was because, debased himself, Pearsall was blind to it in others.

"A lawyer named Girard called last Friday. He said it wasn't a rush. He didn't want to bother you in trial."

Nick Girard had been Seeley's partner at Boone, Bancroft and Meserve in New York. Seeley's last piece of business at Boone, Bancroft had not gone well either for the client or for the firm's partners, and when Seeley left for Buffalo, neither he nor they were unhappy about the move. But, a year later, Seeley was certain that Girard had called to ask if he would return to the partnership.

"I'll call him when I get back." Absently, Seeley continued turning the pages in the sketchbook. At one, his hand froze. He had seen the portrait—the steel-rimmed glasses, the odd, incipient double chin—the first time he went through Pearsall's steno pads, but that was before he met St. Gall's young in-house lawyer in Judge Farnsworth's chambers. What if Dusollier was the stranger with the French accent Lucy Pearsall saw talking to her father at choir rehearsal?

Seeley cursed himself for being so preoccupied with the trial that he failed to make the connection earlier. In the etiquette of a lawyer's life, a company's in-house lawyer rarely speaks to the outside counsel of his adversary. Even if they were colluding, if St. Gall had a message to deliver to Pearsall, it would be through Thorpe or Fischler. Or Dusollier could have spoken with Barnum. If it was Dusollier who talked to Pearsall in the hallway of Lucy's school, there was no good reason for him to do so. And if Lucy had seen him, he had probably seen her.

Mrs. Rosziak said, "This lawyer, Girard, sounded like he'd be glad to talk with you."

Talking like this with Mrs. Rosziak, about Girard, phone calls, and families, Seeley felt a spasm of panic, a sudden premonition of the Ellicott Square Building collapsing into dust, as if consumed by an explosion or a wrecking crew. "How's the building?"

"You mean the office? The usual. The radiator's on the fritz again."

"Call Rudy. Get him to fix it."

Tina was in the doorway and Seeley put his hand over the phone.

"Chris called. The jury's coming back. The judge wants everyone there in an hour."

Seeley held up a hand for Tina to wait. "I'll be back on Monday.

Tell Rudy to get it fixed by then." And, forgetting about Andy Lewandowski, he said, "Remember, tell Harold not to talk to anyone."

He rose and handed the steno pad, open to Dusollier's portrait, to Tina. "Make a copy of this picture and get it to Judy Pearsall. I think Pearsall had a fax machine in his office at home."

Tina nodded. "I have the number."

"Ask her to show it to Lucy. See if she recognizes him. Send it to Lieutenant Phan, too. Tell him it's from me."

"About the jury—should I call Ed Barnum?"

"Please."

"And your brother?"

"Sure," Seeley said. "Call him, too."

In the taxi to the courthouse, Seeley dialed Judy Pearsall's number. The housekeeper said she was at a museum meeting, but when he told her that it was urgent and involved Lucy, gave him her cell number. Five minutes after he left his number on her voice mail, Judy Pearsall called back, her voice a whisper.

Seeley said, "Tina's faxing you a sketch your husband made of someone. I want you to show it to Lucy. It may be the man she saw talking to him at school."

"I appreciate your interest, Mr. Seeley"—though hushed, the voice was annoyed, dismissive—"but I just stepped out of a board meeting. We're not even halfway through our agenda."

"When does Lucy get home from school?"

"Half an hour, forty-five minutes. Really—"

"This is important. You need to be there when she gets home and have her look at the picture. If it's the same man, I want you to call Lieutenant Phan."

"I don't understand—"

"Lucy may be in danger."

The phone went silent. "Thank you. I'll leave right now."

As he snapped the phone shut Seeley tried to remember whether the doorman at their apartment building walked to the bus with Lucy, or merely watched her from his post in the lobby.

TWENTY-FOUR

A trial transcript records every spoken detail of the proceeding. But for the participants, it is the courtroom that accumulates the veneer of incident and memory—the flickering overhead light that needs to be replaced, the edge of counsel's table where the finish has worn off, the clock high above the watercooler that is regularly six minutes fast. This is where the red-haired court reporter and the hoop-earringed court clerk faced each other like bookends and, in the corner next to the jury box, where the bailiff sat virtually motionless for the entire trial. And at 4:30 on a dying autumn afternoon, it was a place that reminded Seeley, coming in through the swinging gate, how irretrievably justice can take a wrong turn.

The bench was empty, but the six remaining jurors were in the box. Seeley recognized most of the faces in the gallery. The lawyers for the investment banks were there, and even a few of the protesters had learned of the jury's return, although apparently not Phil Driscoll. Gail Odum was in the back, scribbling on a notepad. Leonard was in the second row and Barnum was at counsel's table, his back to Palmieri. At the defense table, Fischler turned as Thorpe came through the gate. The clerk called for all to rise and Judge Farnsworth entered the courtroom, robes swirling as she settled in behind the bench. Her sharp glance combed the room, leaving Seeley in no doubt about the outcome of the jury's deliberations.

"Mr. Foreman." There were to be no preliminaries, no courtesies to the gallery nor congratulations to the jurors.

The schoolteacher, a beanpole of a man with a prominent Adam's apple, rose.

"Has the jury reached a verdict?"

"No, Your Honor." The Adam's apple worked furiously. "No, we have not. We've reached a stalemate. Although we tried, we haven't been able to break it."

"Has the jury voted?" Farnsworth's voice was pinched.

"Several times, Your Honor."

She looked directly at Seeley. "And what was the result?"

"The last vote was four in favor of validity, two opposed."

"And the vote before that?"

"It was the same, Your Honor."

"And what was the result of the first vote?"

The foreman looked down at a page torn from a legal pad. "Five in favor of validity, one opposed." He looked at the sheet again. "We didn't vote on infringement. You told us not to unless we agreed that the patent was valid."

"Thank you, Mr. Foreman."

Farnsworth methodically canvassed the jury with her eyes. The foreman, uncertain whether the judge was finished with him, hunched over awkwardly, waiting for a signal from her, and when it didn't come, finally took his seat.

Seeley had been watching the foreman, and now when he looked across the double row of downcast faces, he was startled to find the kid staring at him. Gary Sansone's jaw was set, his lips compressed, but at the corners was the smallest possible smile. He had been the first to vote against the patent, the one, Seeley was sure, who had persuaded the second juror. He was thinking that he defeated Seeley. He had read the news story or been told about it. Or maybe it was just that he resented Seeley, Seeley's client, and the client's celebrity scientist, Alan Steinhardt. Whatever the reason, in defeating them he did just what Seeley expected he would do. Seeley felt diminished, using the kid this way, and the knowledge that there was no alternative did nothing to relieve that feeling.

Farnsworth asked whether any of the jurors objected to the foreman's description of their deliberations, and when three or four shook their heads, she said in the same sad voice, "You have failed in your duty here. Your duty was not just to attend the trial and to deliberate among yourselves, but, at the end of this large expenditure of time and resources by the parties, by the taxpayers, and by this court, your duty was to reach a verdict. A trial cannot conclude without a verdict."

Seeley wondered how much of the reprimand was genuine—this was the judge's first hung jury—and how much was Farnsworth building her legend, and decided it was mostly genuine. He felt a hard look coming from the defense table. It wasn't Thorpe, whose perfectly tailored gray flannel back was to him, but Dusollier. The St. Gall lawyer's expression was bitter around the slash of his mouth. This was not the complacent Swiss lawyer Pearsall had captured in his sketchbook.

"You have disserved the judicial system," Farnsworth said, "and you have disappointed me. I have no alternative but to declare a mistrial." She shuffled the papers in front of her. "The jury is discharged."

This was as much as Seeley hoped for. He had put on too strong a case in the first part of the trial, and Thorpe had mounted too weak a defense, for the jury to vote unanimously against the patent. But, even though the patent survived, the mistrial would mortally weaken it and other companies would attack the patent. The prospect of Vaxtek and St. Gall dividing the market between them had evaporated. Seeley knew that it was grandiose, but for a moment the image passed through his mind of an ocean liner reversing course.

Seeley felt Palmieri's hand grasp his under the table. The grip was strong, and any doubt disappeared about whose side the young partner was on.

When Seeley rose, Barnum was next to him. "We'll win the retrial," he said.

The response was no more than a reflex, and Warshaw would correct Barnum soon enough. "If there's a retrial, you're going to have to win it honestly, and I don't think you can."

The court reporter, who had been conferring with the judge, returned to her table. Leonard came through the gate and grabbed Seeley's arm. He was pale and tiny beads of perspiration had formed above his upper lip.

The judge picked up, then set down, the papers in front of her, this time to address the lawyers. "Counsel will see me in chambers. Just the lead lawyers, Mr. Thorpe, Mr. Seeley. Right now!"

Leonard said, "How long are you staying?"

"Just a few days."

Seeley had already decided to spend time with Lily and then to stop off in New York to see Nick Girard, on his way to Buffalo.

"Mom's coming back from Mexico in four days. Why don't you stay for Thanksgiving?"

Tomorrow there would be margin calls on Leonard's stock purchases. The mistrial would financially destroy him. Yet all he could think of was a family reunion.

Behind the rail, Odum wanted to talk to Seeley.

Seeley said, "I can't stay. I have clients waiting in Buffalo."

"Please," Leonard said. "Come see us before you go."

Farnsworth passed through the doorway to her chambers, and Odum came toward Seeley.

"I have to go, Leonard."

Thorpe disappeared into the doorway at the back of the courtroom.

Odum said, "Did I get it right?"

"You know I can't talk to you." The gag order was still in force, but Seeley owed the reporter for what she'd done. He said, "You're an astute legal observer."

He waited for her smile to be sure she understood the message, then walked away.

When Seeley came into Judge Farnsworth's chambers, he saw at once how rigorously she had controlled herself in the courtroom.

Now, with only him and Thorpe as witnesses, the fury poured off her. These two men had hung her jury and destroyed her perfect record.

"I didn't ask the court reporter to join us. Do either of you gentlemen have any objection?"

There was no way they could object.

The judge leaned against a corner of the desk, her back to the glass wall and its panoramic view of the Civic Center and the bay. She gestured for the lawyers to take the two wooden chairs in front of her, a teacher reprimanding errant schoolboys.

"I saw this coming," she said. "This trial started off course right after your meeting with me, Mr. Seeley." She looked at Thorpe, not Seeley, as she spoke. "You should have objected, Emil. You shouldn't have allowed it."

"It wasn't an easy decision, Your Honor. I was trying to be considerate of visiting counsel." Thorpe wisely didn't add that the judge herself could have refused the meeting.

"Well, your hospitality was misplaced." Her eyebrows lifted, and with them, it seemed, some of the venom. "You had no idea, of course, what Mr. Seeley was going to tell me at our meeting."

"There was a question of perjury, I thought."

"You know, Emil, I have always been a great admirer of your courtroom skills. When I was a young lawyer, I'd come to court on my own time, just to watch you." Her tone had become almost gentle, but Seeley knew it could turn violent in a second, and when it did, it would be directed at him.

"So you will understand me when I say that I can't begin to imagine why you tried this case the way you did. Your thoughts seemed to be somewhere else." She glanced at Seeley, then returned to Thorpe. "Sometimes it looked to me like you were actually helping Mr. Seeley make his case. Or was that just part of your hospitality to strangers?"

The fog that had burned off earlier in the day had returned and now sifted through the domes and turrets of the Civic Center. Thorpe's career trying large cases was over and now he was being humbled by a woman who could have been his granddaughter. But, if these thoughts were on his mind, the old lawyer didn't show it. He appeared relaxed in the wooden chair, legs crossed, black socks drooping negligently around his ankles, exposing white flesh.

"This was not an easy case to try, Your Honor. The stipulation of priority placed an extraordinary tactical burden on my client."

"Then why did your client make the stipulation?"

"Because the facts compelled it. If we contested it at trial, we would have lost credibility with the jury on other issues, like validity, where we had a better shot at winning." Thorpe looked across at Seeley, his eyes asking for support.

"Well, you're going to get your chance to dispute Vaxtek's priority at the retrial. I'm going to want to see some proofs next time. I'm not going to accept the stipulation."

Farnsworth was bluffing. She had read Odum's story in the *Chronicle* and she knew that Thorpe's client wouldn't want a retrial that would force both parties to contest Lily's claim to have discovered AV/AS. The judge wants something from Thorpe and his client, Seeley thought, and from me and mine. And she wants Thorpe to understand that she knows about the clients' collusion.

Thorpe saw it, too. "I was sure we'd won when Mr. Seeley cut Dr. Steinhardt's testimony short on direct. Obviously, though, the jurors were impressed. We were lucky to hang the jury."

"It was only Steinhardt's lies that impressed the jury." Farnsworth rocked angrily against the desk. "You could have crucified him."

Where, Seeley thought, was she taking this?

"Do you think Emil was throwing the case, Mr. Seeley?" She shot a narrow, crooked smile at him. "Why would a man of Emil's experience and integrity do such a thing?"

Was Farnsworth going to betray the confidence of their ex parte meeting? Seeley knew there was nothing he could do if she did.

She said, "Which do you think Emil is guilty of—collusion or incompetence?"

Now Seeley saw what the judge was doing. She was baiting them, maneuvering the two lawyers into a corner of moral irrelevance where neither could influence the ultimate outcome of the case. That was fine with Seeley so long as the result was that neither Vaxtek nor

St. Gall controlled the market for AV/AS. He knew what it would require to get that result, but the decision would have to be Farnsworth's.

When the judge saw that Seeley wasn't going to answer, she said, "I want you gentlemen to inform your clients that they have a choice. They can have a retrial, but I'm going to be the judge and, as I told you, there won't be any stipulations or any other monkey business. And, no, Emil, don't even think about making a motion to recuse me."

Seeley didn't want a retrial any more than Vaxtek or St. Gall did. With Farnsworth's case calendar as tight as it was, it could be more than a year before the case was retried. In that time the two companies could entirely destroy Lily's credibility and reputation.

"The alternative is for your clients to save my time and the taxpayers' money, and settle this case, enter into a licensing agreement."

Fog rubbed against the windows and streetlights switched on against the falling dusk all the way to the bay. Seeley felt a surge of energy in the large room. For the first time, Thorpe leaned forward in his chair, eager. "I expect that my client would find that an interesting option." Wasn't that what Thorpe had implied at lunch at Schroeder's: that the difference between settlement and collusion is no more than a shade of gray?

"The settlement wouldn't have this court's seal of approval," Farnsworth said. "There would be no judicial stamp of validity."

That stamp of validity was why the parties had colluded, and Farnsworth knew that. She also evidently knew that she had frightened Thorpe with her promise of a retrial with no stipulations.

Thorpe said, "I will have to bring this to my client, but in all likelihood, they will be agreeable—"

"That's good, Emil, because you're also going to have to persuade them that it's in their best interest to provide in the license agreement for a reasonable royalty—"

"Reasonable, of course. Reasonable."

"I haven't finished. A reasonable royalty, with the license available on nondiscriminatory terms to any drug company that wants one. No one—not St. Gall, not Vaxtek, not any company—gets a competitive advantage over anyone else."

Thorpe rose. "You can't do that, Ellen. You can't force an open-ended license on a patent owner."

"I'd think that would be the patent owner's concern, Emil, not the infringer's."

Thorpe saw the trap as soon as it closed on him. Awkwardly he retook his seat.

She looked at Seeley. "As the patent owner's counsel, what do you have to say?"

"I'll present this to my client, Judge." Farnsworth's proposal was exactly what Seeley wanted. With open licensing, the price of AV/AS could fall to where the people who needed the drug might actually be able to pay for it. He pictured a jubilant Driscoll pumping his arms in victory. But Warshaw would reject these terms, just as St. Gall would. "My client's going to want to know why it should sign a deal that would effectively give away its crown jewels."

"You're being unusually diplomatic, Counselor. They're going to want to know what leverage Judge Farnsworth has on them. Tell your client that the U.S. attorney for the Northern District of California is in this courthouse every day. If I thought there was some kind of collusion between your client and Mr. Thorpe's, there's no reason, is there, why I shouldn't have a talk with the U.S. attorney about a criminal antitrust violation?" Her eyes twinkled. She was enjoying herself. "And I'm not looking for a free license, just a reasonable one. Vaxtek will in time make back its investment, and then some. Your client—and Mr. Thorpe's client—just won't get the monopoly profits they were hoping for."

Thorpe was out of his chair again, and pacing the chambers. "This is a decision that has to be made in Switzerland—"

"But they're going to listen to you," Farnsworth said. "They'd be fools not to."

Thorpe said, "I'd advise them to take the trial."

"What about you, Mr. Seeley. How are you going to advise your client?"

"I'd advise them to take the license. There won't be a public record. It wouldn't be in the news for more than a day." And, he thought, both sides would do everything they could to appease Lily. "Their stock might even recover."

Thorpe was at the far end of the chambers, studying the bindings on the judge's bookshelf, but he heard Seeley and Farnsworth. He was smart and, for all his objections, he was going to recommend that his client take the license.

"Let me know your clients' decision by five p.m. Friday."

Thorpe coughed to clear his throat, as if he were about to make a pronouncement, but said only, "Of course, Your Honor."

Other than a few late courthouse workers leaving for the day, the plaza was empty. The press, if they had been there, were gone, including Odum, the solitary, earnest reporter still after her story. Late-autumn twilight mixed with the fog and the distant drone of automobiles heading home on the freeway. The fragrance of roasting coffee was again in the air and, improbably, the winey scent of overripe apples.

Thorpe said to Seeley, "You've been practicing law how long— twenty, twenty-five years?" He didn't wait for an answer. "I know it's trite, but the longer you practice, the easier it is to lose sight of the principles that brought you into the profession."

Seeley imagined Thorpe as a skinny law student, in a fever for truth and justice as he rushed from class to class. "What are you getting at?"

"Wherever he thought the equities lay, Jake Ehrlich would never have tried to subvert his own client's case."

"If that's true—and I don't know that it is—it's only because he never had an adversary who tried to make his own case for him."

When they reached the edge of the plaza, Seeley stopped. The gray creased face turned to him. "You mean our little talk at lunch? I was speaking entirely hypothetically—but of course, I told you that. What Ellen said about a collusive lawsuit? I wouldn't have any part of one!" The crafty eyes dulled then flashed. "Would you?"

Thorpe's feint was no surprise. This was a man accustomed to neither confessions nor amends. Nor would the police catch him up in the investigation of Pearsall's death. If Lucy Pearsall could identify

Dusollier, that might make the connection between the collusive law-suit and Pearsall's death, but only if Lieutenant Phan chose to pursue it. And, even if he did, Thorpe would have built an impenetrable wall between himself and his client's wrongdoing.

Seeley said, "You should never have done this."

Thorpe's expression turned contrite, then belligerent, with an actor's ease. "How could I forget—you're the lawyer who never makes a mistake."

To Seeley's astonishment, he felt a smile taking form. "I make mistakes all the time," he said. "One is forgetting that there are people walking the streets, esteemed professionals, who can commit the most monstrous acts, acts that would shame any human soul, yet not suffer a moment's regret."

Such an intense, cold hatred consumed Thorpe's features that for an instant, Seeley shivered. Then the lawyer recovered, returning Seeley's smile with one of his own. "Goodbye, Michael. You have been a . . . splendid adversary."

Seeley watched the lawyer's gray back disappear into the crowd of office workers and tourists thronging toward Market Street. He had no idea what attracted American tourists to San Francisco, other than the receding but carefully burnished corners and echoes of a fabled past. But he now understood what European travelers found here—an indifferent, heartbreaking beauty, one that casually wrapped the deepest cruelties in its embrace—and why they thought of it as America's most European city.

TWENTY-FIVE

Lieutenant Herbert Phan had the *San Francisco Chronicle* open on his lap in Heilbrun, Hardy's thirty-seventh-floor reception area and looked up only when Seeley approached. "We've been trying to find you all morning."

Seeley glanced at his watch. It wasn't even eight thirty. He wondered, Why is it that I can have a level conversation with someone as deeply corrupt as Emil Thorpe, yet if a police detective makes a mild crack, I want to throttle him?

Phan took his time folding the paper before following Seeley up the open staircase, past Tina's empty desk, to Pearsall's office. Seeley took the chair behind the desk and the detective the one across from it, resting a notepad on his crossed knee. He had on the same zippered boots as the last time.

"Why don't you tell us what you know about the murder of Robert Pearsall." The small smile didn't disturb the hairline mustache.

"You've decided it's murder."

"First degree, probably—that's up to the district attorney. But definitely homicide."

"Lucy Pearsall identified Dusollier? The Swiss."

"We spoke with your Swiss colleague yesterday evening at his hotel."

"Adversary," Seeley said, "not colleague." If Lucy made the identification, Phan was playing with him and Seeley didn't know why.

"The night of Pearsall's murder, Mr. Dusollier was in Calistoga, at the mud baths."

"That doesn't mean he didn't arrange it."

Phan opened the notepad, but didn't look at it. "How do you think Mr. Dusollier fits into this?"

Phan was trolling. Seeley said, "I'd only be speculating."

"I like lawyers' hypotheticals. I had a year of law school. USF, here in the city."

"No offense," Seeley said, "but this is for the DA."

"You obviously think St. Gall Laboratories arranged this murder. Why else would you send us after Mr. Dusollier?"

Seeley swiveled his chair to the view outside so that he faced the window. A single sailboat was making its way toward the Golden Gate Bridge.

"In our experience," Phan said, "corporations don't kill off innocent lawyers."

Seeley watched the sailboat's progress. "Corporations don't, but their employees do, particularly if they think their lives are about to fall apart."

"And how was Mr. Dusollier's life about to fall apart?"

"Start higher up. Say you're St. Gall's general counsel, in Switzerland. You're making and spending more money than you ever dreamed possible. Expensive clothes for the second wife, private school for the new kids, cars, a servant or two, the small villa on the Côte d'Azur. You're fifty-five, sixty years old, you don't have a franc in savings and, because you haven't really practiced law for the past twenty years, there's no one who will hire you. You helped your CEO set up a collusive lawsuit in a major case and you've sworn to him that the deal is airtight. Then your opponent's lawyer threatens to wreck the deal. If he does, you know you'll lose your job. So you order someone lower down the ladder, the ambitious young lawyer who's directly responsible for the case, to eliminate the problem. Maybe you point him toward the company's head of security, who might know someone who could help."

The only flaw in Seeley's theory was that Leonard said Pearsall had helped to set up the collusion. Either Leonard was lying or, once having set the collusive lawsuit in motion, Pearsall changed his mind.

Seeley said, "People are fearful. The thought of losing something they value can drive them to acts that, a day earlier, they couldn't even imagine."

"You can't believe—"

"Leaders of countries have started wars for less."

"And you think the person at the bottom was Dusollier?" The detective sounded unimpressed.

"An order from the boss to a bureaucrat."

"Not a bureaucrat," Phan said, "a lawyer."

"Law schools teach ethics, not morals."

When Seeley turned back from the window, Phan's features had slipped into indifference, even boredom.

Phan said, "After the story appeared in the *Chronicle*, we started thinking in the same direction. Except, the way we see it, anything that applies to St. Gall also applies to you."

Seeley said, "If you went to law school, you know I can't talk to you about my client."

Phan's fine features narrowed; the bored expression disappeared. "We don't mean your client. We mean you."

Seeley had never liked the police, their arrogance and unearned authority. But it was a long time since he made the mistake of underestimating their cunning or their power. "This is a wet dream you had, right?"

"We've been watching you since the first time you called us, misrepresenting yourself as Mrs. Pearsall's lawyer. What would that look like to a criminal jury—a complete stranger inserting himself into a murder case, just like that, for no good reason? Then there was that incident in Chinatown. You are brutally attacked, but you make no report to the police. When the desk man at your hotel asks, you tell him it was nothing."

"Your men saw me being beaten and they didn't stop it?"

Phan shrugged. "They said you handled yourself very ably." He gave Seeley another of his miniature smiles. "And—don't ask me why—juries are always impressed when the accused returns to the scene of the crime."

At first, Seeley didn't understand. Then he remembered the dark sedan parked by the train tracks in San Mateo. Phan's people had been there, too.

Through the glass panel next to the office door, Palmieri looked in and, when Seeley shook his head, pointed in the direction of his own office. Seeley nodded.

"And you think I'm involved in the murder of Robert Pearsall?"

"This is one of the questions we are looking into."

"I never even met Pearsall. I was in Buffalo when he was killed."

"But, as you said of Mr. Dusollier, that doesn't mean you weren't in some way responsible."

Dozens of sailboats were on the bay now, a swarm of moths zigzagging toward the Golden Gate.

"And my motive would be, what? To take over his case?"

Phan frowned. "We're fully aware that your law practice in Buffalo barely pays the rent."

"So I kill lawyers to drum up business."

"Possibly. Maybe your life was, as you say, about to fall apart. But the motive we're looking into is that your brother is an employee of Vaxtek. Evidently his entire wealth is tied up in the company. He took a big bet that you would win the case for him."

"And we didn't win."

Phan yawned. "Maybe that's because you're not a very good lawyer." He handed the newspaper across the desk to Seeley.

The story, on the front page beneath the fold, reported that Arnaud Baptiste, a sometime resident of Quebec City, with a record of criminal assaults across Quebec Province, had been arrested by the San Mateo police for the murder of San Francisco lawyer Robert Pearsall. The photograph next to the article was of one of those faces that look out from mug books in station houses around the world: cheeks drawn and sunken by missing teeth, eyes partly closed as if squinting into the sunlight or a police photographer's flash, lank hair falling across a too-narrow forehead.

Seeley was aware of Phan watching him as he read the story. "The first rung of the ladder," he said.

Phan said, "Do you recognize him?"

"No." Seeley remembered the fax that he'd asked Tina to send to Phan. "Did you show him Dusollier's picture?"

"He says he may know him. But he's not going to talk until he thinks we're ready to make a deal."

"Did Lucy recognize Dusollier as the man who was talking to her father?"

"Last night," Phan said. "We had to wait until the doorman came on at six this morning, but he identified both Baptiste and Dusollier. He puts them outside the apartment building one morning last week." In the same flat tone, Phan said, "Dusollier's being taken into custody now."

"And the reason you're talking to me?"

"Because we think you're involved with this."

"Well," Seeley said rising, "call me in Buffalo if you ever get any evidence."

"For right now, we would prefer that you stay in San Francisco."

"Are you arresting me?"

"Not yet."

"Then you can't stop me from leaving."

"We can hold you as a material witness."

Phan was bluffing. "If you want to hold me as a material witness, you'll need a subpoena and, with what you have, you'll never get one." Seeley reached into his jacket for his wallet. "I'll be around for a few days, but after that, you can get me in Buffalo." He took a business card from the wallet. "I'm sure you already have the number."

Phan rose. "We'll be seeing you again."

This time the bluff was so absurd that Seeley laughed. "Not if I see you first."

———

Palmieri was at his desk in the neat white office working at his laptop. Seeley lifted the *Chronicle* off the corner of the desk. "Did you talk with Phan?"

"Friday afternoon," Palmieri said. "After Gail Odum's piece came out."

Seeley returned the paper to the desk. "This guy Baptiste is going to implicate Dusollier."

"Is any of this going to splash onto our client?"

Seeley said, "Phan hinted at it, but he's a cop, and that's what cops do. Did you tell him anything about Vaxtek's part in the collusion?"

"And get disbarred?"

"What was Pearsall's part in it?"

Palmieri pushed back from the desk, but his eyes remained open. In this crisp pink-and-white striped shirt and dark tie, he was as collected as ever. "I finished my grieving for Bob. This doesn't change anything."

"He was part of it, wasn't he?"

"Bob and Emil Thorpe," Palmieri said. "Warshaw and the higherups in Switzerland made the deal, but Bob and Emil executed it."

So Leonard had not been lying. "I wouldn't think that Pearsall was the kind of person who'd do that."

"He wasn't," Palmieri said. "It was one of those drawn-out negotiations where, when you're in the middle of it, it looks like you're just making one small tactical decision after another. Only later, when the negotiations are over and you've moved on to other things, you realize you've made a moral choice. We didn't discover Steinhardt's double bookkeeping, Emil's people did. Emil tried to use it to get Vaxtek to drop the case. But one of our associates had just found the record of Lily Warren's visit to Steinhardt's lab. That gave each side a lock on the other. Bob suggested that the parties settle, and Emil said he'd talk with his client. That's when the two companies came up with the idea of going through the motions of a trial, and getting a judicial stamp of validity on the patent. It didn't seem unreasonable to Bob at the time, so he went along."

But, Seeley thought, if Pearsall was involved in the collusion, why would Dusollier have to arrange for his murder?

Palmieri said, "I can't understand why Bob had to be involved. All he had to do was what any trial lawyer does for his client—prove that the patent was valid. It was Emil who had to pull his punches."

Seeley said, "Someone had to tell Thorpe where the soft spots were in Vaxtek's case so that he could avoid them." Seeley wondered what Palmieri's part was. "Pearsall didn't tell you about the collusion, did he?"

Palmieri shook his head. "A couple of months into depositions, I figured out what was going on. Questions that didn't get asked. Requests for admissions and interrogatories that didn't get served."

"And you confronted Pearsall?"

"Too many people I know have died of AIDS for me to be responsible for any more. I wouldn't repeat this to the lieutenant, but I could have killed Bob myself, I was so furious."

"What did Pearsall say?"

"Bob said I should stop working on the case, but I told him I was going to go to the state bar, and if they didn't do anything, I'd go to the press."

"But instead," Seeley said, "Pearsall went to Warshaw and told him that the firm was withdrawing from the case."

"Worse than that." Tears suddenly filled Palmieri's eyes. "He told Warshaw that if Vaxtek didn't drop the lawsuit, he was going to the press with the story. I don't think he forgave himself for being part of this." Palmieri wiped his eyes with his fingers. "So he got killed instead of me."

"You were very brave."

Palmieri shook his head. "If I were brave, I would have gone to the press myself."

"With what? Your suspicions, and what Pearsall told you? No one would have believed you."

"After Bob was killed, I could have gone to the police."

"You were braver than that. Think of all those things you did to try to sabotage Vaxtek's case."

"They weren't very effective, were they?"

"We got a hung jury, didn't we? I'd say, if there's a hero anywhere in this mess, it's you." And, Seeley told himself, Lily.

"It's nice of you to say that, but—"

"You still have work to do," Seeley said. He told Palmieri about the meeting in Judge Farnsworth's chambers, and explained how the judge was effectively forcing Vaxtek to license AV/AS on reasonable terms to any company that wanted to manufacture it. "You get to close the deal, Chris. Does the firm have an intellectual property transactions group? You'll need someone to draft a license agreement."

"Sure."

"Have them put together a license for Barnum to review. Once he's approved it, send a copy to Emil and get it to the judge by Friday." The party that prepares the first draft of a contract has the upper hand in the negotiations that follow and, after what he'd done to his client in court, Seeley owed it that much.

"What about the royalty rate?"

"Get Nicolas Cordier to fax you a declaration of what he thinks a reasonable royalty should be. Get one from your friend Phil Driscoll, too. Use the lower number."

"And if Vaxtek thinks it's too low?"

"Tell them the judge won't approve anything higher." Seeley nodded at the laptop. "And you can turn that thing off. There won't be a retrial. No appeals. The case is over."

Palmieri turned the screen toward Seeley. It was filled with blue sky, green waters, a white beach, and a jungle of palm trees. "Maui. My partner and I are going for a couple of weeks."

Seeley forgot that Palmieri had been working on the case from the beginning, long before the trial itself began, through unending days of depositions, document review, and legal research. He didn't look it, but he had to be exhausted. Seeley felt a flood of affection for this lawyer who had, by himself, attempted to destroy Vaxtek's case.

Palmieri came from behind the desk. "It's been good working with you, Mike. I never thought I'd meet a trial lawyer as good as Bob Pearsall."

"It was a privilege to work with you." Seeley offered his hand, and resisted the impulse to hug Palmieri, or even to touch his shoulder as a way of embracing what they'd accomplished together. "I couldn't have done this without you."

Palmieri's eyes didn't let Seeley go. He seemed unembarrassed by the quiet intimacy of the exchange. Finally, he withdrew his hand. "I learned a lot from you."

"Like what?"

"How hard it can be to lose a case."

Seeley said, "Only when you're trying."

"You have great timing, Seeley."

For some reason, he liked the sound of Lily calling him by his last name.

"I don't have to be back in the lab until Sunday afternoon. That gives us three days for ourselves."

The night was clear, and from the chaises on Lily's terrace they could see all the way to where a procession of trawlers, their lights strung like Christmas trees, crossed the dark horizon.

"We need to talk about what happened."

"You're the silent one," Lily said. "I don't mind."

"You had a lot of courage, going to the newspaper."

"Not really. Five minutes after you left, I knew I didn't have a choice."

"Why did the story take so long to come out?"

"You're the most impatient person I know!"

"What do you mean?"

"Gail had to check facts and give Vaxtek and St. Gall a chance to return her phone calls. Alan, too."

She rested her fingers on the back of his hand. "You better stick to law. You don't have the patience to make it as a scientist."

Seeley said, "Neither does Steinhardt. He couldn't wait for his own results, so he stole yours."

"What's going to happen to him?"

"In the courts?" It was absurd, but Lily's interest in Steinhardt made him jealous. "Nothing. As much as he wanted to commit perjury, and as close as he came, in the end he didn't."

"Only because you stopped him. Do you regret that?"

As usual, Lily was at least a step ahead of him. "He won't get his reputation back, but he'll try. Don't be surprised if his lawyer calls and offers to put your name next to Steinhardt's on the AV/AS patent."

"If he does, will you be my lawyer?"

"Sure," Seeley said. The thought of helping to attach Lily's name to her discovery pleased him. "The Patent Office also has a procedure for removing a person's name from a patent and replacing it with the name of the true inventor. Yours."

Lily sipped at the jasmine tea that she had brought out to the balcony, but said nothing.

Seeley said, "Think about it."

"I know you can't understand, but there's a part of me that still feels loyal to Alan." After a long moment, she said, "Do it. Don't wait for his lawyer to come to us. Go to the Patent Office and do it."

Seeley knew that there would be no opposition from Vaxtek or St. Gall. Follow-up stories had appeared under Odum's byline and there were others in the national press, but the news of Dusollier's arrest had shut down any plans that the two companies might have had to question Lily's part in the discovery of AV/AS. They now had other battles to fight in the press. This morning's *Chronicle* article had mentioned Lily's role in only a single paragraph, and by the time indictments started coming in and the prosecutions got under way, she would be forgotten.

Seeley said, "What are you going to do next?"

"There've been some phone calls. E-mails. A few of them look serious."

"Any of them interesting?"

"One from Rockefeller University in New York. It's where I got my doctorate. Another from the Scripps Institute in La Jolla."

"Why do I hope you'll choose the Atlantic over the Pacific?"

"There's also a nonprofit in Illinois, near Carbondale, that's talking about giving me my own lab. It's small, but it's well funded. I'm visiting there next week."

Seeley felt the same panicky flutter in his stomach as when he was on the phone with Mrs. Rosziak and imagined the collapse of the Ellicott Square Building. This was a new feeling for him. He knew that he had no claim on Lily, but why did the thought of losing her make him feel this way?

She took his hand in hers.

Seeley said, "What's it like for you, looking at the ocean every day and knowing that your home is on the other side?"

"What was it like for you to look at all those bottles of beer lined up on the wall at Barbara's Fish Trap?"

"I could always take a drink. But I won't. Just like you won't go back to China."

"What are you going to do?"

"I'm not sure," Seeley said. "I'm thinking about moving back to New York." He let her fingers interlace his.

"What about San Francisco? Your brother's here."

Seeley shook his head.

"Are the two of you close?"

The seriousness in her voice forced Seeley to think about the answer, and he realized that, as much as he might want to obliterate it, the bond between Leonard and him would be there forever. "Like two peas in a pod."

"What's going to happen to him?"

"If the government indicted people for being cowards, Leonard would need to hire a lawyer. He knew about the collusion. But nothing will happen." Nothing, Seeley thought, unless he knew of the plan to murder Pearsall.

Neither of them spoke for what seemed like minutes, and then Lily slipped her fingers from Seeley's. "Have you talked with him since the trial?"

"No."

"Where does he live?"

"Atherton."

"It's only a thirty-minute drive." As she spoke, Lily moved her head slowly from side to side. "You weren't planning to say goodbye to him, were you?"

Seeley frowned.

"You need to do that."

"I'll think about it."

"No," she said, "I mean now."

"Why?"

"How many big brothers does he have?" Her face came close to his. "I'll still be here when you get back."

"I don't even know if he's home."

"Come back as soon as you can." She kissed him lightly on the lips. "We'll watch the fog come in."

Water spun from sprinklers on Leonard's lawn, draining into pools on the black pavement. The now-familiar scent of eucalyptus, field grass, and wood smoke reminded Seeley of the pumped-in perfume at a suburban mall. He preferred the yeasty scents of San Francisco, the iodine smell of the ocean.

Leonard must have heard the car because he was at the door.

"I'm glad you came." He had an open bottle of beer in his hand. Behind him, lights burned in the living room and a fire blazed in the huge stone fireplace. "I wish you'd called. Renata's on rounds."

Seeley followed his brother into the room.

"She won't be more than half an hour."

It struck Seeley that Leonard lied even when he had nothing to gain.

"Do you want a drink? Beer? I can get you something stronger."

"I just came to say goodbye."

"Stay until Renata gets back. You're part of the family. She'll want to see you."

"Why do you keep pressing that button, Len?"

Leonard shook off the question. "Well, then, take a good look." He threw his arms wide to encompass the glass-walled room. "This is the last you're going to see of the place. The bank will let us stay for another two, three months, but the equity's gone."

When Seeley looked at Vaxtek's stock price that afternoon, it was down more than forty percent. It might rise a few points on Monday, when the two companies announced the settlement of their lawsuit, but Leonard had bought on margin, and his account had to be wiped out by now.

"Still, with Renata's salary and mine, we're fine. The company, too. We're shutting down Steinhardt's lab—no one's seen him since that newspaper article—but we have other products in the pipeline."

If Leonard believed that, he was kidding himself. In less than a week, disappointed shareholders would begin filing lawsuits against Vaxtek's management and, with AV/AS producing no more than the modest royalties approved by Judge Farnsworth, Warshaw would put the company up for sale for whatever he could get from one of the large multinationals.

"I wouldn't count on it, Lenny."

Leonard winced. "Why not?" He took the hassock by the fire and tilted the green bottle to his mouth. Seeley took the couch opposite him.

"Your chairman's going to be spending more time talking to his lawyers than running his company."

"Criminal?"

"That depends on how high the DA thinks he can go. The killer, Baptiste, is going to try to make a deal by implicating Dusollier. If he does, and if Dusollier's got anything on Warshaw, I'd say your boss is in trouble."

"Joel always lands on his feet."

"I don't think the DA is going to give him special treatment for being a juvenile."

A light snapped on in the entryway, and Seeley started.

"The timer," Leonard said.

"What about you?" Seeley said. "Did you do anything the DA would be interested in?"

"You mean that crack you made about my pushing Pearsall in front of the train? I thought you were kidding."

"You tell me."

"Come on, Mike. Sure, I lied about Steinhardt. I knew about the collusion. But I don't go around killing people."

It wasn't Seeley's best judgment, but he decided to believe his brother.

Leonard drained the beer. "Stay for Thanksgiving. Mom will really be excited to see you."

"You've got to give up on this, Len. It won't work."

"What do you mean? This is family."

"What family?"

"You. Mom. Me. Renata. It's not perfect, the way you always want things, but it's good enough."

"There never was a family," Seeley said.

"Whose choice was that?"

"Why is this so important to you?"

Leonard slumped on the hassock, and Seeley caught a glimpse of what his brother would look like as an old man.

Leonard said, "After everything else is gone—your job, your friends—who else is there but your family?"

"Why does there have to be anyone?"

"I suppose that's the difference between us." For an instant, a spark of acceptance flickered into Leonard's tired eyes, then disappeared. "The story in the *Chronicle*—that was your idea, wasn't it?"

Seeley had told no one, not even Palmieri, what he had done to sabotage Vaxtek's case, and he was not going to start with his brother. "On Friday the judge is going to approve a settlement agreement that will commit Vaxtek to licensing AV/AS to any company that wants to produce it. It's not why I took the case, but I can't say I'm unhappy about the result."

"Why *did* you take the case?"

Seeley started to answer, but the memory of his brother hiding behind their bedroom door stopped him. "Because you asked me to."

Leonard's spirit recovered. "So family does count for something."

"I thought I owed you after walking out thirty-two years ago."

"You count the years, too."

"Did you know that I had my finger on the trigger? That if it weren't for the safety catch, I would have killed him?" Not Father, or even Lothar. *Him.* Seeley reached for his rage—at Leonard, at his father—but found nothing there.

"I didn't know that."

Seeley rose. "I need to go."

Leonard followed him into the hallway. "You realize," he said, "leaving was the best thing you ever did for me."

That jarred Seeley. "How's that?"

"Do you think I liked being your kid brother? You judging me all the time? Always being measured against you? Why do you think I went out for tennis? It was the only sport you didn't play."

"I was only trying to protect you, Len."

"Well, if you want a doctor's opinion," Leonard said, "that's the worst thing you can do to someone. If he messes up, let him fix it for himself."

Seeley smiled to himself. Leonard hadn't lost his alchemist's ability to turn his own faults magically into someone else's responsibility. Seeley looked around the large glass room. The wind had picked up, rattling tree branches across the skylight. He moved to the brightly lit entry, but Leonard was quicker and blocked the door.

Leonard appraised Seeley with the same clinical eye as when he had examined the bruises from his Chinatown beating. "Did you ever think that maybe it was us who abandoned you?"

When Seeley didn't answer, Leonard said, "No, you only think about things that you can fix."

"I'm nothing if not practical."

Leonard grinned. "If you believe that, you're a dreamer. You're the most romantic idealist I'll ever know."

"Then that's another difference between us."

"Are we going to see each other again?"

"I don't know," Seeley said.

"Whatever happened, Mike"—Seeley didn't know if Leonard meant the trial or what happened thirty-two years ago—"it was good to see you. It was good for us to get to know each other again."

Seeley reached out a hand, as did Leonard, but at the last moment—a boxer's fake—Leonard threw his arm around Seeley's neck and drew him into a clumsy embrace. When Seeley tried to pull back, Leonard's lock on him was that of a wild man. Seeley thought, Was this in fact why I came to California? To reconcile with my brother? He looked about, as if the house might reveal an answer, but the windows, the skylight, the hall mirror all reflected back the same baffling image: a grasping thing; some prehistoric being; a benign beast from a dark fable.

ACKNOWLEDGMENTS

For their generous help with this book, I am grateful to friends and colleagues Judge William Alsup, Shantanu Basu, Matt Doyle, Meg Gardiner, Dan Ho, Pam Karlan, Don Kennedy, Gladys Monroy, Alan Morrison, Robert Reinhard, Stephen Sherwin, Jayashri Srikantiah, and Bob Weisberg.

Two books—Jon Cohen, *Shots in the Dark: The Wayward Search for an AIDS Vaccine* (2001) and Patricia Thomas, *Big Shot: Passion, Politics, and the Struggle for an AIDS Vaccine* (2001)—provided useful background, as did Patricia Kahn, ed., *AIDS Vaccine Handbook* (2d ed. 2005). The AV/AS patent—but certainly not the story behind it—is modeled on U.S. Patent No. 6,261,558B1, Synthetic Human Neutralizing Monoclonal Antibodies to Human Immunodeficiency Virus, invented by Carlos F. Barbas, Dennis R. Burton, and Richard A. Lerner.

Gerald Howard and Katie Halleron at Doubleday, and Wendy Strothman at the Strothman Agency, provided valuable editorial suggestions, as did Karla Eoff and Lynne Anderson. Lynne Anderson also typed the manuscript with a timely assist from Mary Ann Rundell.